IMAGES OF CRISIS

GEORGE P. LANDOW

IMAGES OF CRISIS

LITERARY ICONOLOGY,
1750 TO THE PRESENT

ROUTLEDGE & KEGAN PAUL
BOSTON, LONDON AND HENLEY

First published in 1982
by Routledge & Kegan Paul Ltd
9 Park Street, Boston, Mass. 02108, USA,
39 Store Street, London WC1E 7DD and
Broadway House, Newtown Road,
Henley-on-Thames, Oxon RG9 1EN

Set in 10 on 12 pt Baskerville by
Altonprint, Alton, Hampshire
and printed in the USA

Copyright © George P. Landow 1982

Library of Congress Cataloging in Publication Data

Landow, George P.
Images of crisis.
Includes bibliographical references and index.
1. Symbolism in literature. 2. Shipwrecks in
literature. I. Title.
PN56. S9L36   809'.93356   81 - 12086
ISBN 0-7100-0818-X   AACR2

For Bruce B. Redford
and Barton L. St. Armand,

who urged me to build and launch this vessel and, true
friends, pointed out many of the shoals, deceptive currents,
and hidden reefs

But the country which they chop up and burn like a pine-tree, and
    which you see
either in the dark train, without water, the windows broken, night
    after night
or in the burning ship which, as statistics indicate, will surely
    sink,
these things have taken root in the mind and do not change
these things have planted images like those trees
which in virgin forests cast their branches
and these take root in the earth and sprout again;
they cast their branches which sprout again, striding league after
    league –
and our mind a virgin forest of slain friends.
And if I speak to you in fables and parables
it is because you hear it more gently.

George Seferis, 'The Last Stop',
trans. Edmund Keeley and Philip Sherrard

Images are ratios between what is uttered and what, somehow, is
intended, and as Kenneth Burke remarks, you cannot discuss images for
very long without sliding into whole textures of relationships. Cannot
those relationships be charted?

Harold Bloom, 'The Breaking of Form', in
Deconstruction and Criticism

CONTENTS

ILLUSTRATIONS
(between pages 84 and 85)

———————

PREFACE AND ACKNOWLEDGMENTS

During the time that this volume was slowly taking form, I had the benefit of the conversations, doubts, and suggestions of many friends at Columbia, Cornell, and Brown Universities and at the University of Chicago. I am particularly grateful for the interest and encouragement of Hugh Amory, Stephen Brook, Paul Delany, William Galperin, David Hirsch, Linda H. Peterson, Howard Schless, R.C. Tobias, Billy and Barbara Tracy, William Veeder, and Hugh Witemeyer. Elizabeth Beckhard, my former student at Brown University, first introduced me to the importance of bankruptcy as a topos in the nineteenth-century novel, and while at this university I have also had the great advantage of discussing the iconography and iconology of shipwreck with my colleague George Monteiro, whose essay on Stephen Crane's 'The Open Boat' masterfully demonstrates how a nineteenth-century writer manipulated traditional religious commonplaces to his own purposes. I would especially like to thank my good friend Howard M. Helsinger for deluging me with shipwreck metaphors from St Augustine and Gregory the Great to Virginia Woolf.

Portions of this book first appeared in the *Revue de Littérature Comparée, Studies in English Literature,* and *Studies in Iconography*; I would like to thank J. Body, Edward Doughtie, and Thomas C. Niemann, the editors of these journals, for granting permission to reprint these materials, and I would also like to thank the University of California Press for allowing me to reprint portions of my essay on the rainbow, which first appeared in *Nature and the Victorian Imagination.*

I would like to thank the following museums for granting permission to reproduce works of art in their possession: Birmingham Museums and Art Gallery, the Brooklyn Museum, the Forbes Magazine Collection, the Leeds City Art Gallery, the Louvre, the Metropolitan Museum of Art, the Museum de Arte de Ponce, Fundacion Louis A. Ferré, Museum of Fine Arts, Boston, National Collection of Fine Arts, Washington, D.C., National Gallery, Oslo,

Southampton Art Gallery, the St Louis Art Museum, the Tate Gallery, the Walker Art Gallery, Liverpool, and the Whitworth Art Gallery of the University of Manchester.

Grateful acknowledgment is made for permission to reprint extracts from the following copyrighted material. 'Preludes for Memnon, XXXIII' in *Collected Poems* by Conrad Aiken. Copyright © 1953, 1970 by Conrad Aiken. Reprinted by permission of Oxford University Press. 'The Voyage', in *Collected Poetry* by W.H. Auden. Copyright © 1945 by W.H. Auden. Reprinted by permission of Random House and Faber & Faber. 'Ithaka,' by C.P. Cavafy, *Six Poets of Modern Greece*. Copyright © 1960 by Edmund Keeley and Philip Sherrard. Reprinted by permission of Edmund Keeley & Georges Borchardt. 'The Dry Salvages', in *The Four Quartets* in *The Complete Poems and Plays, 1909-1950*. Copyright © 1952 by T.S. Eliot. Reprinted by permission of Harcourt Brace Jovanovich and Faber & Faber. 'Among Islands', in *Minutes,* by Daryl Hine. Copyright © 1968 by Daryl Hine. Reprinted by permission of Atheneum Publishers. 'Australia', 'Conversation with Calliope', 'The End of a Journey', 'Man Friday', 'Observation Car', and 'Wandering Islands,' in *Collected Poems, 1930-1965,* by A.D. Hope. Copyright © 1960, 1962 by A.D. Hope. Reprinted by permission of Viking Penguin. 'Cataclismo', 'La Nave', 'Soliliguo en olas', in *A New Decade (Poems: 1958-1967),* by Pablo Neruda. Copyright © 1969 by Ben Belitt and Grove Press. Reprinted by permission of Grove Press. 'The Last Stop', by George Seferis, in *Six Poets of Modern Greece*. Copyright © 1960 by Edmund Keeley and Philip Sherrard. Reprinted by permission of Edmund Keeley & Georges Borchardt. 'The Sacred Way', by Anghelos Sikelianos, in *Six Poets of Modern Greece*. Copyright © 1960 by Edmund Keeley and Philip Sherrard. Reprinted by permission of Edmund Keeley & Georges Borchardt. 'Notes towards a Supreme Fiction', 'Sail of Ulysses', and 'Sunday Morning,' in *Collected Poems* by Wallace Stevens, Copyright © 1954 by Wallace Stevens. Reprinted by permission of Alfred A. Knopf and Faber & Faber. 'No Horizon', in *The Aggressive Ways of the Casual Stranger,* by Rosemarie Waldrop. Copyright © 1972 by Rosemarie Waldrop. Reprinted by permission of Random House. 'Ballad about False Beacons', in *Stolen Apples,* by Yevgeny Yevtushenko. Copyright © 1971 by Doubleday & Company. Reprinted by permission of Doubleday.

David Cody, Noah Landow, Shoshana M. Landow, Sally Richmond, Debora Sherman, and Richard Schindler (who also contributed the illustration of an erupting volcano which appears on p. 2) helped me read proof, and I am most grateful for this help in time of need.

Once again, my wife has lavished her skills as a professional copy editor upon my work, and once again she is responsible for making of it a clearer, more accurate book.

CHAPTER ONE

IMAGES, SITUATIONS, AND STRUCTURES

The problem . . . is no longer one of lasting foundations, but one of transformations that serve as new foundations, the rebuilding of foundations . . . To say that one discursive foundation is substituted for another is not to say that a whole world of absolutely new objects, enunciations, concepts, and theoretical choices emerges fully armed and fully organized in a text that will place the world once and for all; it is to say that a general transformation of relations has occurred, but that does not necessarily alter all the elements; it is to say that statements are governed by new rules of formation, it is not to say that all objects or concepts, all enunciations or all theoretical choices disappear.

Michel Foucault, *The Archaeology of Knowledge,*
trans. A. M. Sheridan Smith

Like the choice between competing political institutions, that between competing paradigms proves to be a choice between incompatible modes of community life. Because it has that character, the choice is not and cannot be determined merely by evaluative procedures characteristic of normal science, for these depend in part upon a particular paradigm, and that paradigm is at issue.

Thomas S. Kuhn, *The Structure of Scientific Revolutions*

First, the general principles. In order to establish these principles, the fairy tale has to be approached from a standpoint of its environment, that is, the conditions under which it was created and exists. Life and, in the broad sense of the word, religion are the most important for us here. The causes of transformations frequently lie outside the fairy tale, and we will not grasp the evolution of the tale unless we consider the environmental circumstances of the fairy tale.

Vladimir Propp, 'Fairy Tale Transformation',
trans. C. H. Severens

In 'MS. Found in a Bottle' Edgar Allan Poe thrusts us into a situation that has fascinated, even obsessed, artists and writers since the later eighteenth century – into the moment of crisis. Poe's narrator, a wealthy wanderer who had taken passage on a merchant vessel sailing from Java, sets his tale by establishing a mood of complete peace, which he then transforms into a situation of great movement, excitement, and danger. Unable to sleep during one night of almost preternatural calm, he climbed a ladder to the deck.

> As I placed my foot upon the upper step of the companion-ladder, I was startled by a loud, humming noise, like that occasioned by the rapid revolution of a mill-wheel, and before I could ascertain its meaning, I found the ship quivering to its centre. In the next instant a wilderness of foam hurled us upon our beam-ends, and, rushing over us fore and aft, swept the entire decks from stem to stern. . . . Stunned by the shock of the water, I found myself, upon recovery, jammed in between the stern-post and rudder. With great difficulty I regained my feet, and looking dizzily around, was at first struck with the idea of our being among breakers; so terrific, beyond the wildest imagination, was the whirlpool of mountainous and foaming ocean within which we were engulfed. After a while I heard the voice of an old Swede, who had shipped with us at the moment of leaving port. . . . All on deck, with the exception of ourselves, had been swept overboard; the captain and mates must have perished while they slept, for the cabins were deluged with water.

In Poe's tale the moment of crisis takes the specific form of shipwreck in which a vessel and all those upon it are battered by natural forces. The sudden crash of the totally unexpected sea upon the ship produces a moment of crisis, a flash-point, one of those brief instants in time when the primal isolation and helplessness of the human condition are revealed.

Like the analogous situations of becoming a victim of avalanche, deluge, volcano, or alien invasion, that of the man shipwrecked and cast away presents human beings impinged upon by powerful external forces. These forces besiege the perceiving consciousness – here that of a narrator – and threaten him with total loss of existence. Since such experiences are often presented from within the situation (even when it does not result in death, the final crisis), the one who relates it does not yet know the eventual outcome. The essence of this compelling situation, in other words, lies in its isolation and discontinuity, for it is cut off or set off from what precedes and what follows. As Poe's 'MS. Found in a Bottle' makes clear, the situation of crisis creates or generates an entirely new imaginative cosmos for those who experience it. The old world of boredom and monotony that drove Poe's narrator to board the merchant ship in the first place suddenly comes to an end, for he finds himself in a new life, a new situation, a new world. But at the same moment that this new imaginative world comes into being, it also threatens to end – and to end with it the human being who finds himself or herself there.

This situation of crisis and cataclysm, which has so attracted the imaginations of novelists, poets, and painters for the last two hundred years, takes several major forms, all of which are variations upon single basic structure in which human beings are surrounded, assaulted, and often finally engulfed by powerful external forces. This basic intellectual structure appears, for example, in Poe's 'MS. Found in a Bottle' in the form of a literal narrative, but in Anghelos Sikelianos's 'The Sacred Way' the paradigmatic situation takes the form of a complex analogy:

> Through the new wound which fate had opened in me
> it seemed the setting sun entered my heart
> with the impetus of water entering suddenly
> the breach in a sinking ship.
> [trans. Edmund Keeley and Philip Sherrard]

The same structure of crisis and cataclysm also informs J. M. W. Turner's *Cottage Destroyed by an Avalanche* (*c.* 1810, Tate Gallery, Pl. 1), which is also known as *The Fall of an Avalanche in the Grissons*. Turner's image of natural disaster depicts the instant at which a gigantic boulder and mass of snow crash into a small Alpine dwelling. He freezes time at the moment of crisis, for although the rock has already touched the cottage, it has not yet crushed it, and, similarly, the painter has suspended in mid-air the snow and smaller rocks that will obliterate the building and the people inside it. Like Poe's tale, this painting contrasts a quiet, peaceful, essentially static world with one of crisis. 'MS. Found in a Bottle', we recall, begins with the pre-crisis world, and the destroying sea transforms this calm existence into a perilous kinetic one. Turner's *Cottage Destroyed by an Avalanche,* which must work with the means available to the pictorial image, juxtaposes the pre- and post-crisis worlds spatially rather than by temporal succession. The bottom fifth of the picture thus depicts the quiet world of mountain, trees, and cottage upon which the avalanche bursts from above. To this peaceful world, which occupies such a small portion of the image, Turner juxtaposes a series of visually opposing natural forces: the giant boulder that has just reached the cottage inclines on an axis that parallels a line drawn from the picture's upper left corner to lower right, the snowslide behind the boulder forms a sharply opposing diagonal, and the storm in the left distance parallels the axis of the boulder. As Allen Staley has pointed out, this painting has often been compared to the artist's *Snow Storm: Hannibal and His Army Crossing the Alps* (1812, Tate Gallery), another of his many images of the destructive forces of nature:

> Both pictures contain driving storm and huge boulders, but whereas in the *Hannibal* the composition consists of a great swirling vortex which pulls the eye into a deep space, in . . . *[Cottage Destroyed by an Avalanche]* the crossed diagonals of boulder, avalanche, and storm stay near the surface and there is little suggestion of space.[1]

The effect of such flattened treatment of space, one may add, is to reinforce the picture's stopping time at the very instant of crisis.

Curiously, when Turner appended lines of his own composition to the picture when he exhibited it in 1810, he used the same basic situation but emphasized another moment in it:

> The downward sun a parting sadness gleams,
> Portentous lurid thro' the gathering storm;
> Thick drifting snow, on snow,
> Till the vast weight bursts thro' the
>   rocky barrier;

> Down at once, its pine clad forests,
> And towering glaciers fall, the work of ages
> Crashing through all! extinction follows,
> And the toil, the hopes of man – o'erwhelms

Turner's lines do not emphasize or even mention directly the moment when the avalanche hurls itself into the cottage. Instead, they concentrate upon explaining the physical (or natural) causes of this Alpine disaster. The lines build to the moment the 'vast weight burst thro' the rocky barrier', after which they contrast the present moment of destruction to the ages required to create that which is now being destroyed. Unlike the painting, which presents a particularly powerful image of nature destroying man, the verses that accompany it only present this fact in very general terms: 'extinction follows,/ And the toil, the hopes of man – o'erwhelms.' Turner's *Cottage Destroyed by an Avalanche,* then, provides a specific instance of the general phenomenon the lines describe; or to state the relationship between verbal and visual embodiments of the basic situation in a way that is more probably appropriate: after having been attracted to this visual image of the avalanche, Turner then appended his lines to explain how that situation came about. Both the painting and the verse epigraph, however, present a basic structure or situation in which man, or the objects which represent him, are about to be destroyed by surrounding natural forces that burst in upon him.

John Martin, who specialized in cataclysmic and apocalyptic images, employs this same intellectual structure throughout his career in his many representations of biblical history.[2] Turner, of course, also painted similar embodiments of the religious sublime, such as *The Fifth Plague of Eygpt* (1800, John Herron Art Museum, Indianapolis) and *The Angel Standing in the Sun* (1846, Tate Gallery), but he more frequently drew his subjects of catastrophic sublimity from history, classical literature, or his own experience. In contrast, Martin, who was extraordinarily popular in his own time, devoted most of his energies to creating images of divine punishment, though he occasionally painted secular and literary subjects as well. In *The Great Day of His Wrath* (1852, Tate Gallery) this master of the theatrical sublime created an image of the Last Judgment which can stand as a type of his entire career. Using his characteristic elongated horizontal format, Martin follows his usual pictorial strategy of juxtaposing many diminutive human beings to a world whose scale, depth, and energy is about to destroy them. A black chasm opens before the spectator in the immediate foreground, and into this emptiness pour the terror-stricken inhabitants of this doomed world, while down upon them cascade from the left enormous boulders. Lightning flashes across the sky and down on the ground, and this fire from the sky is matched in the right portion of the background by a sea of lava and fire. The curving sides of the hills, the swirling clouds of smoke on the right, and the central blackness all create a vortex that draws spectator and victim into the abyss. By the time Martin painted this image of final crisis, he had already become extraordinarily popular with related images of divine action that drew upon similar intellectual and visual structures, including *The Fall of Babylon* (1819, location unknown), *Belshazzar's Feast* (1820, Mrs R. Knight Col.), *The Seventh Plague of Eygpt* (1823, Boston Museum of Fine Arts), *The Destruction of Pharaoh's Host* (1830, location unknown), *The Fall of Nineveh* (mezzotint; 1829, British Museum), *The Deluge* (1834, formerly Charles Jerdein Col.), *The Destruction of Tyre* (1840, Toledo Museum of Art), and *The Destruction of Sodom and Gomorrah* (1852, Laing Art Gallery, Newcastle upon Tyne). In all these representations of catastrophe and crisis, Martin relies upon the great disparity of scale between his personages and the world in which they find themselves to emphasize man's essential helplessness in the face of natural phenomena. Throughout Martin's work lightning, flood, avalanche, volcanic action, and earthquake destroy human beings and their guilty civilizations, and when he came to paint *The Great Day of His Wrath,* he employed them all, as if to provide a final summation of this situation and of his own career in depicting its various forms.

The fire, lava, and earthquake in *The Great Day of His Wrath* remind us that Martin's visions of crisis and catastrophe, like those of so many other artists and writers of his time, received a powerful impetus from the rediscovery of Pompeii in the previous century. Writing on 'The Impact of Pompeii on the Literary Imagination', Laurence Goldstein has observed that in the destruction of earlier optimism 'during the Age of Revolutions which followed Gibbon ... Pompeii played an important role, as a social phenomenon and as a metaphor.' In particular,

It did so by compelling a personal identification with its

victims. Because it was obliterated in the midst of life, Pompeii revealed to the modern world disturbing images of pathetic individuals stopped in recognizable domestic activities by the volcanic ash. Pompeii became a symbolic code word for what Madame de Stael calls 'death's abrupt invasion.' It fostered a dark literature of premature burial, natural calamity, and universal extinction.[3]

It also encouraged artists to create images of the instant, as Pablo Neruda puts it in 'Cataclismo',

> que cuando
> cayó el humo y el mar, la lava, el miedo
> allí cayeron, enredándose en un nudo de espinas
> que rodaba temblando sobre el dia
> con una cola de agua hirsuta y piedras que mordian . . .

> [when
> the smoke fell, the lava, the seas, the terror
> rained down, spun the knots in the shuddering thorn,
> circled the days
> with a hairy backlash of water and the tooth of the stone.
> trans. Ben Belitt]

Not surprisingly, Martin contributed a painting of Pompeii's end. His *The Destruction of Pompeii and Herculaneum* (c. 1821, University of Manchester, Pl. 2) follows the lead of Jacob More's *Mount Vesuvius in Eruption: The Last Days of Pompeii* (1780, National Gallery of Scotland, Edinburgh), which was apparently the first to join 'a close, low viewpoint that exaggerates the height and bulk of the volcano with a scene of figures fleeing the crumbling city.'[4] Like his more famous visions of catastrophe, Martin's version of Mount Vesuvius destroying the ancient city employs an essentially oval visual field whose curves embrace and capture these victims of nature. Characteristically, the painter drops off his corners into shadow, thus creating a vortex or tunnel-shape that draws the spectator into the picture space. The incandescent cone of Vesuvius, which is shooting forth fiery ash and lava, appears in the farthest visible distance, and it is thus spatially and tonally opposed to the many small figures who people the foreground. The immediate landscape foreground and many of the costumes of the people in it have dark coloration and tone. Hence the Pompeiians fleeing their city's destruction are sharply contrasted visually to the glowing mountain, lava, and lightning that threaten them. They have assembled beside the water of the Bay of Naples, which the painter depicts reaching in from the left margin to the left middleground of the picture. Trapped between a rough sea and a fiery sky, the pathetic inhabitants of the doomed city try to defend themselves by lifting arms, cloaks, and soldier's shields to ward off the coming destruction.

Like so many other images of crisis and catastrophe, Martin's painting of the destruction of Pompeii employs a parallel intellectual and pictorial structure, for its sweeping curves and threatening masses visually embody the way natural forces surround and threaten human beings with painful death. A slightly different version of this structure of engulfment appears in the American painter James Hamilton's *The Last Days of Pompeii* (1864, Brooklyn Museum, Pl. 3). Using a vertical format to present man and his objects destroyed by natural forces, Hamilton creates an image of Pompeii that apparently draws more upon views of Rome than upon Pompeii itself. A column surmounted by a statue, presumably that of a Roman emperor, extends up through the middle of the picture among a series of colonnaded buildings set upon a hill. This silhouetted form of the statue stands contrasted sharply to the fiery, incandescent cone of the volcano, which appears at the centre of a vortex surrounding both it and the statue, an emblem of man's pretences to power and glory. This static opposition of statue and volcano provides one of the painting's major emphases, but the spectator's greatest impression is, however, one of movement, for Hamilton uses a swirl of volcanic clouds and falling rocks to create a particularly powerful image of natural energies descending upon man and his world. Unlike Martin, Hamilton chooses a single visual emphasis to contrast helpless man and powerful nature, and the American painter also lavishes more care on creating the effect of swirling energies. None the less, both painters create images whose forms communicate a situation in which human beings are engulfed by natural forces totally beyond their control.

Edward Bulwer-Lytton's novel, *The Last Days of Pompeii* (1834), which was enormously popular in the nineteenth century, provides a catalogue of such structures of cataclysm and crisis. After building towards the volcano's eruption, *The Last Days of Pompeii* then devotes considerable space to presenting it in detail. Bulwer-Lytton follows

Pliny the Younger and reports that the inhabitants of Pompeii were first surprised by 'a vast vapour shooting from the summit of Vesuvius, in the form of a gigantic pine-tree; the trunk, blackness, – the branches, fire!' (bk 5, ch. 4). Suddenly, the citizens of the doomed city

> Felt the earth shake beneath their feet; the walls of the theatre trembled: and, beyond, in the distance, they heard the crash of falling roofs; an instant more, and the mountain-cloud seemed to roll towards them, dark and rapid, like a torrent; at the same time it cast forth from its bosom a shower of ashes mixed with vast fragments of burning stone! Over the crushing vines; over the desolate streets; over the amphitheatre itself; far and wide, with many a mighty splash in the agitated sea, – fell that awful shower! . . . Darker, and larger, and mightier, spread the cloud above them. It was a sudden and more ghastly Night rushing upon the realm of Noon! [bk 5, ch.4]

After the first stages during which the inhabitants of Pompeii see the eruption and feel the corollary earthquakes and then see the volcanic cloud advancing upon them, a third stage occurs: clouds of volcanic smoke and ash cover the scene, thus transforming Pompeii into a nightmarish phantasmagoric prison:

> The cloud, which had scattered so deep a murkiness over the day, had now settled into a solid and impenetrable mass. It resembled less even the thickest gloom of a night in the open air than the close and blind darkness of some narrow room. But in proportion as the blackness gathered, did the lightnings around Vesuvius increase in their vivid and scorching glare. Nor was their horrible beauty confined to the usual hues of fire; no rainbow ever rivalled their varying and prodigal dyes. Now brightly blue as the most azure depth of a southern sky; now a livid and snake-like green, darting restlessly to and fro as the folds of an enormous serpent. . . . Sometimes the cloud appeared to break from its solid mass, and, by the lightning, to assume quaint and vast mimicries of human or monster shapes, striding across the gloom, hurtling one upon the other, and vanishing swiftly into the turbulent abyss of shade; so that, to the eyes and fancies of the affrighted wanderers, the unsubstantial vapours were as the

bodily forms of gigantic foes, – the agents of terror and of
death. [bk 5, ch.7]

Next, after relating the repertoire of terrifying sounds that besieged
the Pompeiians – the rumbling of the earth, the groaning of the sea,
and the hiss of escaping gases – the novelist tells how the city was
gradually inundated by ashes and poisonous vapours, and how
falling rocks either crushed all beneath them or, breaking into
pieces, set fire to all that was combustible nearby. Finally, after
describing how the elements of civilization disappeared in this night
flight to self-preservation, Bulwer-Lytton narrates the final horror of
the lava flow, which transforms Pompeii and its environment into a
scene from Hell – into a scene, that is, very like that portrayed in
Martin's *The Great Day of His Wrath:*

> Suddenly, . . . the place became lighted with an intense and
> lurid glow. Bright and gigantic through the darkness, which
> closed around it like the walls of hell, the mountain shone,
> – a pile of fire! Its summit seemed riven in two; or rather, above
> its surface there seemed to rise two monster shapes, each con-
> fronting each, as demons contending for a world. These were
> of one deep, blood-red hue of fire which lightened up the
> whole atmosphere far and wide; but *below*, the nether part of
> the mountain was still dark and shrouded, save in three
> places, adown which flowed, serpentine and irregular, rivers
> of the molten lava. Darkly red through the profound gloom
> of their banks, they flowed slowly on, as towards the . . . city.
> Over the broadest there seemed to spring a cragged and stupen-
> dous arch, from which, as from the jaws of hell, gushed the
> sources of the sudden Phlegethon. And through the stilled air
> was heard the rattling of the fragments of rock, hurling upon
> one another as they were borne down the fiery cataracts.
> [bk 5, ch. 8]

As these selected passages demonstrate, Bulwer-Lytton devoted
considerable attention to communicating the experience of the
inhabitants of Pompeii during that city's last terrifying hours.

None the less, although the novelist's narration of the last hours of
Pompeii takes a far more detailed form than does Poe's presentation
of the initial moment of crisis in 'MS. Found in a Bottle', it shares
essentially the same structure. Both works, in other words, present
human beings suddenly assaulted by powerful forces – forces that

exist on a scale far vaster than the human – that threaten to destroy them. The structure or situation in which these people find themselves, moreover, immediately separates their old, everyday existence from the new terrifying one that has just sprung into being.

The fact that situations as apparently different as shipwreck and the destruction of Pompeii can share a common structure in part explains how artists and writers could use them as equivalents for each other. Obviously, many artists, such as Turner, Martin, Coleman, and Miller, who found themselves attracted to a particular kind of crisis-subject painted others as well. Thus, James Hamilton, who painted *The Last Days of Pompeii,* also created a powerful image of the imperilled ship in *Old Ironsides* (1863, Philadelphia Academy of the Fine Arts), and similarly, Johann (or Jens) Christian Dahl, a Norwegian landscapist, painted both the powerful *Shipwreck on the Coast of Norway* (1832, National Gallery, Oslo, Pl. 4) and *Eruption of Vesuvius* (c. 1823, National Gallery, Oslo), as well as numerous other first-hand studies of the volcano. Turner, a great master of scenes of shipwreck and other natural disasters, also painted a *Vesuvius in Eruption* (1817, Yale Center for British Art, New Haven). Of course, the fact that a man who painted shipwrecks also painted other instances of natural disaster does not necessarily signify anything more than that he was attracted to exciting subjects. But as the example of Turner's avalanche picture and the various representations of Pompeii suggest, artists often use what are in essence visual puns to convey the effect of natural forces surrounding the personages who populate their images of disaster. Comparing Turner's many shipwreck pictures with his paintings of snowstorms and avalanches in the Alps, or Martin's *The Destruction of Tyre*, which is a sea piece, with *The Great Day of His Wrath,* one perceives that these artists rely upon many of the same visual forms. Moreover, flowing lava, falling snow, and volcanic ash are often treated as if they were equivalents to the waters that submerge an ocean vessel – as in part they are. The degree to which artists intentionally treat these elements as if they were water is of course difficult to demonstrate to a healthy scepticism.

Fortunately, the fact of such transformation or equivalence is much clearer in literature. For example, when Victor Hugo describes God's punishment of guilty humanity in 'Le Deluge', he imports non-biblical material about earthquakes and lightning that seems more literally appropriate to depictions of Pompeii or the Last Judgment:

Un sourd gémissement sorti du sein des mers
D'un horrible fracas remplit soudain les airs;
De la terre aussitôt les abîmes s'entr'ouvrent,
Des enfers étonnés les plaines se découvrent,
Et du fond de ce gouffre un tourbillon affreux
Repánd et la fumée et la flamme en tous lieux,
L'Air paraît s'embraser.

[A dull groan issuing from the bosom of the sea
Fills the air with a horrible din;
The abysses of the earth at once gape open,
The plains of astonished hell are exposed,
And from the depth of this pit pours out a
Frightful whirlwind, and smoke and fire everywhere,
The air seems to catch on fire.]

Similarly, Bulwer-Lytton, who relates that the volcanic ash and smoke poured from Vesuvius 'like a torrent' (bk 5, ch. 4), uses this water analogy when he describes 'steams of burning dust' (bk 5, ch. 8) in the wind and the lava moving in either 'rivers' or 'fiery cataracts' (bk 5, ch. 8). Since one almost inevitably describes the flow of lava in terms of a river or stream, such a description as that employed by the novelist does not tell us very much about any possible transference of terms derived from one situation to another. The description of the smoke pouring from the crater towards the city and the dust moving through the air, however, does suggest more clearly that Bulwer-Lytton was employing implicit analogies to shipwreck and sea disaster. The novelist's drawing upon an analogy to this other form of natural crisis and disaster also appears in an unexpected form in the scene when the volcano first sends forth fire and smoke. Immediately before Vesuvius erupts, the mob in the amphitheatre surges towards the evil Arbaces, and Bulwer-Lytton describes him as about to perish beneath 'the waves of the human sea' (bk 5, ch. 4). The sudden appearance of smoke and flame pouring forth from the crater temporarily spares him by distracting the mob so he can escape, but in the end he is killed by a bolt of volcanic lightning which overturns an imperial statue that in turn crushes him to death. Bulwer-Lytton's use of the commonplace analogy of mob and ocean, which appears in so many nineteenth-century novels, thus permits him to make an infuriated mass of people appear in the guise of a natural force and hence like the volcano itself. By likening both the mob and Vesuvius to a third term – a sea or mass of water – he makes them appear as comparable agents of divine justice.

The recognition that various apparently different situations share a common structure has much to offer the student of cultural history, ideas, the arts, and the relations among them. For example, when one perceives that literary and artistic presentations of shipwreck, invasion, avalanche, the Deluge, and the last days of Pompeii contain the same basic pattern or structure, they appear as equivalents or transformations of one another. Such a recognition, which makes it possible to identify the culturally important elements in each structure, also permits one to identify both the unifying themes of an age and the relation between various culturally dominant themes, ideas, and metaphors.

Artists and audiences clearly took such situations of extreme crisis to be relevant because they could see them as analogous to their own situations in some way. Thus, Turner's imagined avalanche in the Alps and Bulwer-Lytton's imagined history of Pompeii's last hours were understood to exist not solely as either works of art or re-creations of fact. Rather, they were perceived as referring beyond themselves, for they were interpreted as paradigms, synecdoches, analogies, and metaphors – as representative images or codes that conveyed something of importance to artist and audience alike. Such transformations of a literal thing (or event), or something within a work of art that purports to be such, permitted the situations of avalanche, shipwreck, and Pompeii to serve as cultural codes. They permitted, in other words, members of a particular society to communicate something of interest to one another. Obviously, one can learn much about a society, nation, or age both by examining the situations and structures its members adopt as codes or figurations and by observing how they manipulate, qualify, and adapt them.

By thus perceiving that certain basic structures function as cultural codes that communicate culturally relevant information, one can begin to construct an archeology of imagination capable of at least partially re-creating the way artists and audience experienced the paintings, novels, poems, political speeches, and sermons of an age. Such a proposed archeology of imagination would proceed by showing how apparently opposed or disparate images or situations

15

might be seen as unified, and at the same time it would permit the modern student of an earlier culture – or of his or her own – to differentiate more precisely than otherwise possible apparently similar applications of such structures. Although such an approach would permit us to enter the imaginations of another age by making us sensitive to its voices, codes, and inflexions, it would not fall prey to essentially unsupported and unsupportable generalizations about the mind of an age or its *Zeitgeist*.

Furthermore, treating such structures as codes that can be manipulated and qualified permits us to study the interesting problems of tradition and innovation. Such an approach permits one, for instance, to inquire how avalanches, Pompeii, and ship-wrecks became so popular, how they relate to earlier cultural codes, and how they function within individual paintings and literary works. In fact, the structure of crisis that lies at the heart of so many popular nineteenth- and twentieth-century metaphors, situations, and images turns out to be a transformation of a previously dominant cultural paradigm. As Borges has suggested in his essay on Pascal, 'perhaps universal history is the history of the diverse intonation of a few metaphors.'[5] The journey of life is one of those few metaphors whose variations should command the attention of the student of Western culture. The notion that life is a journey has provided one of the most pervasive commonplaces of Western thought for two and a half millennia, and it is easy to see why.[6] The figures of voyage, progress, or pilgrimage all enable us to spatialize – and hence visualize – our existence. (I had almost written that they enable us to spatialize our *movement through time,* or our existence *in* it, so difficult is it to escape using the forms of space to express those of time, quality, and abstract idea.)[7] One intonation increasingly characterizes Western culture from the late eighteenth century to the present day: the man shipwrecked and cast away. For Augustine, for Dante, for Chaucer, the journey of life was primarily a movement towards God, a voyage to the second Eden and City that has foundations. Renaissance authors retain this idea, yet add as their favourite variations the Ship of State and the Ship of Fools.[8] But by the last years of the eighteenth century shipwrecks and castaways enter poetry, fiction, and painting with increasing frequency until at last the disaster in mid-voyage compels more than the voyage itself.

Clearly, this intonation of the cultural code answered to the needs of many in the age to figure forth the new universe in which they found themselves. These images and situations are born of a sense of crisis, the sense, in particular, that one has seen the old guides, the old destinations, the old truths vanish. In contrast, when the shipwreck topos appears in earlier work, it functions as a metaphor for (1) punishment; (2) test or trial; or (3) means of spiritual education. Thus, when Dante threatens Florence, all Italy, and the Church with shipwreck, he is using this commonplace to suggest that they deserve divine punishment. Such traditional Christian uses of course do not disappear from Western culture, and, for example, when Turner paints a typhoon about to destroy the evil vessel depicted in *The Slave Ship* (1840, Boston Museum of Fine Arts, Pl. 5) he is applying the situation in a traditional manner. Drawing upon the stories of the Flood and Jonah, the Christian tradition has long used this situation to provide an image of punishment. Frequently, however, one comes across more complex earlier uses of shipwreck as code. Defoe's *Robinson Crusoe,* for example, clearly exemplifies a work in which all three basic uses of the situation coincide, for after this most famous of castaways is wrecked on his desert island as punishment for his sins, he proves himself worthy through his trials – and, finally, he becomes a true Christian.

One might say, therefore, that whereas the traditional shipwreck takes place in the *presence* of God, it is precisely the point of the modern one that it occurs in His *absence*. This radical difference between the two versions of the shipwreck, which also exists in other situations of crisis, such as the end of Pompeii, arises out of the way that the shipwreck transforms the journey-of-life metaphor. According to St Augustine, who provides the classical statement of this metaphor, Adam's fall exiled all his descendants from their proper home, which is with God, and their task – our task – is to strive to return to Him. Much like Swinburne and Stevens, St Augustine first presents his vision of life in terms of a hypothetical analogy:

> Suppose, then, we were wanderers in a strange country, and could not live happily away from our fatherland, and that we felt wretched in our wanderings, and wishing to put an end to our misery, determined to return home. We find, however, that we must make use of some mode of conveyance, either by land or water, in order to reach that fatherland where our enjoyment is to commence. But the beauty of the country through which we pass, and the very pleasure of the motion,

charm our hearts, and turning these things which we ought to
use into objects of enjoyment, we become unwilling to
hasten the end of the journey, and becoming engrossed in
a factitious delight, our thoughts are diverted from that
home whose delights would make us truly happy. Such is a
picture of our condition in this life of mortality.[9]

Comparing St Augustine's metaphor of the life-journey with that of
the shipwreck in its modern intonation, one perceives a series of
diametrical oppositions. First of all, according to this classic
Christian statement of the topos, if we fail to survive the journey, the
cause must lie entirely with us. In contrast, what I have termed the
modern or post-Christian version of the shipwreck situation makes
the situation of sea disaster the responsibility of external forces.
Furthermore, although the journey of life presents man exiled from
God and his heavenly home, he yet voyages with some sort of divine
sponsorship, if he can only recognize that fact. At the very least, man
is driven by the needs of his human nature to return to God. The
shipwreck, however, presents man deprived of such a nurturing, if
unseen divine presence, for he is completely isolated, and, as
Wallace Stevens states in 'Sunday Morning', 'unsponsored, free'.
Moreover, whereas the Christian voyage topos obviously possesses a
clear goal or teleology, the shipwreck is unmotivated and unmeaning.
In part, its very randomness makes it so terrifying and disorienting.
Similarly, whereas the Christian conception of life as a journey
consists in movement towards that clear goal, the shipwreck consists
in the interruption of movement, the breaking of a progress.
Consequently, whereas the Christian life-journey emphasizes
meaningful continuity, connection, and duration, the shipwreck
communicates an experience of discontinuity, for the shipwrecked
voyager, like the inhabitant of Pompeii or that Alpine cottage, is
suddenly cut off from his past and thrust into a terrifying new
existence.[10] Finally, whereas the Christian voyager belongs to the
community of fellow believers, a community of which God is the
centre, the shipwrecked voyager finds himself in a condition of
essential isolation and helplessness.

Both the Christian conception of a journey of life and the post-
Christian one of shipwreck function much in the manner of what
Thomas S. Kuhn calls scientific paradigms.[11] Like these paradigms,

they impose a sense of order upon the formlessness and sheer multiplicity of existence in this world. Furthermore, like such paradigms, such images or metaphors have major cultural values for those who accept them, since they become the 'ordinary' or dominant way of considering reality. They also become, of course, a chief means of communicating that way of considering reality. A scientific paradigm has the important function of sealing off certain areas of dispute and thus allowing scientists to go about their main endeavour, which, says Kuhn, is solving problems of a particular sort. Both the journey of life and the shipwreck again work in the same way, for by proffering a ready-made interpretation of the human condition, they effectively seal off areas of dispute to permit other kinds of thought and action to flourish.

If both the Christian conception of the journey of life and the modern vision of shipwreck function so efficiently and satisfyingly, one wonders how one could have developed from the other. In particular, since Christian uses of the shipwreck take it to be test, education, or punishment, one wonders how the modern intonation of the ancient topos could have acquired this very different structure and significance. Erwin Panofsky's explanation of how medieval artists developed new types, motifs, and images from classical ones provides us with a valuable clue. According to him,

> As a rule such re-interpretations were facilitated or even
> suggested by a certain iconographical affinity, for instance
> when the figure of Orpheus was employed for the represen-
> tation of David, or when the type of Hercules dragging
> Cerberus out of Hades was used to depict Christ pulling Adam
> out of Limbo. But there are cases in which the relationship
> between the classical prototype and its Christian adaptation is a
> purely compositional one.[12]

In other words, when a certain visual structure created for a certain purpose fulfils requirements for another application, medieval artists adapted it to their own ends. Sometimes obvious intellectual or symbolic affinities prompted such transference of visual patterns from one application to another, but in other instances the presence of an available image was enough to prompt such adaptation. Such a process has much in common with Darwinian conceptions of biological adaption and natural selection, for in each case a structure (physical or visual) develops, and once developed proves to have a function. Since it thus has a function, it becomes reproduced and hence more prevalent. Of course, whereas biological structures evolve through genetic variation, these artistic and intellectual ones first develop for one purpose or within one context which then disappears. None the less, considered from the vantage-point of the application of an existing structure and not its genesis, the processes are strikingly similar.

Returning to the question of how one paradigm or cultural code could have evolved into another, we can now suggest a mechanism. As St Augustine's eloquent presentation of the Christian vision of the life-journey makes clear, this paradigm always allows for the possibility that the voyager will fail. The human being travelling back to his heavenly home can become so enthralled by the pleasures of the journey that he may lose sight of his eventual goal. Moreover, as the stories of Jonah and the Deluge, as well as countless later hymns, also make clear, God can punish man with shipwreck and death by water. These failed voyages and shipwrecks, unlike what I have termed the post-Christian ones, are presented from a divine perspective – from the vantage-point, that is, of a present God. In fact, however terrifying earlier shipwreck images may have been, they always come assimilated to the basic structure of the divinely sponsored, continuous, meaningful pilgrimage to God. None the less, like many other situations and structures originally formulated within a religious context, such as the Pisgah sight, this one of shipwreck possessed an entire range of potentially ironic or ultimately subversive features.[13] As long as this situation was only associated closely with the journey-of-life topos, none of these features could develop, but once the shipwreck moved out of the shadow of the previously dominant structure, authors and artists began to make use of those elements of it that are diametrically opposed to the original paradigm. Thus, a structure first arises within a particular context, and from the vantage-point of those who no longer accept that context it appears empty and ready to be filled with new ideas and feelings, or else unemployed and ready to be used in some new way. Such a mechanism not only permits the student of iconology and culture to observe the gradual changes that lead eventually to radical departures from a point of origin or oppositions to it, it also has the crucial virtue of necessarily avoiding any sort of teleology or smuggled-in hindsight that would turn history into a prerecorded tale known only to the critic.

Having thus observed the way that the shipwreck metaphor or paradigm evolved from its diametrical opposite, the Christian vision of a journey to God, we can now examine a related situation of crisis, that of mariners on a drifting hulk or castaways on a desert island. After Poe's narrator in 'MS. Found in a Bottle' recovers from the state of shock and hopelessness that first afflicted him when the ocean crashed into his ship, he realizes that he and his companion, the old Swede, have been spared immediate death but will almost certainly have to endure a lingering one. The two men, in other words, remain trapped in a situation of peril and crisis but one different from that experienced in the moment of shipwreck:

> The main fury of the blast had already blown over, and we apprehended little danger from the violence of the wind; but we looked forward to its total cessation with dismay; well believing, that in our shattered condition, we should inevitably perish in the tremendous swell which should ensue. But this very just apprehension seemed by no means likely to be soon verified. For five entire days and nights . . . the hulk flew at a rate defying computation, before rapidly succeeding flaws of wind . . . more terrific than any tempest I had before encountered. . . . We awaited in vain for the arrival of the sixth day – that day to me has not yet arrived – to the Swede never did arrive. Thenceforward we were enshrouded in pitchy darkness, so that we could not have seen an object at twenty paces from the ship. Eternal night continued to envelop us . . . . We neglected all care of the ship, as worse than useless, and securing ourselves as well as possible, to the stump of the mizzen-mast, looked out bitterly into the world of ocean. We had no means of calculating time, nor could we form any guess of our situation. . . . In the meanwhile every moment threatened to be our last. . . . I could not help feeling the utter hopelessness of hope itself.

In contrast to the situations of shipwreck, avalanche, or the other versions of crisis one encounters in George Stubbs's *Lion Attacking a Horse* (1770, Yale University Art Gallery) or Elie Delaunay's *The Plague at Rome* (1869, Louvre), this equally important paradigm is not particularly kinetic. Thus, whereas the shipwreck and analogous forms of the situation of crisis present the instant at which powerful forces first impinge upon the victim, this situation has an essentially different structure. The men on the drifting hulk, like those in the analogous situations of being trapped on a desert island, lost in a labyrinth, or shut in prison, are held in, contained, circumscribed by forces that block their aims and constrain free action.[14] This basically static situation obviously bears a less intense emotional charge than the situations of sudden crisis, such as shipwreck. This paradigm (or what Paul Ricoeur terms a 'schema of existence')[15] appears in a Christian or traditional form far less commonly than does that of the shipwreck, and its primary meaning seems to be as an image of primal isolation – of isolation from both God and other human beings. Its relation to the Christian topos of the life-journey, like that of the shipwreck, takes the form of diametrical opposition, but the chief emphasis falls, not upon the cataclysmic interruption of the voyage, but upon simple cessation of movement and consequent deprivation. Poe's application of this paradigm in 'MS. Found in a Bottle' both traps the survivors on the floating hulk, thus threatening their lives, and also deprives them of freedom, food, and even light and a sense of time passing. The significance of the shipwreck and castaway paradigms, then, is that by transforming the Christian metaphor of the life-voyage, they provided a superbly appropriate analogy to the way many men and women experienced their world these past two centuries. The full explanation for this changed use of basic cultural paradigms during this period would require something very like a complete history of recent Western civilization. Although such a history clearly lies beyond the bounds of this study and the capabilities of its author, let me tempt the charge of rashness by suggesting a few of the more central factors that have called this imaginative landscape into being.

The crisis of Christianity and its drawn out death-struggles over the past few centuries certainly provide the chief reason why these two paradigms became important. The medieval historian Lynn White has proposed (during a seminar at the Society for the Humanities, Cornell University, in autumn 1969) that in the future when students of history find the periods into which we divide the years since the Middle Ages increasingly cumbersome and increasingly unsatisfactory, they will call the centuries from the sixth to the twentieth the 'Christian Ages'; for during this time the beliefs of Christianity, which were generally accepted as divine revelation, formed and informed the morality, philosophy, science, economics, and politics of the West. In thus suggesting the sixth and twentieth centuries as outer limits of the Christian Ages, Professor White sets his boundaries as wide as possible, for, as R. H. Tawney has shown in *Religion and the Rise of Capitalism* (1926), the unified view of God and man which typified the Middle Ages had already begun to disappear with the Reformation and the rise of Protestantism, capitalism, and nationalism. And one should add that as early as the seventeenth century, the ideas of Descartes, Hobbes, and Locke were beginning to erode the philosophical bases of Christianity, a process continued by the philosophes, the emotionalist moral philosophers of the Scottish school, and the sciences of geology and biology. At the same time that older conceptions of man's place in a hierarchically ordered universe began to weaken, new models of the human mind, new attitudes towards society, and new conceptions of politics wore away at Christian belief. With the French Revolution, perhaps the central event of modern history, the imaginative landscape of Europe, now politicized in an entirely new way, had changed for ever. Then, in the next century Darwinian theories of natural selection, the new philology, and German Higher Criticism further undercut belief in the literal truth of the Scriptures and their relevance to contemporary life, as did the writings of Marx and Freud.

By claiming that the increasing secularization of America, Britain, and Europe caused the genesis and subsequent popularity of these new paradigms or non-religious schemes of existence, I do not mean either that Christianity completely disappears from Western civilization at a particular date or that the student of culture can easily recapture the imaginative tone of individual minds with casual references to secularization. In fact, although Western thought becomes increasingly more secular between the late Middle Ages and the present – which is to say that non-Christian or anti-Christian cultural codes and ideas become increasingly more important – that change is especially difficult to chart. One reason for such difficulty lies in the fact that until quite recently secularization rarely took the form of the abandonment of Christian positions and their replacement by explicitly non-Christian ones. Furthermore, major instances of religion's loss of previous ideological dominance frequently appear to the agents involved as necessary combinations of retreat and advance. For example, every time a group of independent Christians has abandoned what had once been a fundamental doctrine or attitude, its members have announced that they were abandoning false belief as a way of purifying Christianity. Thus, the American Unitarians abandoned the divinity of Christ, the Broad Church Anglicans the literal truth of the Bible, and the seventeenth-century Calvinists earlier prohibitions against usury. Similarly, to Evangelical Protestants of all denominations their de-emphasis or even complete abandonment of church tradition and church hierarchy, like their emphasis upon subjective emotional states, seemed – and to many still seems – to signify the advance, rather than the retreat, of faith in everyday life. None the less, one can justifiably argue on two grounds that such changes in the Christian religion constitute evidence of progressive secularization in Western society. First, they in fact opposed earlier forms of Christian belief that had more completely permeated Western culture. There can be no doubt that during the past several centuries, Christianity, which once so completely dominated European thought, has played an increasingly smaller role in political ideology and action, economic theory, and the arts; and any form of Christianity, such as funda-mentalist Protestantism, which supports such lessening influence, *de facto* contributes to secularization. Second, when viewed at a distance, most of these changes obviously appear as signs of Christianity's lessening power and influence because they did not in fact fulfil their early claim to revivify Christian belief and thence restore it to its earlier position of pre-eminence. After all, had *Essays and Reviews* (1860), Bishop Colenso's *The Pentateuch and the Book and Joshua Critically Examined* (1862), and Broad Church abandonment of earlier belief in Verbal inspiration actually created a major and long-lasting religious revival, then one would have to grant that their narrowing of traditional bases of religious faith successfully produced a new stage of Christianity, equal in influence and power to that of the Middle Ages. As one who has devoted considerable attention to the generally unrecognized major role that scriptural interpretation had upon Victorian culture, I am the last to claim that Christianity completely lost its power over men's minds in the last century. On the other hand, I am also forced to recognize that, despite apparent anomalies like Victorian typology, the broad history of Christianity during the past two centuries is one of sporadic advances amid general retreat and even surrender.

A further difficulty in charting the de-Christianization of Western thought lies in the fact that secularization has often taken the path of adapting religious forms to new uses. Indeed, as M. H. Abrams has so convincingly demonstrated in *Natural Supernaturalism* (1971), the defining characteristic of German and British Romanticism consists precisely in such transference of the most detailed patterns of religious thought to secular purposes. Conceptions of history, prophecy, symbolism, interpretation, inspiration as well as those of redemption and apocalypse all were adapted to systems of thought in which the mind of man or some other entity replaced that of God. According to Abrams,

> The tendency in innovative Romantic thought (manifested in proportion as the thinker is or is not a Christian theist) is greatly to diminish, and at the extreme to eliminate, the role of God, leaving as the prime agencies man and the world, mind and nature, the ego and the non-ego, and self and the not-self, spirit and the other, or (in the favorite antithesis of post-Kantian philosophers) subject and object. . . . The notable fact, however, is that this metaphysical process does not delete but simply assimilates the traditional powers and actions of God, as well as the overall pattern of Christian history. . . . In this grandiose enterprise, however, it is the subject, mind or spirit which is primary and takes over the initiative and functions which had once been the prerogatives of deity.[16]

Attempting, in the absence of God, to employ a structure or paradigm originally based upon the coming together of man and his maker has certain obvious difficulties, the most basic of which is that one party, and that the least able, now has to do all the work. Abrams's description of the grandiose enterprise of British and German Romanticism again demonstrates how codes, paradigms, or structures originally developed as part of orthodox Christian belief then became applied to a secular programme; and one may add that when nineteenth-century thinkers perceived that limited time-bound, relatively helpless humanity could not in fact assume the power and glory of a deity, then the ironic and subversive capacities of the originally Christian paradigms became particularly compelling.

Although the modern or post-Christian versions of the situation of crisis become increasingly important during the nineteenth century, they never become completely dominant – at least not in the sense that medieval Christianity and its codes became dominant enough to triumph completely over classical pagan thought, however much of it it subsumed, assimilated, or reinterpreted. In fact, as the interpretation of any single metaphor or situation of crisis will suggest, for the past two centuries we have existed in the face of competing code systems. For example, whereas some literary and artistic interpretations of the destruction of Pompeii present it as an instance of essentially inexplicable catastrophe, others, such as Bulwer-Lytton's novel and Summer Lincoln Fairfax's poem *The Last Night of Pompeii* (1832), employ it as an instance of God's vengeance upon sinners. Similarly, some paintings and poems employ the shipwreck to communicate the post-Christian sense of existence in a Godless universe while others do so to communicate traditional beliefs about divine punishment of the guilty. As we shall observe in the next chapter, what is particularly interesting about the position of any particular paradigm in this situation of competing codes is that its users can emphasize this radical ambiguity; that is, taking the shipwreck as an initially opaque or uninterpretable event, writers like Coleridge, Tennyson, and Hopkins intentionally employ its capacity to move the reader back and forth between opposing cultural codes and the imaginative universes they create. The most orthodox employment of the journey of life can be transformed into a new metaphor of isolation and helplessness, and, conversely, an image of shipwreck that first appears to present the speaker in a Godless universe can, with equal suddenness, be converted into reassurances of divine presence. As Tennyson puts it, a wandering, helmless bark may turn out to be, after all, an ark of grace and deliverance. For these and many other authors, then, paradigmatic imagery and structure, like the human condition it is supposed to help us understand, may first appear in the guise of ambiguous revelations. Matthew Arnold, following Carlyle's 'Characteristics', describes modern man as

> Wandering between two worlds, one dead,
> The other powerless to be born.
> ['Stanzas from the Grande Chartreuse']

In fact, the situation of so many men and women of the past two hundred years is better described as having to choose between two fully developed codes and the imaginative worlds they create. Once again, the condition of artist, writer, and audience faced with having to choose between alternative applications (or meanings) of such situations and structures of crisis has much in common with that of the scientist during a period of scientific upheaval. According to Kuhn,

> The transition from a paradigm in crisis to a new one from which a new tradition of normal science can emerge is far from a cumulative process, one achieved by articulation or extension of the old paradigm. Rather it is a reconstruction of the field from new fundamentals, a reconstruction that changes some of the field's most elementary theoretical generalizations as well as many of its paradigm methods and applications. . . . Others who have noted this aspect of scientific advance have emphasized its similarity to a change in visual gestalt: the marks on paper that were first seen as a bird are now seen as an antelope, or vice versa. . . . Just because it is a transition between incommensurables, the transition between competing paradigms cannot be made a step at a time, forced by logic and neutral experience. Like the gestalt switch, it must occur all at once (though not necessarily in an instant) or not at all. . . . The transfer of allegiance from paradigm to paradigm is a conversion experience that cannot be forced.[17]

Kuhn's description of what takes place during scientific revolutions well describes what occurs during spiritual, religious, or philosophical ones as well. His pointing out that a conversion takes place when a person exchanges paradigms certainly matches what we have observed when people lose or acquire religious faith. Since, however, the paradigms (or paradigmatic structures and metaphors) at which we have been looking are also cultural codes, they have the capacity to reproduce the basic experience of conversion. By employing such an essentially problematic situation, the artist and writer can remind us that one assigns values to it only by declaring allegiance to a particular cultural code and conception of the human condition. Prompting the audience thus to assign a value or spiritual interpretation to a problematic situation – be it a shipwreck, the invasion of Rome, or the destruction of Pompeii – also leads its members to undergo something roughly analogous to a religious conversion, the difference between this artistic conversion and a real-life one being that here the audience assigns value upon discovering which paradigm the author has accepted and not the one that they would have chosen.

By now the reader will have observed that in the preceding pages I have used a variety of terms, including 'situation', 'figure', 'analogy', 'structure', and 'paradigm', to refer to what are often called images, and now is the time to explain the reasons for employing such a diverse vocabulary and the advantages it has for the student of iconology. The prime reason for avoiding the term 'image' is that, like so many critical terms, it is essentially an analogy and therefore often potentially misleading.[18] Turner's *Cottage Destroyed by an Avalanche* (Pl. 1) and Martin's *The Destruction of Pompeii and Herculaneum* (Pl. 2), which are paintings, provide examples of literal images or visual representations. The scene at which we have looked from Poe's 'MS. Found in a Bottle' does not; and furthermore, since it does not function in any obvious manner as an analogy, metaphor, or figuration, we cannot usefully employ the terms 'image' or 'imagery' in their accepted senses as referring to figurative language. According to the section on imagery in the *Princeton Encyclopedia of Poetry and Poetics,* the term is used in criticism to mean (1) mental images; (2) figures of speech; and (3) imagery and image patterns as embodiments of symbolic vision or of non-discursive truth. Although there is obviously some sort of major relation between the shipwreck passage in Poe, the analogy in Sikelianos's 'The Sacred Way', and Dahl's *Shipwreck on the Coast of Norway* (Pl. 4), the terms 'image' and 'imagery' taken in any of these meanings will not help us investigate it. Each of these three works does, however, employ or depict the same *situation*, and therefore I have used this term as most clearly and efficiently communicating that fact. Furthermore, the situations in Turner's *Cottage Destroyed by an Avalanche,* Dahl's *Shipwreck on the Coast of Norway*, and Martin's *The Destruction of Pompeii and Herculaneum,* which are paintings, share with the situation in Bulwer-Lytton's *The Last Days of Pompeii*, which is a literary work, a common *structure*, or what Ruskin would have called an 'idea of intellectual relation'. This term has the important virtue of permitting the student of iconology to perceive common elements in both different arts and different situations. Furthermore, the conception of structure, which emphasizes the elements and relations that constitute a situation, also permits the student of iconology to trace the genesis and development of such situations. Many, though not all, of these situations function as tropes, which is to say that they serve as metaphors, analogies, synecdoches or other figurations, and to do so they may take the form of similes or metaphors, or some signal in text or painting can prompt the audience to interpret the situation as such. In addition, certain of these troped situations, ones employed symbolically or metaphorically, also function as *paradigms* to organize, focus, and communicate a society's ideas and attitudes about a range of culturally significant subjects, such as man's relation to God and eternity, the nature of work, politics, and sexuality, and so on. When discussing their capacity to organize thoughts and feelings about such subjects, I have generally employed the term 'paradigm,' though when concentrating on their communicative function, I have often emphasized their role as *codes*. Of course, in different contexts the shipwreck can function as a structure, analogy, metaphor, paradigm, or code: or rather, the shipwreck, which always possesses a definable, describable structure, may also function as a figuration, which may or may not be paradigmatic.

Since the shipwreck has had such a long and rich history in Western culture, I have chosen to use it as a test case in the following chapter, which will offer additional schema and hypotheses for examining figurative and non-figurative situations in narrative, lyric, and other forms. Since, as we have already observed, such situations can be profitably studied as equivalents to other ones, the third chapter will offer examples of different kinds of relations and equivalencies. Finally, the concluding chapter will examine the kind of relationships that such situations have to other aspects of literary form, including point of view, lyric organization, and narrative structure. However, before proceeding to set forth a typology of shipwreck and related situations, which will be the concern of the next chapter, I wish to suggest more precisely than I have done thus far the range of subjects included in a complete iconological approach. A useful place to begin such a survey is an autobiographical account of shipwreck that Poe scholars have suggested as a possible basis for his fictional ones. According to Captain Aubin, whose sloop *Betsy* sank off the coast of Dutch Guiana on 5 August 1756, the disaster came without warning as he and his mate were relaxing on deck:

The vessel suddenly turned with her broadside to windward:
I called to one of the seamen to put the helm a weather, but

he replied that it had been so for some time. . . . At this
moment the vessel swung around with her head to the sea,
and plunged; her head filled in such a manner that she could
not rise above the surf, which broke over us to the height of
the anchor stocks, and we were presently up to our necks
in water; every thing in the cabin was washed away. Some of
the crew, which consisted of nine men, were drowned in
their hammocks, without a cry or groan.[19]

Like the shipwreck scene in 'MS. Found in a Bottle', Captain Aubin's
takes the form of a narrative of fact, but whereas Captain Aubin was
engaged to record an event that had actually happened to him, Poe's
narrator only follows fictional convention. Neither shipwreck
narrative, however, takes the event as a paradigmatic one. As in so
many cases of actual disaster, the traumatic event so impressed itself
upon the survivor's imagination that the event remains uninterpreted
and essentially opaque.

None the less, no matter how opaque an event or situation in
narrative may at first appear, the very fact that it appears within a
narrative provides it with some sort of figurative status or function.
At the very least, if a narrator presents an event as totally opaque,
mysterious, or without meaning, it thereby becomes representative
of that class of events which are totally opaque, mysterious, and
without meaning. Of course, the narrative situation that we label
uninterpreted and uninterpretable lacks only a particular kind of
meaning. Captain Aubin's tale, for example, tells us about the
dangers of the sea, the way even good seamanship could not save
him, and the fact that he finally did survive. Furthermore, in a later
part of his story we learn that the Carib Indians treated him with
great kindness and that some of their herbs saved his life. The actual
situation of shipwreck, however, remains uninterpreted in spiritual
terms. Neither Poe's narrator nor Aubin perceives any spiritual
meaning in his experience, for he does not take it as a paradigmatic
event. Shipwreck narratives, religious records of deliverance at sea,
Bible commentaries, and hymns had long taught believers to
perceive such situations in religious terms, that is, as part of a
religious code; and several decades after Aubin's experience writers
began to use the situation as part of an explicitly non-Christian code.
But neither the narrator of a 'MS. Found in a Bottle' nor Captain
Aubin sees the relevance of any such cultural code to his situation.

In contrast, Tennyson's 'The Wreck' exemplifies a literary employment of the shipwreck in which the narrator perceives it to be paradigmatic. The heroine of Tennyson's poem describes the identical situation we have already observed in narratives by Poe and Aubin, for she also emphasizes that instant

> the ship staggered under a thunderous shock
> That shook us asunder, as if she had struck and crashed on a rock;
> For the huge sea smote every soul from the decks of The Falcon
> but one;
> All of them, all but the man that was lash'd to the helm had gone.
> [11. 106–9]

Unlike Poe's narrator, the speaker in this dramatic monologue explicitly makes the sea disaster a metaphor for her life:

> My brain is full of the crash of wrecks, and the roar of waves,
> My life is itself a wreck, I have sullied a noble name,
> I am flung from the rushing tide of the world as a waif of shame.
> [11. 4–6]

Thus the shipwreck she experienced literally, physically, becomes metaphoric as well, and she sees it as the central moment in her life, encompassing and characterizing all. Her role in society, her child, her lover, all have vanished. She did not perish physically in the shipwreck, but everything that mattered to her died then, and she sees her life in terms of this disaster. When Tennyson has her cry that her 'brain is full of the crash of wrecks, and the roar of waves,' he is using the shipwreck both as a commonplace means of conveying the experience of a mind in crisis and an equally commonplace means of summing up a life. In addition, the poet combines these uses of the situation with another conventionally employed as a figure for the fallen woman – the waif or castaway. By ringing these changes on the theme of shipwreck, Tennyson is able to make the literal sea disaster experienced by his character take on additional meanings and quickly come to appear as the centre and significance of her life.

Tennyson's 'The Wreck', which exemplifies a metaphoric use of the situation, presents it in the form of narrative. In contrast, the same poet's 'Despair', 'The Two Voices', and *In Memoriam* employ it solely as a figure, essentially condensing the narrative elements into an emblematic analogy. 'The Wreck' uses the situation as a paradigm of divine punishment, 'Despair' as one of post-Christian spiritual hopelessness, and 'The Two Voices' and *In Memoriam* as a transformational paradigm that moves the reader from the experience of one imaginative cosmos to another. Every one of these poems, however, presents the situation to communicate the experience of a first-person narrator. Matthew Arnold's 'A Summer Night', on the other hand, employs it to generalize about the human condition. Realizing that 'most men in a brazen prison live' and languidly give their lives to 'unmeaning taskwork', he has a vision of the fate of the few who

> Escape their prison and depart
> On the wide ocean of life anew.
> There the freed prisoner, where'er his heart
> Listeth, will sail;
> Nor doth he know how there prevail,
> Despotic on that sea,
> Trade-winds which cross it from eternity.
> Awhile he holds some false way, undebarred
> By thwarting signs, and braves
> The freshening wind and blackening waves.
> And then the tempest strikes him; and between
> The lightning-bursts is seen
> Only a driving wreck,
> And the pale master on his spar-strewn deck
> With anguished face and flying hair
> Grasping the rudder hard,
> Still bent to make some port he knows not where,
> Still standing for some false, impossible shore.
> And sterner comes the roar
> Of sea and wind, and through the deepening gloom
> Fainter and fainter wreck and helmsman loom,
> And he too disappears, and comes no more.
>
> [11.51–72]

In addition to such explicit deployments of the shipwreck situation as paradigm, art and literature also make use of subtle forms of allusion. For example, at the beginning of Charlotte Brontë's *Jane Eyre,* the lonely orphan child finds herself unloved, isolated, threatened, and deprived in the Reed household. She exists, in other words, in a situation analogous to that of the shipwrecked mariner. Stendhal, at the opening of the twenty-seventh chapter of *The Red and the Black,* describes the similar isolation of Julien Sorel at the seminary by pointing out that 'he was alone like a boat abandoned in the midst of the ocean'. Brontë makes the same point with more subtlety when she has Jane describe the way she used to hide in the window-seat and read Bewick's *History of British Birds*. She read with fascination descriptions of arctic bleakness and found herself drawn to Bewick's vignettes of the 'rock standing up alone in a sea of billow and spray; to the broken boat stranded on a desolate coast; to the cold and ghastly moon glancing through bars of cloud at a wreck just sinking'. The reader who is aware of some of the usual significance of such scenes of shipwreck soon perceives that those at which Jane is looking function as analogues for her condition. Much in the manner of Tennyson's 'Mariana', *Jane Eyre* here expressionistically makes the objects described by a narrator – here literally images – communicate that narrator's inner world.

CHAPTER TWO

SHIPWRECKS AND CASTAWAYS

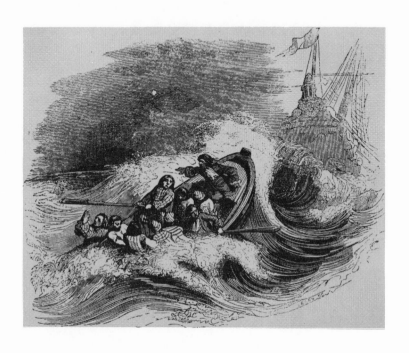

A typology of shipwrecks and imperilled mariners

The Bororo myth, which I shall refer to from now on as the key myth, is, as I shall try to show, simply a transformation, to a greater or a lesser extent, of other myths originating either in the same society or in neighboring or remote societies. I could, therefore, have legitimately taken as my starting point any one representative myth of the group.

A myth may well contradict the ethnographic reality to which it is supposed to refer, and the distortion nevertheless forms part of its structure. Or it may be the case that the myth perpetuates the memory of customs that have disappeared or still persist in another part of the tribal territory.

> Claude Lévi-Strauss, *The Raw and the Cooked:*
> *Introduction to a Science of Mythology: I,*
> trans. John and Doreen Weightman

From the very start, Lévi-Strauss recognizes that the Bororo myth which he employs in the book as the 'reference myth' does not merit this name and this treatment. The name is specious and the use of the myth improper. This myth deserves no more than any other its referential privilege. . . . There is no unity or absolute source of the myth. The focus or the source of the myth are always shadows and virtualities which are elusive, unactualizable, and nonexistent in the first place. Everything begins with structure, configuration, or relationship.

> Jacques Derrida, 'Structure, Sign and Play
> in the Discourse of the Human Sciences', *Writing*
> *and Difference,* trans. Alan Bass

The moment of actual shipwreck is not the only form in which the situation of the imperilled mariner appears. There is, first of all, the moment when the sailor realizes that he is lost and can obtain no bearings. Then, after he has drifted hopelessly, there comes the instant his ship crashes upon a rock or is overwhelmed by raging seas; and this is followed by the moment the mariner strikes the water, a swimmer in the waste, cold ocean. Last comes the time when he drags himself ashore only to find himself on a hostile desert island.

This typology, which proceeds by arranging different situations and structures to make up a hypothetical master narrative, can be illustrated by many nineteenth- and twentieth-century paintings. Thus, Winslow Homer's *Lost on the Grand Banks* (1885, John S. Broome Coll.), which portrays several figures in a dory peering anxiously through the gray world surrounding them, exemplifies the first stage, while his *Gulf Stream* (1899, Metropolitan Museum of Art, Pl. 6) depicts a drifting, damaged vessel about to be destroyed by final disaster, which we see approaching in the form of a waterspout. John Sell Cotman's *Dismasted Brig* (c. 1823, British Museum) offers another variation on this theme: the painter presents his stricken ship, which has already lost one of its masts, in profile against an enormous iceberg that dwarfs it, and Delacroix's *Shipwreck on the Coast* (c. 1862),[1] carried a vessel even closer to final disaster, showing it after it has become completely dismasted and nothing more than a drifting hulk – a situation presented with even more power in Clarkson Stanfield's *The Abandoned* (1856, location unknown).[2] The Scandinavian artist J. C. C. Dahl takes us one step farther, as it were; his *Shipwreck on the Norwegian Coast* (1832, National Gallery, Oslo) presents a dismasted vessel which smashes itself against a rocky coast that curves round the left side of the canvas. Dark, stormy skies look down upon the disaster, creating a powerful image of the ways the sea and the heavens crush man's ships and his hopes. This situation of the ship destroyed against the coast is always laden with irony because it demonstrates how even the approach to land, which should be an approach to safety, can cause final destruction. Variations upon this very popular pictorial subject appear in George Morland's undated *Shipwreck* (private coll.) and identically entitled works by Francis Danby (1843, James White Coll., Dublin) and Eugène Isabey (n.d., Museum of Art, Rhode Island School of Design), Homer's *Wrecked Schooner* (c. 1903, St Louis Art Museum, Pl. 7), and Turner's *Wreck of a Transport Ship* (c. 1810, Gulbenkian Foundation, Lisbon). This last painter's *Shipwreck* (1805, Tate Gallery, Pl. 8) moves the victims farther out to sea but still in sight of land, while his *Fire at*

Sea (*c.* 1835, Tate Gallery) portrays the disaster on the open, empty ocean. Clarkson Stanfield's *Wreck of the 'Avenger'* (n.d., Whitworth Art Gallery, Manchester, Pl. 9) depicts the stricken vessel, which fills most of the canvas, from the stern as it heels at forty-five degrees in raging wind and seas. Beneath dark skies streaked by lightning the crew scrambles to secure hold on the port rail to keep from being carried overboard. A mast and other wreckage already float free, and we know it will not be long before the ship goes down. John Brett's *Shipwreck* (n.d., Bournemouth Museums) and Danby's *Shipwreck against a Setting Sun* (*c.* 1850, Paul Mellon Coll.), which also take place on the open sea, represent the next stage of maritime disaster since the sailors have already taken to the lifeboats and abandoned their doomed ships.

The next stage, that of the castaway, is represented by I. K. Aivazovskii's *The Ninth Wave* (n.d., Leningrad). Heavy fog obscures the upper portion of the scene, and in a mist-free section below we glimpse several figures hanging and sitting on the remains of a mast amid high waves. This figure of the castaway or swimmer, which is related to representations of the dying Ophelia by Millais (1852, Tate Gallery) and Delacroix (1853, Louvre),[3] also appears in Turner's *Slave Ship* (1840, Boston Museum of Fine Arts, Pl. 5) and Delacroix's *Bark of Dante* (or *Dante and Virgil*; 1822, Louvre).

Géricault's *The Raft of the 'Medusa'* (1819, Louvre, Pl. 10), one of the most important and influential images created by the Romantic imagination, provides another version of the castaway situation. Having been saved from immediate death when their vessel went down, the survivors boarded a raft and were then abandoned by the lifeboat towing them, and afterwards many of them perished from hunger, thirst, and exhaustion. Géricault has chosen to portray that instant the survivors struggled desperately but in vain to attract the attention of a passing rescue vessel. *The Raft of the 'Medusa'*, then, depicts, not the moment of the imperilled mariners' salvation, but that in which their hopes were crushed.[4]

A third variation upon the theme of the ironies of being saved appears in Philip de Loutherbourg's *Survivors of a Shipwreck Attacked by Robbers* (1793, Southampton Art Gallery, Pl. 11), for having escaped the dangers of nature the victims are destroyed by their fellow men.[5] Like de Loutherbourg's painting, Homer's *After the Hurricane* (1899, Art Institute of Chicago) presents a grimly ironic image of the castaway, the survivor of shipwreck, who has reached land but has not survived. This version of death by water thus resembles George Frederic Watts's *Found Drowned* (*c.* 1866, Walker Art Gallery, Liverpool) and Vassily Grigorievich Perov's *The Drowned Woman* (1867, Tretyakov Gallery, Moscow).

Yet another intonation of this image of man's fate appears in many nineteenth- and twentieth-century pictures of wreckage on the shore, such as James Clarke Hook's *Wreckage from the Fruiter* (n.d., Tate Gallery). Edward Wadsworth's *Requiescat* (1940, Leeds City Art Gallery, Pl. 12) portrays the aftermath of war, presenting an image of a shore strewn with the ribs of shattered boats which resemble nothing so much as the rib cages of dinosaurs and other extinct monsters. This wreckage and those shattered hulks are all that remain of life's journey.

One may take the German painter Caspar David Friedrich's *Sea of Ice* (or *Arctic Shipwreck*; 1823-4, Kunsthalle, Hamburg, Pl. 13) as a type of this theme in nineteenth-century painting: only the stern of the vessel remains visible among the crushing heaves of jagged ice which mark the desolation of an arctic wasteland.[6] Bits and pieces of shattered masts lie wedged in among the pyramids of ice which rise into an empty, pale-blue sky, creating a powerful emblem of life's end amid the failure of hope, of hope crushed by destiny and the forces of nature. All is cold, dead, jagged – and the sun shines brightly on the crushed hopes of man.

This arrangement of these various situations of maritime disaster to form a hypothetical master narrative is a useful critical tool for the iconologist, for it permits him to relate widely differing situations to one another. Furthermore, by treating them as discrete stages, he preserves the individuality and uniqueness of each particular situation. Such a procedure, in other words, permits one both to perceive the general relation of individual situations and structures to some overall paradigm and then, once this general relation has been perceived, it then encourages one to discriminate carefully among the various forms or stages in which the imperilled mariner appears. By thus placing various situations in this kind of narrative progression, I do not mean to imply that artists and authors who employed them regarded their images, metaphors, and subjects in this manner. My arrangement, in other words, is hypothetical – a research tool that promises to allow and even encourage the student of iconology to study such matters more efficiently. It certainly does not pretend to describe a nineteenth- or twentieth-century planbook or handlist of tropes and subjects.

The principle of transformation, which underlies all my attempts to relate various situations, structures, and tropes, here takes a chronological (or diachronic) form, whereas when I tried to demonstrate a common structure underlying the very different situations experienced by the victims of shipwreck, avalanche, and Etna, the transformation appeared in a non-chronological (or what structuralists somewhat misleadingly call a synchronic) form. The principle of transformation, moreover, also appears in this second form when one relates any individual stage of maritime disaster to the main cultural paradigm, which in this case is the Christian conception of life as a journey. Each individual form of the situation of maritime disaster exists as a transformation – specifically, an inversion and denial – of the entire Christian paradigm, but it also frequently turns out to be a transformation of a stage, or sub-paradigm, of the Christian journey of life. For example, as I shall demonstrate in the following pages, the post-Christian situation of the lost and drifting mariner and vessel serves as precisely such a transformation of the commonplace Christian metaphors of Christ guiding one's vessel. Similarly, the moment when the voyager's destination disappears transforms the entire Christian notion of a purposeful journey or pilgrimage.

The reality of shipwreck

The terrific storms of the preceding twelve months have been productive of the most unprecedented disasters in the seas and on the shores of the United Kingdom. A terrible record of shipwreck and loss of life will be found in the 'Board of Trade Wreck Register.' This states that the increase in these disasters is mainly to be traced to the very heavy storms of October 25 and 26, and of October 31 and November 1 and 2 last. In the former gale there were 133 total wrecks and 90 casualties, resulting in serious damage, and 798 lives were lost. This number, however, includes the loss of 446 lives in the *Royal Charter,* which will always be remembered as one of the most melancholy shipwrecks that ever occurred on British shores. . . . It appears that in one voyage out of 175 voyages made by British ships employed in the overseas-trade a casualty has happened, while in only one voyage out of 335 has a casualty happened to a foreign ship similarly employed. . . . It appears that, exclusive of passengers, there were 10,538 persons on board these 1416 wrecks, and that of these 3977 were actually imperilled, and 2332 have been saved from a watery grave by life-boats and other craft; the remainder 1645 having unhappily been drowned.

'The Wreck Register of 1859', *Illustrated London News,*
20 October 1860

41

Although 1859 may have been a particularly perilous year for British sailors, shipwreck was an ever-present threat to sailors of all nations. As anyone who has visited the maritime museums of old and New England can attest, disaster in mid-ocean or upon a coast ended the careers of an astonishingly high percentage of nineteenth- and twentieth-century vessels. Looking at a sampling of well-known ships from this period, one observes how many were lost at sea. For example, the *Benjamin W. Latham,* a particularly handsome Grand Banks fishing vessel built in 1902, foundered at an advanced age off the coast of San Juan in 1943; the Gloucester, Massachusetts, fishing schooner *Elsie* was built in 1910 and sank in the Gulf of St Lawrence in 1935; the New York pilot boat *Phantom* was built in 1868 and was lost with six crew members when driven upon the New Jersey shore during the blizzard of 1888; the steam-paddle cutter *Harriet Lane* of New York, which was built in 1857, foundered in 1884 off Pernambuco; and the American revenue cutter *Roger B. Taney,* which was built in 1833, was destroyed by lightning near Savannah, Georgia, in 1857.

Such sea disasters occurred frequently enough during the past two centuries that many artistic and literary figures not only could have encountered them in newspaper accounts and other published shipwreck narratives but also could have been acquainted with them more intimately. In fact, many artistic and literary figures had experienced shipwreck at first hand, had observed them taking place or had friends or family who perished in them. William Falconer, whose poem in three cantos, *The Shipwreck* (1762), did much to popularize the subject, himself drowned at sea, as did Shelley, whose poetry makes frequent use of such situations.[7] Stephen Crane survived shipwreck on the *Commodore* in 1897 and lived to base a newspaper article, short story, and poem upon his confrontation with a coldly indifferent nature. Margaret Fuller, the American critic and journalist, drowned in a storm off Fire Island, New York, as she was returning to America. 'She was drowned', wrote Emerson to Carlyle, 'with her husband and child on the wreck of the ship Elizabeth on the 19 July, at 3 in the P. M. after sitting all day, from morning, in plain sight of the shore'.[8] Nine years before the death of Margaret Fuller, Carlyle had interrupted a letter to Emerson when a ship met with disaster before his eyes.

– Good Heavens! Here comes my Wife, all in tears, pointing out to me a poor ship, just tumbled over on a sandbank on the

Cumberland Coast, men still said to be alive with it! – a Belfast steamer doing all it can to get in contact with it! Moments are precious (say the people on the beach), the flood runs at ten miles an hour. Thank god, the steamer's boat is out: 'eleven men,' says a person with a glass, 'are saved; it is an American timber-ship coming up without a pilot.' And now, – in ten minutes more – there lies the melancholy mass alone among the waters. [p. 307]

Joseph Conrad, whose experience of rescuing a similar endangered vessel taught him much about himself and the sea, drew upon his experience throughout his career as a novelist. As is well known, a maritime disaster similarly affected William Wordsworth, whose beloved brother John, a captain of a merchant vessel, perished with his ship on 6 February 1805.

For three months, Wordsworth stopped work on *The Prelude.* The loss of his brother is as major an event in Wordsworth's poetry as in his life. Directly due to it are the powerful lines that form Wordsworth's palinode on his gospel of Nature, the *Elegiac Stanzas,* better known as *Peele Castle.*[9]

Gerard Manley Hopkins also wrote about an actual shipwreck in *The Wreck of the Deutschland*, and, as Elizabeth Schneider has pointed out, he and his family had long shared a deep interest in sea disaster. His brother had exhibited paintings of shipwrecks and

Wrecks, it will be remembered, were a main part of the business of his father, who as head of a firm of marine average adjusters not only wrote technical works on marine insurance but, only a short time before the *Deutschland's* disaster, had published *The Port of Refuge, or Advice and Instructions to the Master-Mariner in Situations of Doubt, Difficulty, and Danger* (1873), a book practical in purpose but adorned, beyond the alliterative title, with quotations from *The Ancient Mariner.* . . . The whole family seems to have been a company of horrified amateurs of maritime disaster, too high-minded to rejoice in others' misfortune but vividly interested.[10]

Granted, shipwrecks were common enough that they provided an obvious example of dramatic disaster and crisis. The commonness or cultural availability of such events does not, however, explain why this situation should take on new meanings when employed as an analogy and paradigm. Although the physical conditions that made this situation of crisis particularly popular may have provided a *necessary* condition for its use, they could not provide a *sufficient* condition, one whose presence completely explains its cultural significance.

Thoreau's *Cape Cod*, a fugue on the theme of shipwreck, exemplifies such distinctions. This work also gives us a far better idea of the human cost of such disaster than does any 'Wreck Register' or list of foundered vessels, for although examples and statistics suggest how commonly sea voyages ended beneath the waves rather than in port, they do not convey what it was like either to experience a shipwreck or to observe its aftermath. In the first sentence of *Cape Cod* Thoreau informs us: 'Wishing to get a better view than I had yet of the ocean, which, we are told, covers more than two-thirds of the globe. . . I made a visit to Cape Cod in October, 1849, another the succeeding June, and another to Truro in July, 1855.' It immediately becomes clear that having wished to obtain this 'better view' of the sea, Thoreau does so by gazing on its victims. Arriving in Boston on 9 October 1849 on his way to the Cape, he discovers that a severe storm has delayed the boat he had planned to take to Provincetown and that the same storm took one hundred and forty-five lives at Cohasset, which then became his destination. 'The brig *St. John,* from Galway, Ireland, laden with emigrants, was wrecked on Sunday morning.' Passing the graveyard, he observes a large hole, like a cellar, being prepared for a mass burial; and arriving at the beach, Thoreau encounters the sea and its victims:

> I saw many marble feet and matted heads as the cloths were raised, and one livid, swollen and mangled body of a drowned girl, – who probably had intended to go out to service in some American family, – to which some rags still adhered, with a string, half concealed by the flesh, about its swollen neck; the coiled-up wreck of a human hulk, gashed by rocks or fishes, so that the bone and muscle were exposed, but quite bloodless, – merely red and white, – with wide-open and staring eyes, yet lustreless, dead-lights; or like cabin windows of a stranded vessel, filled with sand. Sometimes there were two or more children, or a parent and child, in the same box, and on the lid would perhaps be written with red chalk, 'Bridget such-a-one, and sister's child'.

Turning to the rubble that litters the beach, Thoreau begins to comprehend the ocean's power from the way it has shattered the brig's masts, largest timbers, and iron braces.

The wreck of the *St John* was not a unique event on these shores, Thoreau soon discovers, and it has not even disturbed the daily routine of farmers who gather seaweed to fertilize their fields, while others gather the bodies that are also cast up by the sea. Later he visits Truro where, despite the lighthouse,

> after every storm we read of one or more vessels wrecked
> there, and sometimes more than a dozen wrecks are visible
> from this point at one time. The inhabitants hear the crash
> of vessels going to pieces as they sit round their hearths, and
> they commonly date from some memorable shipwreck. ['The
> Highland Light']

These people live with the sound and memory of shipwrecks, and almost every family has lost some of its members in them. Continuing his attempt to get a 'better view' of the ocean, Thoreau catches sight of this monument:

> Sacred
> to the memory of
> 57 citizens of Truro,
> who were lost in seven
> vessels, which
> foundered at sea in
> the memorable gale
> of Oct. 3d, 1841.

Thoreau reports that the names and ages of the victims appeared on different sides of the stone, arranged by families. 'I was told that only one vessel drifted ashore on the backside of the Cape, with the boys locked into the cabin and drowned.' The homes of all these victims lay within two miles of one another. So many fishermen were lost, Thoreau adds, that the company which owned many of the boats failed for want of crews.

> But the surviving inhabitants went a-fishing again the next
> year as usual. I found it would not do to speak of shipwrecks
> here, for almost every family has lost some of its members at
> sea. 'Who lives in that house?' I inquired. 'Three widows,'
> was the reply.

Such a response prevents all dialogue, since it would be cruel to speak of the realities of shipwreck with those who have suffered so much from it.

Thoreau, however, can confront the bleak, undignified, unheroic, almost infinitely pathetic facts associated with these sea disasters because he places them in a religious context and accepts that these Irish emigrants may have perished a brief mile from shore;

> but before they could reach it, they emigrated to a newer world than ever Columbus dreamed of. . . . We have reason to thank God that they have not been 'shipwrecked into life again.' The mariner who makes the safest port in Heaven, perchance, seems to his friends on earth to be shipwrecked, for they deem Boston Harbor the better place. ['The Shipwreck']

Until Thoreau abruptly introduces this Christian reading of an actual event, the reader of his text has received no indication that such might be this shipwreck's meaning for him. By unexpectedly considering this actual disaster from the vantage-point of a well-known Christian commonplace, Thoreau manages to transform a horrifying scene of slaughter into a place of good fortune. The Christian paradigm, then, functions in the manner of a magic lens, for it permits him to show the reader an otherwise invisible world of spirit inhering in the things of this one.

Thoreau's procedure in *Cape Cod* demonstrates that any particular fact or event does not in itself possess a meaning. The meaning derives from the context of these codes that define it. At first, Thoreau's objective, even chilling descriptions of the emigrants' bodies seduces his reader into interpreting the shipwreck of the *St John* as an instance of either a meaningless event or one that reveals nature's essential indifference to man – and that of God as well. By inserting this historical event into the cultural code provided by Christian notions of the journey of life, he unexpectedly defines the event in his chosen terms. He transforms an apparently tragic voyage into a supposedly happy one.

Of course, had Thoreau not seen the victims of this particular shipwreck, he could not have written *Cape Cod* in this way. None the less, as his procedure brilliantly demonstrates, no event has its own meaning; it must receive one from a human agent, who defines it by placing it in one or another context. Thoreau's point, we recognize is that, as a seer, as a man who can see better than most in his audience, he claims to be able to interpret such matters for us better than we can do ourselves.

Turning back to some of the situations of crisis discussed earlier, we observe that the same principles obtain. For example, although Pompeii is unlikely to have become a paradigmatic event had it not been rediscovered in 1745 – contemporary accounts of its destruction by Pliny the Younger and others had not sufficed to make it one – the fact of Pompeii brought with it no one meaning. Some interpreters perceived it to be an instance of divine punishment of paganism and others took it as a slaughter of the innocents. Although certain events may prove so shocking as to lead a believer to abandon his faith, no event, in itself, can necessarily do so, for the eye of faith can always, as it has so many times, perceive any disaster as a punishment, test, or means of spiritual education.[11]

Indeed, as the following pages will demonstrate, any particular situation of crisis, whether considered primarily as an historical event or metaphor, could be interpreted as a paradigm belonging to one or two diametrically opposed codes or systems, those I have termed the Christian and the post-Christian. The Christian eye of faith claims implicitly – and often explicitly as well – that to see a shipwreck or a destroyed Pompeii as an instance of man's isolation in an indifferent universe is to suffer spiritual blindness. The sceptical post-Christian eye, in contrast, claims similarly that to take them as instances of divine justice is wilfully to blind oneself to human suffering in order to preserve a desperate belief in a non-existent world of the spirit.

The destination disappears

> La nave o proa entonces
> surgió de los desiertos,
> navegaba hacia el cielo:
> una punta de piedra dirigida
> hacia el insoportable infinito,
> una basílica cerrada
> por los dioses perdidos. . . .
> Sólo hasta allí llegó mi viaje:
> más allá empezaba la muerte.
>
> Pablo Neruda, 'La Nave'

[It was then that the ship, or a ship's prow
hove to on the desert
sailing into the sky:
a flint pinpoint aimed
at the unbearable infinite,
a basilica closed
by the perishing gods. . . .
But the voyage led me no farther:
death began in the distance.
                    'The Ship', trans. Ben Belitt]

The first problem faced by so many men and women during the past two hundred years was to locate the safe harbour, where the destination lay, or, in the words of Tennyson's prefatory sonnet to the *Nineteenth Century,* 'If any golden harbour be for men/ In seas of Death and sunless gulfs of Doubt.' Certainly, many agreed with Lamartine that 'l'homme n'a pointe de port' ('Le Lac'), or with Baudelaire that 'Singulière fortune où le but se déplace,/ Et, n'étant nulle part, peut être n'importe où!' ('Le Voyage'). Centuries before Chaucer's ideal parson might have been able to claim that he could

show yow the wey, in this viage,
Of thilke parfit glorious pilgrymage
That highte Jerusalem celestial.
                    ['Parson's Prologue', ll. 49-51]

And, of course, many writing in the last century remained confident that they knew both that a port existed and how to find it. For instance, in Longfellow's 'The Building of the Ship', the worthy pastor – 'shepherd of that wandering flock,/ That has the ocean for its wold,/ That has the vessel for its fold' – assures his parishioners that

if our souls but poise and swing
Like the compass in its brazen ring,
For ever level and true
To the toil and the task we have to do,
We shall sail securely, and safely reach
The fortunate isles.

The American sage Emerson similarly employs the ancient Christian topos confidently to convey his sense at being at home in a purposeful, coherent world. In 'Terminus', a poem that begins with the realization that he has arrived at the 'time to be old,/ To take in sail', the poet calmly rejoices that a divine presence still guides him to his goal:

> I man the rudder, reef the sail,
> Obey the voice at eve obeyed at prime:
> 'Lowly faithful, banish fear,
> Right onward drive unharmed;
> The port, well worth the cruise, is near,
> And every wave is charmed.'

Such American optimism appears across the Atlantic Ocean as well. Newman, for example, opens the fifth chapter of his *Apologia Pro Vita Sua* by describing the 'perfect peace and contentment' he had enjoyed since converting to the Roman Church in terms of the traditional comparison: 'I was not conscious of firmer faith . . . but it was like coming into port after a rough sea.' Such are the joys and real comforts of belief: confidence that a spiritual goal, be it heaven or true faith, really exists; the happy feeling that one has arrived at safe harbour or will doubtlessly do so; and, perhaps most important, the sense that God has created a nurturing universe after all.

On the other hand, when many in the last century look around them in mid-voyage, they no longer know in which direction to steer – or, indeed, if there is any direction in which one can steer. Once doubt began to wear away at the Christian beliefs that had given direction to men's lives for more than thirteen centuries, people began to find themselves in a new, puzzling, and occasionally terrifying imaginative landscape. Generally, however, the recognition that the destination of the life-journey has disappeared or been called into question does not produce the severe emotional impact that informs the shipwreck situation. Doubt, dissatisfaction, and ennui, rather than terror, characterize the literary appearances of this intonation of the journey-of-life metaphor. Similarly, one encounters a characteristic tone of worldly disillusionment, for those who speak within such situations, or employ them for objective correlatives for their spiritual condition, do not find themselves captured by panic. Thus, the questioner in Auden's 'The Voyage' is certain, even as he asks, that such journeyings have no goal, no purpose.

> alone with his heart at last, does the traveller find
> In the vaguer touch of the wind and the fickle flash of the sea
> Proofs that somewhere there exists, really, the Good Place,
> As certain as those the children find in stones and holes?

No, he discovers nothing; he does not want to arrive.
The journey is false.

The basic structure of this situation, then, is formed by a recognition that the goal, the intended end, of a pattern of movement has disappeared, and therefore the one moving loses suddenly a previous certainty about what to do. Things have lost their apparent meaning, but they have not yet begun to threaten one. One feels dissatisfied and disillusioned, but one does not feel particularly endangered. Having lost one's earlier certainty, one feels anger and resentment at being cheated out of such a comforting possession; but having thus lost this dear possession, one willingly assumes the posture of the disillusioned and the worldly-wise.

One of the corollaries of such radical disillusionment is that it tends to emphasize the less attractive conditions of the journey. For example, in George Seferis's *Mythical Story* the questioner cannot avoid a general discomfort and decay that permeates all:

> What do our souls seek journeying
> on the decks of decayed ships
> crowded with sallow women and crying infants
> unable to forget themselves, either with the flying fish
> or with the stars which the tips of the mast indicate,
> grated by gramophone records
> bound unwillingly by non-existent pilgrimages
> murmuring broken thoughts from foreign tongues?
>
> What do our souls seek journeying
> on rotten, sea-borne timbers
> from harbour to harbour?
>
> [trans. Edmund Keeley and Philip Sherrard]

Once the goal has disappeared, the journey becomes irksome and even grotesque rather than heroic. Indeed, to return to St Augustine's basic analogy which presented the pilgrim in danger of becoming an idle tourist, one may observe that those who find that the goal of the life-journey has vanished are in the positions of tourists unexpectedly finding themselves condemned to remain in countries they had wanted only to visit briefly. Having proclaimed that these alien lands were nice places to visit but one would not want to live there, they find themselves having to live there in exile. What had been picturesque, now seems sordid; what had been a condition of adventure, now seems an unending cause of boredom.

Like the structure that informs the moment of shipwreck, this one also takes various non-nautical guises. Carlyle, for example, frequently sets the suddenly destinationless life-journey in the desert as well as the ocean. A particularly common twentieth-century intonation of the basic metaphor employs the train trip, rather than the ocean voyage, as the means of conveying the imaginative world in which the goal has vanished. In Auden's 'Caliban to the Audience', from *The Sea and the Mirror: A Commentary on Shakespeare's 'The Tempest'*, that character summons all the sordid, depressing details that Seferis had employed to argue against any coherence and purpose on this train trip.

> The Journey of Life – the down-at-heels disillusioned figure can still put its characterisation across – is infinitely long and its possible destinations infinitely distant from one another, but the time spent in actual travel is infinitesimally small. The hours the traveller measures are those in which he is at rest between the three or four decisive instants of transportation which are all he needs and all he gets to carry him the whole of his way; the scenery he observes is the view, gorgeous or drab, he glimpses from platform and siding; the incidents he thrills or blushes to remember take place in waiting and washrooms, ticket queues and parcels offices: it is in those promiscuous places of random association, in that air of anticipatory fidget, that he makes friends and enemies, that he promises, confesses, kisses, and betrays until, either because it is the one he has been expecting, or because, losing his temper, he has vowed to take the first to come along, or because he has been given a free ticket, or simply by

misdirection and mistake, a train arrives which he does get into: it whistles – at least he thinks afterwards he remembers it whistling – but before he can blink, it has come to a standstill again and there he stands clutching his battered bags, surrounded by entirely strange smells and noises – yet in their smelliness and noisiness how familiar – one vast important stretch the nearer Nowhere, that still smashed terminus at which he will, in due course, be deposited, seedy and by himself.

Sea voyages have always had a kind of glamour that has generally been absent from most travel by rail, and therefore the train trip as voyage of life has appeared to many the particularly appropriate way in which to invest the old topos with a wry disillusionment.

A. D. Hope, the fine contemporary Australian poet, thus emphasizes in 'Observation Car' the element of boredom, for although, he says, he may have once found the travelling novel and even 'fun',

> now I am tired of the train. I have learned that one tree
> Is much like another, one hill the dead spit of the next
> I have seen trailing off behind all the various types of country
> Like a clock running down. I am bored and perplexed.

Not only does the terminus change or vanish, so do the other passengers in a quite maddening way, for

> The schoolgirl who goes to the Ladies' comes back to her seat
> A lollipop blonde who leads you on to assault her,
> And you've just got her skirt round her waist and her pants round
> her feet

> When you find yourself fumbling about the nightmare knees
> Of a pink hippopotamus with a permanent wave
> Who sends you for sandwiches and a couple of teas,
> But by then she has whiskers, no teeth and one foot in the grave.

Such changes, such temporal devastation, lead him to confess, 'I have lost my faith that the ticket tells us where we are going.' He does not, however, find himself terrified by such disillusionment, for although there are 'rumours the driver is mad', that we are being shipped to slaughter-houses somewhere, or that 'the signals are jammed and unknowing/ We aim through the night full speed at a wrecked viaduct', he refuses to countenance such hysterical fears. 'The future is rumor and drivel.' He is the man of disillusion, and his is the world of ennui, not fear.

The pole-star vanishes

We, like the disciples, are toss'd,
By storms on a perilous deep;
But cannot be possibly lost,
For Jesus has charge of the ship:
Though billows and winds are enrag'd,
And threaten to make us their sport;
This pilot his word has engag'd
To bring us in safety to port.

John Newton, 'The Disciples at Sea', from
The Olney Hymns

We know not where we go, or what sweet dream
May pilot us through caverns strange and fair
Of far and pathless passion, while the stream
Of life, our bark doth on its whirlpools bear,
Spreading swift wings as sails to the dim air;
Nor should we seek to know, so the devotion
Of love and gentle thoughts be heard still there.

Percy Bysshe Shelley, *The Revolt of Islam,* Canto 6, st. 29

We, the weak mariners of that wide lake
Where'er its shores extend or billows roll,
Our course unpiloted and starless make
O'er its wild surface to an unknown goal.

Percy Bysshe Shelley, *The Witch of Atlas,* st. 63

. . . *and those far, elusive lights plunged the souls of seamen into darkness, offering them false hope* . . .

From an ancient pilot's manual

We've been bewitched by countless lies,
by azure images of ice,
by false promises of open sky and sea,
and rescued by a God we don't believe.

Like coppers rattling from a beggar's plate
guiding lights have fallen on our days
and burned and died.
                                    We've pressed our ship
a pilgrimage of nights toward such lights
as, always elusive, lured and tricked
the keel upon the rocks and ripped
the helmhold from the hand and I shed
the beggared palm to scraps.
Ice tightens at the bow and breath.
To dock, to drop the anchor to its rest,
to drift (a dream!) on waters quieted
and calmed. We can't. We're after a mirage. . . .
Beacons can't be trusted. Trust instead
the will of your own hand and head.
Again the captain waves his glass,
sights a beacon, turns and cries
'Helmsman! There's a beacon. Are you blind?'
But Helmsman, with the truer eye
thinks mutiny and grumbles,
                                    'A mirage.'
Yevgeny Yevtushenko, 'Ballad about False Beacons',
                              trans. Anthony Kahn

Like the loss of one's heavenly destination, the disappearance of one's heavenly guide forms another part of the typology of shipwreck. Perhaps because the journey's goal and end is so far removed from wherever the voyager finds himself at the present, its disappearance does not produce moments of extreme crisis, and therefore this situation serves as a figure to communicate ennui and disillusion rather than crisis. When the traveller perceives that the stars by which he guides his course have vanished, however, then he feels something akin to panic, for the loss of these guides leaves him disoriented and in danger. Such moments of recognition occur to believers and unbelievers alike. In 'Le Pont', for example, Victor Hugo, a man of faith, feels himself lost in the silent, mute infinity of the abyss, but, suddenly, 'Au fond, à travers l'ombre, impénétrable voile,/ On apercevait Dieu comme une sombre étoile' (In the depths, across the shadows, through the impenetrable veil, God is seen like a sombre star). With such a star to provide his bearings, the otherwise helpless worshipper can then use prayer, which is the 'bridge' of the title, to reach his Lord.

Characteristically, when a non-believer employs this figure, he moves in an opposing direction, for rather than begin with a sense of disorientation and then find a guiding star, he will first mention a star and then suddenly recognize that it is missing. When Conrad Aiken presents this situation in 'Preludes', he thus describes how he

> turned for terror,
> Seeking in vain the Pole Star of my thought;
> Where it was blown among the shapeless clouds,
> And gone as soon as seen, and scarce recalled,
> Its image lost and I directionless;
> Alone upon the brown sad edge of chaos,
> In the wan evening that was evening always.

This disorienting loss of one's guiding star, then, creates one of those moments, like that of the actual shipwreck itself, in which one realizes one's isolation and helplessness. The goal of the life-journey, of course, always existed necessarily at some remove from the pilgrim, but the guide or guiding star always existed within one's sight, and when it vanishes the shock is far greater than when the heavenly destination becomes cast into doubt.

The disappearance of Aiken's 'Pole Star', like the disappearance of all such heavenly guides, provides a particularly effective structure therefore to communicate the emotional shock of encountering what one may term a primal absence – an absence of that divinity who founds one's entire sense of order and coherence. St Augustine's original metaphor does not mention any guiding star or other assistance for the pilgrim voyaging back to God and his heavenly home, but the very fact that in his vision of things the pilgrim senses both his state of exile and an essential need to be with God means that St Augustine believes that man possesses some sort of inner guide. That guide, that essential longing for God and the essential recognition that one is incomplete, is, in effect, the divine presence in Everyman. When Aiken and others, such as Shelley, Nerval, and Moore, find no such guide, they also encounter a sudden absence of their God, of any God.

This disappearance of the pole-star has served many British and American writers of the last hundred years as a particularly effective way of emphasizing spiritual crisis precisely because the Evangelical

Protestant revival that has such profound influence upon the culture of England, Wales, Scotland, and America made figures of the divine presence so popular. The situation that we may call 'the pole-star vanishes' thus acts as an inversion, a denial, of commonplace images and analogies which countless hymns, sermons, tracts, emblem books, and the like had established as a popular cultural code.

Hymns, for example, frequently emphasized that no matter how endangered the Christian voyager believed himself, he still had some sort of divine presence with him in his vessel. William Hiley Bathurst's 'Great God, when I approach Thy throne' provides an unusually abstract version of such assurance when it presents the Christian confiding that

> My course I could not safely steer
> Through life's tempestuous sea;
> Did not this truth relieve my fear,
> That Jesus died for me.

Far more common is the situation in which Christ or His voice turns out to be in the endangered ship. Thus, James Grant's 'O Zion, afflicted with wave upon wave' explains that although Christians are 'With darkness surrounded, by terrors dismay'd', they do not have to fear, since 'skilful's the Pilot who sits at the helm'. Then, after offering such comfort, the hymn presents Christ Himself providing words of needed assurance:

> 'My promise, My truth, are they light in thy eyes?
> Still, still I am with thee, My promise shall stand,
> Through tempest and tossing, I'll bring thee to land.'

Charlotte Elliott's 'When waves of trouble round me swell' similarly figures forth the divine presence as a voice, as does John Newton's 'Pensive, doubting, fearful heart'. Several of his other immensely popular hymns instead simply assert the presence of God as guide or pilot. In 'The Lord will provide' (or 'Though troubles assail'), Newton thus reassures us:

> We may, like the ships,
> By tempests be tost

On perilous deeps,
But cannot be lost: . . .
For though we are strangers,
We have a good guide.

This Christian assurance that God was present with him during the course of the life-journey meant that the Lord, a being existing out of space and time, was both the believer's guide and goal, for He sustained the Christian during his pilgrimage and yet awaited him at its close. God, in other words, was both present and absent, or at least the believer could not fully enjoy His presence until he joined Him in heaven, the Christian's true home.

As John Newton's 'The Disciples at Sea', which I have placed as an epigraph to this section, reminds us, the notion of Christ as pilot, guide, or vocal presence derives in part from the sixth chapter of the Gospel of St John. Old Testament incidents similarly supported such a conception of God's guiding presence since the sacred history recorded in its various books was accepted by Christians of all denominations until quite late in the last century as containing divinely intended anticipations of Christ and His dispensation. Thus, Moses' sight from Mount Pisgah of the unattained Promised Land was commonly interpreted as a prevision of the Christian heaven, while the pillars of fire and cloud that led the Hebrews through their desert wanderings were similarly taken as types of Christ's presence to the believer. Newman's 'The Pillar of the Cloud', which is usually known as 'Lead, Kindly Light' from its opening words, makes the common assumption that the things and events of the Old Testament not only prefigure matters of importance to the Christian but also refer to his life as well. Employing the language of the typologist, one can say that individual types and shadows of Christ in the Old Testament saw completion (or were fulfilled) both in the life of Christ Himself and also in the lives of his followers, who constitute Christ Mystical.[12]

Unlike hymns, which were only accepted by High Anglicans in the second half of the nineteenth century, biblical typology was shared by Roman Catholics, High and Low Church Anglicans, and a great many Evangelical denominations throughout the Western world. Liturgies, the church calendar, stained-glass windows, eucharistic vessels, altar frontals, Bible commentaries, sermons, and, where employed, hymns all taught believers to read their Bibles in terms of types and shadows of Christ. This once almost universal hermeneutic mode provided particularly strong support for the notion that one could perceive God's presence in this world. Personal types, such as Moses, Samson, or Melchisedek, each anticipate some portion of Christ's history and message. Types (or 'figures' as they are also known) endow biblical history with major spiritual value in several ways. First of all, they together form a system of progressive revelation that gradually announces Christ's appearance in human history. Second, types, which provide a kind of hidden structure to scriptural events, demonstrate God's orderly plan for His children – the so-called Gospel Scheme. Third, they demonstrate dramatically that God, Who is in some way present in each type, has appeared countless times in human history. Fourth, types constitute a semiotics of the divine presence, for they individually serve as the signifying elements in a divine code impressed on history. Types, in other words, are God's writing in human events, and as such they offer yet another form of the divine presence. In effect, each individual type serves as the believer's guide and pilot, for each not only bears the often unexpected stamp of God's presence in complex and occasionally hard-to-understand events but also establishes a proper Christian vantage-point.

Since biblical typology relied upon a belief that the Bible was literally, even in translation, the word of God, it gradually lost its attraction for all but the most conservative Evangelical groups. Geology, comparative philology, archeology, and other disciplines that tended to discredit the literal veracity of the Scriptures undermined typology, and by the late nineteenth century it was already a generally outmoded form of thought and biblical interpretation. Typology, which was an extraordinarily complex cultural code, did far more than merely relate Old and New Testaments: it conveyed an entire conception of divine presence and divine significance. The loss of these basic attitudes about the nature of reality proved far more traumatic than the loss of a powerful repository of complex literary and artistic allusions.

Against such a background, therefore, the situation of the pole-star's disappearance stands out with particular force, for, as we have seen, it represents, not just a loss of certainty or a shaken faith, but an entirely new sense of being in the world; or stated differently, such a topos communicates the experience of finding oneself with a world radically different from that described in the various Christian structures of assurance. The sheer emptiness of a cosmos in which an *expected* God turns out to be missing appears a central fact. As Gerard de Nerval describes this emptied universe in the second part of 'Le Christ aux oliviers',

> Partout le sol désert côtoyé par des ondes,
> Des tourbillons confus d'océans agités . . .
> Un souffle vague émeut les sphères vagabondes,
> Mais nul esprit existe en ces immensités,
>
> En cherchant l'oeil de Dieu, je n'ai vu qu'une orbite
> Vaste, noire et sans fond, d'où la nuit qui l'habite
> Rayonne sur le monde et s'épaissit toujours.

[Everywhere the desert soil bordered by waves, by the confused eddies of rough oceans . . . An uncertain breath moves the wandering spheres, but no spirit exists in those vast spaces. Seeking the eye of God, I saw only a huge black bottomless socket, whence the night that dwells in it radiates over the world and becomes ever more dense.

trans. Anthony Hartley, ellipsis in original]

Obsessed by the emptiness, the absence he encounters, Nerval proceeds by inverting all the usual emblems of watching divinity: the seeing eye of a present God becomes the unseeing, empty socket of a skull, which is the remains of a now absent life. God's light, which, according to the Gospel of St John, illuminates the entire creation, becomes a darkness that similarly penetrates and permeates everything. All the qualities of caring, life-creating, guiding Presence become transformed into their opposites.

Like Nerval, Thomas Carlyle, the first and most influential of the Victorian sages, employs this same intonation of the life-journey to create an entire imaginative world. We have already observed how this paradigmatic metaphor emerged from within (and against) various Christian ones, and we have also observed the uses to which several poets have put it. Now I would like to trace this paradigmatic moment of recognition through the works of a single author, Carlyle, who returns to it frequently.

Carlyle as sage concerns himself chiefly with the spiritual life – and particularly the spiritual ills – of his time. In *Sartor Resartus,* his experimental combination of autobiography, satire, *Bildungsroman,* and fantasy, he therefore uses the disappearance of the pole-star to dramatize a crucial moment in the life of his representative man, Diogenes Teufelsdröckh. In the days before Carlyle's hero attains a post-Christian faith, he finds himself lost and alone, and he suffers terribly in his isolation:

> Whither should I go? My Loadstars were blotted out; in that canopy of grim fire shone no star. Yet forward must I; the ground burnt under me; there was no rest for the sole of my foot. I was alone, alone! ('Sorrow of Teufelsdröckh')

Like so many nineteenth- and twentieth-century wanderers and would-be pilgrims, the Clothes-Philosopher presents his experience of crisis in terms of a pattern that begins with the search for the pole-star, mentions its absence, and ends with the recognition that the earth has suddenly become transformed into a desert, universe of death, and hell-on-earth. As Carlyle explains in *The Life of John Sterling,* his tribute to one imperilled voyager, when the modern traveller looks heavenward for guidance, he finds no stars by which to chart his way because in the 'wild dim-lighted chaos all stars of Heaven [have] gone out. No star of Heaven visible, hardly now to any man.' Instead, the would-be pilgrim, the nineteenth-century Everyman, finds that 'pestiferous fogs, and foul exhalations' have 'blotted-out all stars: will-o'-wisps, of various course and colour, take the place of stars.' The way, if there is a way, quickly becomes lost, and the pilgrim must stumble along as best he can through 'his pathless wanderings'. Such is the world of Carlyle, and such, he says, is the nineteenth-century world in which Sterling found himself:

> No fixed highways more; the old spiritual highways and recognized paths to the Eternal, now all torn-up and flung in heaps, submerged in unutterable boiling mud-oceans of Hypocrisy and Unbelievability, of brutal living Atheism and damnable dead putrescent Cant; surely a tragic pilgrimage for all mortals; darkness, and the mere shadow of Death, enveloping all things from pole to pole; and in the raging gulf-currents, offering us will-o'-wisps for load-stars, – intimating that there are no stars, nor even were except some Old-Jew ones which have now gone out. Once more, a tragic pilgrimage for all mortals, and for the young pious soul,

winged with genius, and passionately seeking land and passionately abhorrent of floating carrion withal, more tragical than for any! – A pilgrimage we must all undertake nevertheless, and make the best of it with our respective means. Some arrive; a glorious few: many must be lost, – go down upon the floating wreck they took for land.

Carlyle's concluding figure makes one perceive how much the significance of disaster on the life-journey has changed. The image of the sailors who meet their destruction when they mistake something perilous for dry land is an old one: Physiologus tells the tale of the mariners who mistake Leviathan for secure haven and drown when this embodiment of Satan dives beneath the surface. Milton similarly likens the devil to this illusory isle in the first book of *Paradise Lost*.[13] In both cases the voyagers on the journey of life perish because they sin, but in Carlyle's terrifying vision of the human condition one perishes merely because such risk, such peril, is an essential part of the unguided voyage.

In the essay entitled 'Boswell's Life of Johnson', Carlyle traces the origins of this modern world of the unguided life-journey back to the eighteenth century. For then, says Carlyle, men first began to doubt the existence of the Everlasting City; then sheets of fog first began to obscure the stars that had always guided man's life-voyage, as it seemed that they paled and, one by one, went out. Since most men journey through this life in large groups, never questioning either the route or the destination, it took a long time for them to perceive how perilous their voyage had become. Almost all

sail their Life-voyage in huge fleets, following some single whale-fishing or herring-fishing Commodore: the log-book of each differs not, in essential purport, from that of any other: nay, the most have no legible log-book (reflection, observation not being among their talents); keep no reckoning, only *keep in sight* of the flagship, – and fish.

The lives of the majority of men do not, therefore, interest Carlyle as much as the histories of those who steer their own courses – whether as commodores or as solitary, endangered mariners.

Beginning in the eighteenth century, these heroic men (as Carlyle deems himself to be) find themselves adrift, castaway, becalmed, or verging on shipwreck. They clutch at literature, 'wonderful Ark of the Deluge, where so much that is precious, nay priceless to mankind, floats carelessly onwards through the Chaos of distracted times.' Moreover, since the history of literature during the past two centuries 'is our proper church History' – the 'other Church, during that time, having more and more decayed from its old functions and influences' – Carlyle turns to the lives of literary men for tales of spiritual voyagers, for tales of both those who make port and those who perish in the waste ocean.

In 'Diderot', for example, he discusses a man brave, sincere, but mistaken – one who exemplifies the isolated, defeated traveller. Originally, he did not sail alone, for he had D'Alembert, his fellow *philosophe,* as companion, but after the Revolution his friend abandoned him. 'Sad it was to see his fellow-voyager make for port, and disregard signals, when the sea-krakens rose round him!' Diderot courageously forged on alone until he had 'sailed through the Universe of Worlds and found no Maker thereof.' Like the lost Teufelsdröckh, like Nerval, he finds himself in a Universe of Death. He looked for 'the DIVINE EYE, and beheld only the black, bottomless, glaring DEATH's EYE-SOCKET; such, with all his wide voyagings, was the philosophic fortune he had realized.' 'It is', says Teufelsdröckh, 'but the common lot in this era. Not having come to spiritual majority prior to the *Siècle de Louis Quinze.* . . . thou hadst no other outlook. The whole world is, like thee, sold to Unbelief' ('The Everlasting No', *Sartor Resartus*). Unlike the Clothes-Philosopher, Diderot finds no salvation. He becomes one of the failed voyagers from whom we can learn courage but from whose lives we can learn nothing else that will aid us on our own life-journey.

Of far more interest to him are the lives of those like Samuel Johnson, who make port despite the roughest seas. According to the Victorian seer, Boswell's *Life*, 'our English *Odyssey*', reveals the major significance of 'that great Samuel Johnson . . . the far-experienced, "much-enduring", man, whose labours and pilgrimage are here sung.' Though this English 'Ulysses', like Diderot, finds himself a solitary voyager on the waste ocean of life, he yet manages to complete his journey successfully. One can imagine the great Cham nodding approval at Carlyle's description of him, for as he himself wrote in *The Rambler,* no. 184:

We set out on a tempestuous sea, in quest of some port, where we expect to find rest, but where we are not sure of admission;

we are not only in danger of sinking in the way, but of being misled by meteors mistaken for stars, of being driven from our course by the changes of the wind, and of losing it by unskillful steerage.

Perhaps Carlyle had this very passage in mind when he wrote, in 'Boswell's Life of Johnson', that when Johnson

looked up to Religion, as to the polestar of his voyage, already there was no *fixed* polestar any longer visible; but two stars, a whole constellation of stars, each proclaiming itself as the true. There was the red portentous comet-star of Infidelity; the dim-fixed star, burning ever dimmer, uncertain whether or not an atmospheric meteor, of Orthodoxy.

Thus, in terms that, by intention or coincidence, closely match Johnson's own, Carlyle describes this hero-as-man-of-letters in mid-journey. One should incidentally point out how significant are the differences in the way each employs the topos of the perilous voyage: although both conceive of the journey of life as difficult and dangerous, Dr Johnson holds that man goes astray through his own weakness – through weakness that may at last prevent his admission to port. Carlyle, on the other hand, emphasizes that the stars – the heavenly guides – and not the voyager are most at fault.

Drifting on the waste ocean

> Her place discovered by the rules of art,
> Unusual terrors shook the master's heart;
> When Falconera's rugged isle he found,
> Within her drift, with shelves and breakers bound;
> For, if on those destructive shallows tost,
> The helpless bark with all her crew are lost. . . .
> Dire was the scene, with whirlwind, hail and shower;
> Black Melancholy rul'd the fearful hour!
>
> William Falconer, *The Shipwreck,*
> canto II. ll, 581-6, 599-600

The brig was a mere log, rolling about at the mercy of every wave; the gale was upon the increase, if any thing, blowing indeed a complete hurricane, and there appeared to us no earthly prospect of deliverance. For several hours we held on in silence, expecting every moment our lashings would give way, that the remains of the windlass would go by the board, or that some of the huge seas, which roared in every direction around us and above us, would drive the hulk so far beneath the water that we should be drowned before it could regain the surface.

Edgar Allan Poe, *Narrative of A. Gordon Pym,* ch. 9

When the stars by which one navigates go out or disappear into the mist, when God withdraws or seems to have died to man, the voyager finds himself drifting lost and alone. St Augustine described human life as a voyage towards God, and he warned that man had to take care lest the journey so fascinate him that he forget his final destination, and dally so long in the pleasures of tourism and exploration that he would, at last, lose all chance of making port. But once the way of reaching this port vanishes, and with it the safe haven as well, those embarked on the journey of life drift aimlessly, unsure of their bearings, unsure where to head, unsure indeed if there is anywhere to head. In one version this situation merges with those in which the voyager realizes that the destination and guiding stars have disappeared; this is the moment when one feels lost, alone, and helpless. In another version, however, the mariner finds himself drifting helplessly on a damaged vessel; this is the moment, exemplified by the epigraphs to this section, when one feels lost, helpless, alone – and in immediate danger of death. This is the situation, we recall, faced by Poe's narrator in 'MS. Found in a Bottle', who, having survived the initial disaster that left his ship a battered hulk, now realizes that he is helplessly drifting to his destruction. The drifting topos, therefore, presents a situation of extreme crisis in which the final moments, the final agonies, are tantalizingly deferred.

A series of political and intellectual cataclysms from the late eighteenth century until the present day have left many feeling thus cast adrift, and this situation has struck many who believed either they or their cultures were in crisis as paradigmatic. According to Albert Hancock's *The French Revolution and the English Poets* (1899), such perilous drifting was the fate of all in the aftermath of that catastrophic event:

Cut loose from the contemplation of heaven and hell,
divorced from faith in a beneficent supernatural being, and
convinced, too, that the divinely appointed delegates, those
priests and kings, were imposters and tyrants, men were flung

back upon themselves. . . . They felt like a shipwrecked crew, adrift amid the winds and waves and threatened with instant destruction.

Such, warned Lamennais, the great nineteenth-century Catholic apologist, such must be the fate of man without God, for 'when the faith which once united man with God and raised him to God's heights begins to fail, something terrible happens': no longer able to anchor himself, man therefore 'drifts without rest amid the whole of creation like a battered vessel tossed hither and thither by the waves on a deserted ocean.'[14] What makes Lamennais such a representative man of the nineteenth century is not just that, like so many others, he should conceive the situation of man without God as that of a drifting, endangered vessel. No, what makes him most characteristic of his age is that after writing these lines, he should have abandoned his faith and left the Church, thereby joining the ranks of those whose condition he had so well described.

Lamennais became, in other words, like the hero of Charles Kingsley's *Alton Locke,* a man who confesses that after abandoning his mother's Evangelical Protestantism he finds himself drifting 'rudderless' (ch. 2). Or like Arthur Hugh Clough, one of the most famous Victorian victims of spiritual crisis, who described himself in 'Blank Misgivings' with

> sails rent,
> And rudder broken, – reason impotent, –
> Affections all unfixed.

These images of drifting well convey the imaginative world which the end of Christian belief revealed to many.

In the late eighteenth century, long before such widespread religious crisis in the West, Burke's *Reflections on the Revolution in France* had accurately warned that 'when ancient opinions and rules of life are taken away, the loss cannot possibly be estimated. From that moment we have no compass to govern us; nor can we know distinctly to what port we steer.' Many, like Burke, who have sensed that disaster threatens once we lose our bearings, blame what Locke in another context termed the busy, meddling mind of man. For those who had experienced the gradual dissolution of Christianity and with it the gradual disappearance of God, it often seems that the search for truth, itself such an apparently noble enterprise, would bring man to shipwreck. The protagonist of James Anthony Froude's *The Nemesis of Faith,* one of many nineteenth-century novels of religious crisis, thus explains how the worthy effort to remove absurd belief and foolish superstition led him to spiritual disaster:

> The notion of inspiration was no more satisfactory than that of the Church's infallibility; and if the power of the keys, and sacramental grace, and apostolic succession, were absurdities, the Devil was at least equally so. And with the Devil fell sin, and the atonement fell, and all revelation fell; and we were drifting on the current of a wide ocean, we knew not where, with neither oar nor compass. ['Confessions of a Sceptic']

In *The Birth of Tragedy,* Nietzsche had similarly pointed to the dangers of what he called 'Alexandrian culture' with its ideal of 'theoretical man equipped with the greatest forces of knowledge, and laboring in the service of science, whose archetype and progenitor is Socrates.' Having observed the inability of most men to live in doubt, Nietzsche claimed that 'Modern man is beginning to divine the limits of this Socratic love of knowledge and yearns for a coast in the wide waste of the ocean of knowledge.' Necessarily, the contradictions implicit in a society based upon this quest for knowledge will lead it towards horrifying destruction. The basic flaw of nineteenth-century political structure, according to Nietzsche, is that this

> Alexandrian culture, to be able to exist permanently, requires a slave class, but with its optimistic view of life it denies the necessity of such a class, and consequently, when its beautifully seductive and tranquillizing utterances about the 'dignity of man' and the 'dignity of labor' are no longer effective, it gradually drifts toward a dreadful destruction.

Further aggravating the problem is that 'in the face of such threatening storms, who dares to appeal with any confidence to our pale and exhausted religions?' (sec. 18, trans. Walter Kaufman). The extent to which Western society is already drifting surely appears in Nietzsche's reference not to religion but to religions.

A. C. Swinburne, who frequently uses the destruction of late pagan belief by a young, vital Christianity as an analogy for Christianity's own death throes after contact with modern secular thought, none the less rejoices in the loss of what Nietzsche terms 'our pale and exhausted religions'. In the 'Prelude' to *Songs before Sunrise,* his volume of political poems, Swinburne expresses his belief that man necessarily drifts to disaster if he looks heavenward for guidance. The poet, however, does not find unnerving the idea that religious beliefs which had long supported man no longer can aid him in life's journey. Calmly dismissing the older faiths, he urges self-reliance:

> Save his own soul's light overhead,
> None leads him, and none ever led,
>   Across birth's hidden harbour-bar,
>   Past youth where shoreward shallows are,
> Through age that drives on toward the red
>   Vast void of sunset hailed from far,
> To the equal waters of the dead;
>   Save his own soul he hath no star,
> And sinks, except his own soul guide,
> Helmless in the middle turn of tide.

Although Swinburne often seems obsessed with the notions of being shipwrecked and cast away (they are among his most common images), he here appears to have reached that state of acceptance which comes after the initial shock of recognition. Believing that 'man's soul is man's God', he emphasizes that man has no other deity and that man can expect no other guide: all becomes a matter of personal responsibility. Of course, for Swinburne, who considered himself a disciple of Mazzini, such acceptance of responsibility meant that he had to work for the causes of Italian freedom and unification. He therefore devoted considerable energy to winning support for the Risorgimento and for his own notions of humanistic democracy with his political poetry.

Bracing and attractive as Swinburne's challenge might be, it had struck many, like Nietzsche, as a recipe for disaster. For example, in his last days, N. S. Rubashov, the protagonist of Arthur Koestler's *Darkness at Noon,* recognizes that precisely such a programme had led him and the masses to their destruction. As he waits in his cell for the arrival of his executioners, he thinks to himself that perhaps the mistake

lay in the precept which until now he had held to be uncontestable, in whose name he had sacrificed others and was himself being sacrificed: in the precept, that the end justifies the means. It was this sentence which had killed the great fraternity of the Revolution and made them all run amuck. What had he once written in his diary? 'We have thrown overboard all conventions, our sole guiding principle is that of consequent logic; we are sailing without ethical ballast.'

Perhaps the heart of the evil lay there. Perhaps it did not suit mankind to sail without ballast. And perhaps reason alone was a defective compass, which led one on such a winding, twisted course that the goal finally disappeared in the mist. ['The Grammatical Fiction', pt 2, trans. Daphne Hardy]

As he gropes his way down the dark steps towards the prison depths where he will be shot, Rubashov, 'now nearly blind' after his pince-nez accidently breaks, still wonders about the fate of 'these masses . . . this people', which for 'forty years had been driven through the desert, with threats and promises, with imaginary terrors and imaginary rewards. But where was the Promised Land?' Wondering if any 'such goal' in fact exists for 'this wandering mankind', Rubashov desperately wants an answer but knows he has not received one and never will.

Having employed the paradigmatic situations of the wandering vessel and the desert wanderings of the Hebrews after the Exodus, Rubashov, who naturally considers himself a Moses-figure, compares his Pisgah sight to that of his predecessor:

> Moses had not been allowed to enter the land of promise either. But he had been allowed to see it, from the top of the mountain, spread at his feet. Thus, it was easy to die, with the visible certainty of one's goal before one's eyes. He, Nicolas Salmanovitch Rubashov, had not been taken to the top of a mountain; and wherever his eye looked, he saw nothing but desert and the darkness of night. ['The Grammatical Fiction', pt 3]

The Pisgah sight, which marks the coming together of human and divine, serves in older Christian terms as a type either of heaven or a truly Christian deathbed.[15] Here, in contrast, this inverted Pisgah sight serves as an analogue to the disappearance of the pole-star and communicates the bitterness of dying in this new post-Christian 'faith'.

Fittingly, Koestler closes the novel with the situation of drifting, for immediately after Rubashov thus compares himself to Moses on Mount Pisgah, he is shot and finds himself drifting, passively allowing himself to be carried toward death:

A dull blow struck the back of his head. He had long expected it and yet it took him unawares. . . . He lay crumpled up on the ground, with his cheek on the cool flagstones. It got dark, the sea carried him rocking on its nocturnal surface. . . . A second, smashing blow hit him on the ear. Then all became quiet. There was the sea again with its sounds. A wave slowly lifted him up. It came from afar and travelled sedately on, a shrug of eternity.

Thus, Nicolas Salmanovitch Rubashov, who would lead the people to their Promised Land by depending on his own inner chart, finds himself at last groping through darkness until he is shot and drifts to eternity.

Koestler's compact, skilful manipulations of several commonplace Christian paradigms do more than implicitly contradict Swinburne and secular humanists like him. These effective intonations demonstrate, of course, how modern writers use older cultural codes ironically, and they also show how much of the ideological and ideational drama of this novel takes the form of juxtaposing these codes or paradigms with modern life. In particular, the pretensions of Russian communism to create a better life for the masses are subverted by placing them within the context – or against the background – of traditional Christian ways of speaking about such desires for attaining paradise. As Koestler demonstrates, the Christian solutions may no longer pertain, but the search for drastic new ones, such as that found in Soviet Marxism, still leaves man adrift.

The mind a wandering bark

And ever louder the voices grew,
        And the tramp of men in mail;
Until my brain it seemed to be
As though I tossed on a ship at sea
        In the teeth of a crashing gale.
Dante Gabriel Rossetti, 'The King's Tragedy',
            ll. 550–4

Thus far we have observed only those metaphors of drifting which explicitly figure forth the situation of the person who finds himself without purpose, without direction, because his religious faith has vanished. The related situations of drifting and actual shipwreck, however, frequently appear in a second form as a paradigm of severe mental crisis not necessarily connected with the problems of religious belief. For instance, the speaker in Baudelaire's 'Les Sept Vieillards' uses this image of drifting to convey his feeling when he came upon the seventh of the identical men encountered in the fog-filled streets. Wandering through the swarming city, he comes upon a grotesque, horrifyingly evil cripple, and immediately catches sight of a second, third, fourth – each the same – until at the seventh he flees this horrifying absurdity and returns home:

> Vainement ma raison voulait prendre la barre;
> La tempête en jouant déroutait ses efforts,
> Et mon âme dansait, dansait, vieille gabarre
> Sans mâts, sur une mer monstrueuse et sans bords!

> [My reason vainly sought to seize the helm;
> The blowing storm foiled all its efforts,
> and my soul danced, danced, an old hulk
> without masts on a sea monstrous and without shores.]

Wounded by mystery and absurdity, he discovers himself to be an old barge battered by forces too great for him to resist.

When Thomas Moore describes Zelica's mental state after she has been mistakenly informed that her lover Azim is dead, the poet employs a similar analogy:

> The mind was still all there, but turn'd astray; –
> A wandering bark, upon whose path-way shone
> All stars of heav'n, excepting the guiding one! [*Lalla Rookh*]

Zelica therefore becomes 'a wreck, at random driven,/ Without one glimpse of reason or of heaven.'

These psychological versions of the shipwreck structure present the conscious intelligence, and not just the person's physical being, surrounded and impinged upon by alien forces. In Baudelaire's application of the commonplace figure, the sight of something horrible thus threatens his reason, while in Rossetti's and Moore's versions sounds and voices are the analogous agents. Baudelaire's image of the battered hulk, like that of Moore, emphasizes that the element of external, overwhelming force conquers reason – conquers, in other words, what is human. Such psychological applications of the ship-in-danger topos continue the ancient attempt to explain the effect upon the self of the unexpected and irrational. In *The Greeks and the Irrational,* E. R. Dodds explains that Homeric man had no unified concept of what we call soul or personality. Furthermore, Homer had

> a habit of explaining character or behaviour in terms of knowledge . . . not only the possession of technical skill . . . but also what we should call moral character or personal feelings. . . . If character is knowledge, what is not knowledge is not part of the character, but comes to a man from outside. When he acts in a manner contrary to the systems of conscious dispositions which he is said to 'know', his action is not properly his own but has been dictated to him. In other words, unsystematised, non-rational impulses, and the acts resulting from them, tend to be excluded from the self and ascribed to an alien origin.[16]

Nineteenth- and twentieth-century conceptions of the human mind do accept that irrational impulses belong to the person experiencing them. None the less, the conscious mind is often portrayed as if it were being battered, a vessel in peril, by alien forces. The effect is implicitly to reduce the self to a consciousness while treating powerful feelings as exterior powers. The effect of such a conception of the mind's relation to itself and the exterior world is to reverse that progressive interiorization that has characterized Western thought since Periclean Athens, and which has been the subject of commentary by twentieth-century authors as different as Werner Jaeger and Paul Ricoeur.

It is difficult to say whether these descriptions of the mind in crisis are simply extensions of the metaphors mainly associated with problems of religious faith or whether they are the natural result of the new attitudes towards emotions and mental processes which accompany Romanticism. Baudelaire's 'Les Sept Vieillards' of course exemplifies a situation that is clearly a secularized version of the similar metaphors employed by both religious authors and those describing loss of faith. Suddenly encountering himself in a world in which natural laws do not hold, the speaker in Baudelaire's poem discovers precisely that threatening, senseless cosmos experienced by those who lose their religious belief, for like them he finds himself impinged upon by external forces beyond his control. The crucial feature of both metaphysical and psychological versions of the shipwreck topos, in other words, lies in the fact that they both present the human intelligence abandoning claims to full responsibility for man's fate. The Christian version of the journey-of-life and shipwreck metaphors gives man the dignity of deciding his fate; or more accurately, it presents man deciding his fate on those spiritual matters that it conceives as the most important portion of his life and end. The modern version of these commonplace situations and metaphors in contrast declines such responsibility, ceding it, instead, to some external cause, condition, or force.

Moore's many uses of the shipwreck situation in *Lalla Rookh* reminds us, however, that there had long existed one popular application of it that emphasized precisely just this basic lack of responsibility for one's fate. The Irish poet employs the analogy of maritime disaster to convey the intense psychological trauma of Zelica, who has lost her lover; and in fact, erotic and amatory verse has always used such images of shipwreck either to compliment the beloved or to emphasize the supposedly undeserved sufferings of the unrequited lover. Here, for example, the anonymous twelfth-century Goliard poet who wrote 'Dum Diane vitrea' describes the characteristic plight of the lover in terms of the many shifting moods he endures:

> Ut vaga ratis per equora
> dum caret anchora,
> fluctuat inter spem emtumque dubia.

George F. Whicher's edition (1949) of *The Goliard Poets,* from which these lines are taken, renders them:

> No ship that drifts
> With anchor lost
> Can match the shifts
> Of hope and fear
> Wherewith he's crossed.

Such medieval representations of the mind in turmoil differ from nineteenth- and twentieth-century ones in two ways: first of all, they tend to have an obvious moral emphasis, something quite appropriate to an age that conceived of the mind in terms of moral, rather than a faculty, psychology. In fact, immediately after describing the lover in terms of the anchorless, drifting vessel, the author of 'Dum Diane vitrea' draws the moral that such is the fate of all who become soldiers of Venus. Second, the lover's mental stress is often conveyed by the psychomachia, almost a logical debate, rather than by any attempt to re-create psychological experience.

In essence, the speaker in many such erotic poems places God and the rest of the world in brackets, thereby making his beloved the centre of the universe and the only true divinity. Such an intentional isolation of the lovers of course permits the speaker in seduction poems to employ delightful hyperbole. Such hyperbole, in turn, permits him to urge that the beloved's cruel unwillingness to yield, and not his own desires, bears full responsibility for his sufferings. Thomas Carew thus instructs his desired one in 'To *Celia,* on Love's Ubiquity' that she is the sole power responsible for his unhappy destiny:

> Whilst in the bosom of the waves I reel,
> My heart I'll liken to the offering Keel,
> The Sea to my own troubled fate, the Wind
> To your disdain, sent from a soul unkind.

Throughout his poetry Carew rings many witty changes on this basic conceit, elaborately comparing himself, for example, to an imperilled mariner in 'To her in Absence – *A Ship',* while in 'My Mistress commanding me to return her letters' he represents himself as 'th'advent'rous Merchant' who throws the 'long toil'd for treasure' into the angry sea to save himself from destruction. Although Carew may claim he most desires his mistress's letters, his previsions of safe journey always end in the less literary pleasures of her 'arms, which are my port'. The poet's strategy is to pretend to a passive relation to the beloved in the hopes of in fact placing her in a passive relationship to him. Of course, both the poem and its argument are playful, and the hyperbolic imagery of shipwreck is used largely as a means of complimenting the mistress, who appears in the position of a deity or natural power.

Such a witty exchange of the beloved for God at the centre of one's imaginative cosmos, which characterizes much Renaissance amatory verse, is crucially tied to the erotic genres as such. Naturally enough, all the other key terms of the journey-of-life topos can be transformed as well. John Donne makes the usual Christian application of the topos in 'The Progresse of the Soule' when he asserts that 'though through many streights, and lands I roame,/ I launch at paradise', but the paradise at which most erotic poets set their courses turns out to be very much in this world. Carew's 'A Rapture' thus promises a happy voyage indeed:

> Thou like a sea of milk shalt lie display'd
> Whilst I the smooth calm ocean will invade,
> With such a tempest, as when *Jove* of old
> Fell down on *Danae* in a stream of gold;
> Yet my tall pinnace shall in th' *Cyprian* straight
> Ride safe at anchor, and unload her freight:
> My rudder with thy bold hand, like a tried
> And skilful pilot, thou shalt steer, and guide
> > My bark into Love's channel, where it shall
> > Dance, as the bounding waves to rise or fall.

The erotic poet, furthermore, can transform even the more paradoxical uses of Christian shipwreck as happy disaster to his own uses. Drawing upon the Christian belief that true life, one's full existence, begins only after death when one joins God, many believers, including Coleridge, Thoreau, and Hopkins, claim that physical shipwreck can mark a spiritually successful end to one's life-voyage by bringing one directly to one's heavenly destination. As Emily Dickinson, who did not always write so hopefully, put the paradox:

> If my Bark sink
> 'Tis to another sea –
> Mortality's Ground Floor
> Is Immortality – [no. 1,234]

Making the erotic poet's transformation of the original Christian paradox, the anonymous early eighteenth-century author of 'The Enjoyment' describes how he and his lover were

> Tost with a tempest of Desire;

Till with utmost fury driven,
Down, at once, we sunk to heaven.

As these examples reveal, the amatory and erotic author frequently employs all the structures, situations, and analogies associated with traditional religious discourse. The particular importance for this study of literary iconology of such a recognition lies in the fact that it illuminates another stage in the development of a culturally important code, for although what I have termed modern paradigms of metaphysical shipwreck only begin to appear in the late eighteenth century, erotic writing traditionally had employed very similar structures for centuries before. Whereas the modern uses of the shipwreck and similar situations to figure forth man's fate tend to do so with extreme earnestness, erotic ones, of course, generally take a far lighter tone, since they are often employed for witty hyperbole. Such erotic applications of an entire set of cultural codes that were originally religious – or at least had been so since the end of the classical world and the beginning of the Christian one – show us, therefore, one way in which society developed potentially subversive versions of religious paradigms. By bracketing God and the universe and thus making the lover's world all that mattered, such erotic applications of Christian metaphors made it possible that someone, sooner or later, would decide that this imaginary cosmos in which God did not exist usefully described the world that he had experienced. One would not have to insulate the universe of the speaker from the supposedly truer one of religious discourse if religion turned out to be false. Ironically, erotic writing, which thus parodies modes of religious discourse, seems to have at least some role in creating modern versions of these more earnest modes.

William Falconer and the meaning of shipwreck

O first-born daughter of primeval Time!
By whom transmitted down in every clime,
The deeds of ages long elaps'd are known,
And blazon'd glories spread from zone to zone;
Whose breath dissolves the gloom of mental night,
And o'er th'obscur'd idea pours the light!
Whose wing unerring glides thro' time and place,
And trackless scours th'immensity of space;

> Say, on what seas, for thou alone canst tell,
> What dire mishap a fated ship befel,
> Assail'd by tempests, girt with hostile shores? –
> Arise! approach! unlock thy treasur'd stores!

William Falconer, *The Shipwreck,* canto 1, ll. 109–20

After the mariner's vessel has drifted hopelessly, there comes the feared moment when it crashes upon a hidden reef or founders in raging seas – the moment of actual shipwreck. This is the moment one encounters in Poe's 'MS. Found in a Bottle', Tennyson's 'The Wreck', Baudelaire's 'Le Voyage', and Stanfield's *The Wreck of the 'Avenger'* (Pl. 9). This is also the moment that William Falconer, himself a survivor of sea disaster, presents at length in his auto-biographical poem *The Shipwreck;*

> The ship hangs hovering on the verge of death,
> Hell yawns, rocks rise, and breakers roar beneath! – . . . .
>
> Uplifted on the surge, to heaven she flies,
> Her shatter'd top half-buried in the skies,
> Then headlong plunging thunders on the ground,
> Earth groans! air trembles! and the deeps resound!
> Her giant bulk the dread concussion feels,
> And quivering with the wound in torment reels.
> So reels, convuls'd with agonizing throes,
> The bleeding full beneath the murd'rer's blows –
> Again she plunges! hark! a second shock
> Tears her strong bottom on the marble rock:
> Down on the vale of Death, with dismal cries,
> The fated victims shuddering roll their eyes
> In wild despair; while yet another stroke,
> With deep convulsion, rends the solid oak:
> Till like the mine, in whose infernal cell
> The lurking demons of destruction dwell,
> At length asunder torn, her frame divides;
> And crashing spreads in ruin o'er the tides. [bk 3, ll. 612-13, 632-49]

Immediately after thus describing the moment the vessel strikes the rocks that cause its final destruction, Falconer turns away from the action and wishes that he had Vergil's poetic skill, so that he could 'wake to sympathy the feeling heart', present his subject in all the 'pomp of exquisite distress', and 'deplore/ Th'impervious horrors of a leeward shore' (ll. 651, 653, 656–7). Both Falconer's choice of poetic model and his statement of his poetic purposes reveal much about the intensely problematic nature of the shipwreck and similar situations of disaster and crisis for Western culture. Falconer's once extraordinarily popular poem, which first appeared in 1762, does not fully present the shipwreck as the modern situation of man's essential isolation and helplessness, but at the same time it does not convincingly present it as an instance of divine punishment either. In fact, the poet's major difficulties in endowing his narrative of maritime disaster with a proper significance – with a meaning, that is, which will satisfy him – can serve as a type of the problems such crises occasion for the artist in an age of transition.

To begin with, Falconer, like so many poets of the following century, wishes to find modern equivalents for epic subject, and, again, like many of the Romantic and post-Romantic generations, he wishes to find that subject in his own life and experience. Unfortunately, unlike Wordsworth, Tennyson, and Hopkins, he does not realize that an epic subject requires the poet to use it as part of something very like a theogony, for what makes the subject important is precisely that it permits, or rather requires, the poet to justify the ways of God to man or otherwise propound a view of the human condition. Characteristically, although Falconer employs epic devices frequently to endow his subject with epic dignity, the Muse he invokes is not Calliope, the epic Muse, but memory. Such a procedure characterizes his poem because, having set out to memorialize the events of which he had been a victim, he never knows quite what to make of them. Part of the difficulty arises in the fact that this barber's son who went to sea as a purser was not all that skilful as a poet, and yet his occasional patches of satisfying verse show that his problems derive from more than lack of poetic technique.

Falconer's poem takes the form of three cantos, each of which has more than nine hundred lines. Although he describes the stages of the sea disaster in considerable detail, this narration still takes up a fairly small proportion of the entire work, and therefore all the other material in the poem must lead up to this maritime disaster and make us sympathize more with its victims. The first canto sets the scene and presents the cast of characters, which in Falconer's narrow class-bound view consists entirely of the officers of the merchant ship *Britannia* and their families at home; the poet briefly mentions the rest of the crew as 'th'inferior naval train' (bk 1, l. 420) and swiftly consigns them to deepest oblivion. Once the officers have been introduced and the vessel described, Falconer devotes the remainder of the canto to narrating the tale of the love of Palemon, the youngest officer, for Anna, the daughter of the captain. This love interest, which occupies considerable space in the poem, is obviously intended to make us feel more sympathy for the sea's victims, and to create it the poet draws upon pastoral convention for Palemon's name and both pastoral and fiction for the tale of young love. At the same time, the first canto also repeatedly compares man's battle with the sea to sieges and other episodes in war. Such traditional means of poetic aggrandizement serve to suggest that Falconer's subject, the shipwreck of a merchant vessel, possesses epic dignity.

The poem's second canto begins with everyone thinking of home. A storm comes up and then clears, after which Rodmond, the crude first mate, kills a dolphin for no apparent reason. A second storm then overtakes the ship, and Falconer describes it in detail while also providing elaborate, awkward instruction on seamanship. As the third canto opens, the ship, which has narrowly avoided drifting onto the rocks at Falconera, drifts helplessly towards Greece. Falconer interrupts the narrative to provide a political history of Greece, after which he presents the ship's final moments and the deaths of many in its crew. Falconer, who had lived through one such disaster and was to perish in another, describes the final slaughter effectively and in detail. For example, he explains that, knowing they were about to crash upon the rock-bound shore, the crew climbed the rigging in the hopes that they would there better their chances of survival:

> As o'er the surge the stooping main-mast hung,
> Still on the rigging thirty seamen clung;
> Some, struggling, on a broken crag were cast,
> And there by oozy tangles grappled fast,
> Awhile they bore th'o'erwhelming billows' rage,
> Unequal combat with their fate to wage;
> Till all benumb'd and feeble they forego
> Their slippery hold, and sink to shades below.
> Some, from the main-yard-arm impetuous thrown
> On marble ridges, die without a groan. [bk 3, ll. 658-67]

At last Arion, the character who represents Falconer himself, makes it safely to the shore but discovers that his friend Palemon has been severely injured by being thrown against the rocky shores. After a long death speech Palemon dies, and Arion promises to memorialize his death and that of the ship and its crew.

The intensely problematic nature of his task appears in the poem's final inability to provide any final meaning for the shipwreck. Falconer's lack of intellectual or philosophic focus appears with particular clarity in those many places where he assigns a significance to something and then apparently forgets it. For instance, early in the poem he speaks of his life as one afflicted by a 'vindictive Fate' (bk 1, l. 73), but it soon appears only that he had had a hard time of it. He does not, in other words, seem to believe that any greater plan or fate pursued him, and therefore this supposedly 'vindictive Fate' does not play any role in the destruction of the vessel and those on board. Similarly, when Falconer describes the ocean in the manner of hymn-writers as 'the faithless main' (bk 1, l. 714), he not only neglects to amplify this notion but he also does not make clear how or with whom the sea could conceivably have broken faith. Again, when he mentions 'the faithless tides' (bk 2, l. 23) upon which the ship sails for home from Candia, he does not show the reader how tides, which are a natural force and certainly follow (and 'keep faith') with natural law, could be faithless, for the mere fact that they do not suit the needs of men does not seem enough to make them thus 'faithless'.

A major part of Falconer's problems with his subject arise from his attempting to do something with a literary form, diction, verse form, and allusiveness not entirely appropriate to them. His basic attempt to endow their experienced shipwreck with epic (or tragic) grandeur thus leads him to use forms, particularly epithets, that may at first strike one as appropriate but which, upon consideration, have implications that ill accord with what he is apparently trying to communicate. His characteristic difficulties in attempting to achieve epic dignity appear, for example, in the long description of the *Britannia* which closes the first canto. After describing the ship's beauties at length, Falconer ends with a characteristically ambiguous mention of the Union Jack:

> High o'er the poop the flattering winds unfurl'd
> Th'imperial flag that rules the watery world.

Deep blushing armors all the tops invest;
And warlike trophies either quarter drest:
Then tower'd the masts, the canvass swell'd on high,
And waving streamers floated in the sky.
Thus the rich vessel moves in trim array,
Like some fair virgin on her bridal day.
Thus, like a swan, she cleaves the watery plain,
The pride and wonder of th'Ægean main!

[bk 1, ll. 932–41]

In fact, neither England's flag nor that of any human power rules the 'watery world' – something we are to learn from Falconer at great length. Falconer gives no indication that he writes ironically, and he apparently means only that of all naval powers his nation is the greatest. To state that Britain rules the naval and merchant vessels of other nations in this form suggests, however, that it rules the ocean itself. In other words, Falconer's desire to employ usual means of poetic compliment leads him to ironies of which he seems unaware.

One such potentially ironic passage appears in the poem's closing pages when Arion looks at Palemon's corpse and, transfixed by the sight, renews his earlier oath to tell his friend's beloved Anna all that has happened, for at this point in the action he essentially forgoes any attempt to understand the meaning of what has just happened to Palemon, himself, and the rest of the ship's company:

Disastrous day! what ruin hast thou bred!
What anguish to the living and the dead!
How hast thou left the widow all-forlorn,
And ever doom'd the orphan child to mourn;
Thro' life's sad journey hopeless to complain!
Can sacred Justice these events ordain?
But, O my soul! avoid that wondrous maze
Where Reason, lost in endless error, strays!
As thro' this thorny vale of life we run,
Great CAUSE of all effects, *Thy will be done!*

[bk 3, ll. 899–908]

By simply accepting the will of God and yet by abandoning any attempt to demonstrate the presence of God in this terrible event, Falconer obviously declares his own inability to explain either for himself or the reader the value, the meaning, of what has just occurred. Upon encountering events and an external nature too difficult to decipher, the poet simply turns away from this source of puzzlement and throws himself upon the bosom of God.

By failing to derive any metaphysical, moral, or religious value from this sea disaster, Falconer has none the less been true to his original commitment to his Muse, which is memory, since he has presented what happened as he saw it. His frequent citations of epic convention, however, demonstrate that he has not just preserved traces of these terrible deaths in his memory, for he has tried to endow the entire event with dignity and high seriousness and he has continually suggested, moreover, that it possesses importance for the audience. Furthermore, he also draws the reader's attention to the event's significance, and to effect a successful poetic closure he must resolve some of the problems he has raised. Had Falconer never in the poem made any attempt either to open such questions or to provide answers, his final resignation might conceivably have ended the poem successfully. But, in fact, he has offered so many contradictory partial explanations in the course of *The Shipwreck* that the final stance of unquestioning humility violates all that has preceded it.

His lack of poetic control over this crucial issue of the shipwreck's meaning and relevance also appears in his own response to this speech about accepting God's will and abandoning his own judgment, for after promising Palemon that he would tell his end to Anna, he has written a poem that does not focus upon the ill-fated lover. Indeed, immediately after recalling his promise to memorialize these tragic events, Falconer's speaker proceeds in true neo-classical fashion to generalize. Rather than elaborate upon all the sad implications of his friend's death and Anna's consequent unhappiness, he immediately turns his attention to unnamed other sufferers. Having shown that he conceives of his task of memorialization as more than just the tale of Palemon's fate, he raises an issue that he cannot answer.

Such basic difficulties in ending *The Shipwreck* would not have arisen at all, one suspects, if Falconer had not permitted himself to hint so many times and in so many ways that he knew the meaning of the sea disaster. The poem several times suggests that the sea or tides were faithless and that in some way these natural forces are to blame in some way, that is, more than the one of purely physical causation. Falconer's use of inappropriate epithets thus forces the reader's attention to issues that might otherwise have remained dormant. He also applies such inappropriate epithets to the ship itself, for shortly after mentioning that the wind 'betray'd' the unwilling vessel, he describes the ship 'caparison'd in gaudy pride' (canto 2, ll. 228, 237), as if to suggest that it or, by implication, its officers are guilty of pride; but nothing else in the poem makes such an assignment of value seem in the slightest convincing. His similar comparison of the plunging ship to Satan, which demonstrates that Falconer is a good eighteenth-century Miltonist, also strikes one as singularly inappropriate:

> As that rebellious angel who, from heaven,
> To regions of eternal pain was driven;
> When dreadless he forsook the Stygian shore,
> The distant realms of Eden to explore;
> Here, on sulphureous clouds sublime upheav'd,
> With daring wing th'infernal air he cleav'd;
> There, in some hideous gulf descending prone,
> Far in the rayless void of night was thrown.
> Even so she scales the briny mountain's height,
> Then down the black abyss precipitates her flight.
>
> [canto 3, ll. 97-106]

The major difficulty in assigning blame for the deaths of so many people either to the supposedly faithless sea or the pride of the vessel and its men is that nothing else in the poem makes such explanations seem appropriate or convincing. In fact, as the obvious opposition of the two contrasting explanations suggests, they seem to cancel each other out; and if one wished to employ some more complex explanation, say, in which the vessel's pride allowed it to destroy itself within the faithless waves, one would have to make a far greater effort to establish an explanation than does Falconer.

He several times does make attempts to explain the meaning of this sea disaster in traditional terms. For example, near the opening of the poem, he suggests that the shipwreck to come will be caused by greed and that the victims therefore will be punished by their own allegiance to Mammon. But even as he obliquely makes such a suggestion, he characteristically manages to undercut it, thus making this assignment of value problematic and hence intensely puzzling to the reader:

> The watchful mariner, whom Heaven informs,
> Oft deems the prelude of approaching storms.

True to his trust when sacred duty calls,
No brooding storm the master's soul appals;
Th' advancing season warns him to the main:-
A captive, fetter'd to the oar of gain!
His anxious heart, impatient of delay,
Expects the winds to sail from Candia's bay;
Determin'd from whatever point they rise,
To trust his fortune to the seas and skies.

[canto 1, ll. 206–15]

As this representative passage suggests, Falconer holds two potentially contradictory views of the merchant seaman's life and does not have any governing idea that might permit him to reconcile them or subordinate one to the other. On the one hand, he firmly believes that the sailor's dangerous calling, his obedience to duty, and his willingness to take personal risks as part of his occupation make him truly heroic. The seaman's battles with natural forces of current, sea, and storm, Falconer repeatedly demonstrates, deserve epic, heroic treatment as much as do the siege of Troy and similar mythic struggles; and that, of course, explains why he so frequently uses epic similes to aggrandize his subject. On the other hand, the poet also seems to believe that the need to make money, whether for oneself or the ship's owners, leads to terrible disaster, and that, moreover, the shipwreck comes in part as punishment. Unfortunately, when looked at closely, this explanation does not make much sense, for the men who perish on the ship – and upon whose deaths Falconer concentrates in the poem's long climactic scenes – do not themselves seem liable to the charge of greed; they are only earning their livings, and hard, dangerous livings they are. In contrast, the ship's owners, the economic system that prompts such mercantile adventuring, or Britain as a whole might be guilty of such greed, but none of these perishes in this shipwreck.

Another intriguing, but equally unconvincing, reason for the shipwreck appears when the unsympathetic first mate Rodmond kills a dolphin. This cruel, essentially absurd act does not finally explain anything, both because it seems out of keeping with what follows in the poem and because it is never again mentioned. Unlike Coleridge's fable of sin against nature and expiation, Falconer's *The Shipwreck* takes place in a realistically conceived universe; and whereas *The Ancient Mariner,* which takes the form of a fantasy, continually emphasizes that human reason cannot understand the magical connections between events, Falconer's poem remains, despite its epic pretensions, completely in a very ordinary world.

What is so intriguing about Falconer's *The Shipwreck* is the way it offers so many possible explanations, fails to integrate them into any larger one, and finally turns away from the task of explanation altogether. The poet offers so many oblique, implicit, hinted interpretations of the shipwreck that one can easily imagine a skilful assembler of interpretations who would claim to locate the 'meaning' of the poem in its statements about pride and greed. The experience of reading the poem, however, shows clearly that although Falconer makes some game attempts to offer a meaning for the events he describes, no interpretation commands his imagination enough to dominate the poem. The emphasis of the poem, therefore, rests upon his carefully narrated scenes of disaster at sea, which remain too large for the poet's intellect. He can relive them, but he cannot explain them. Unfortunately, such explanation proves to be essential to this kind of subject, in part because it had so long served as a cultural code or paradigm that provided religious explanations for disasters.

Furthermore, *The Shipwreck* also seems to demand such metaphysical or spiritual explanations because Falconer, having no other mode into which to cast his painful experience, sought to aggrandize it, to give it poetic dignity and importance, by casting it in epic and tragic modes, modes which traditionally offer some sort of fundamental explanations. As the Australian poet A. D. Hope has the epic Muse inquire in 'Conversation with Calliope',

> since society has ended
> Its ancient pact with the divine,
> The public actions which depended
> On common faith to make them shine
> Once gone, what use is left the splendid
> Impetus of the epic line?

Falconer, who attempts to use epic devices to aggrandize his subject, does not realize that such devices themselves function as signals or codes. Although he remains unaware of the spiritual and poetic crisis described by Hope, Falconer none the less serves as an excellent instance of it, for although traditional interpretations of the nautical disaster do not attract him enough to make them the centre of his poem, he has no alternative ones to offer.

1 J. M. W. Turner, *Cottage Destroyed by an Avalanche (The Fall of an Avalanche in the Grisons)*, c. 1810. Oil on canvas; 35½ × 47½ in.

2 J. Martin, *The Destruction of Pompeii and Herculaneum*, after 1821. Oil on canvas; 33 × 48 in.

3   J. Hamilton, *The Last Days of Pompeii*, 1864. Oil on canvas; 60⅛ × 48⅛ in.

4   J. C. Dahl, *Shipwreck on the Norwegian Coast*, 1832. Oil on canvas;
28¹/₃ × 43³/₁₀ in.

5   J. M. W. Turner. *Slavers Throwing Overboard the Dead and Dying – Typhon Coming
On (The Slave Ship)*, 1840. Oil on canvas; 35³/₄ × 48 in.

6   W. Homer, *The Gulf Stream*, 1899. Oil on canvas; 28⅛ × 49⅛ in.

7   W. Homer, *The Wrecked Schooner, c.* 1903. Watercolour and charcoal;
15 × 21½ in.

8   J. M. W. Turner, *The Shipwreck*, 1805. Oil on canvas; 67½ × 95 in.

9   C. Stanfield, *The Wreck of the 'Avenger'*, undated. Watercolour, gouache and pencil; 10¼ × 15¼ in.

10   T. Géricault,
*The Raft of the
'Medusa'*, 1819.
Oil on canvas;
193 × 282 in.

11 P. de
Loutherbourg,
*Survivors of a
Shipwreck
attacked by
Robbers*, 1793.
Oil on canvas;
43¾ × 63⅛ in.

12   E. Wadsworth, *Requiescat*, 1940. Tempera on panel; 25 × 34 in.

13   C. D. Friedrich, *The Sea of Ice* (or *Arctic Shipwreck*), *c.* 1823–4. Oil on canvas; 38½ × 51⅛ in.

14   F. Danby, *The Deluge*, 1837–40. Oil on canvas; 112 × 178 in.

15   N. Poussin, *The Four Seasons: Winter (The Flood)*, 1660–4. Oil on canvas; 46½ × 63 in.

16 L. Bassano, *The Flood*, *c.* 1600. Oil on canvas; 75 × 107 in.

17 J. M. W. Turner, *The Deluge*, 1813. Oil on canvas; 57 × 93 in.

18   G. Doré, *The World Destroyed by Water*. Engraving from *The Holy Bible*.

19   A. Grimshaw, *The Seal of the Covenant*, undated. Oil on canvas; 28 × 36 in.

20   J. T. Linnell, *The Rainbow*, 1863. Oil on canvas; 44 × 63½ in.

21   D. Maclise, *Noah's Sacrifice*, 1847. Oil on canvas; 80 × 100 in.

22   J. E. Millais, *The Blind Girl*, 1856. Oil on canvas; 32½ × 24½ in.

23   J. M. W. Turner, *The Wreck Buoy*, 1849. Oil on canvas; 36½ × 48½ in.

24   J. Shroeder, *The Rainbow Dancers*, 1975. Oil on canvas; 27 × 34 in.

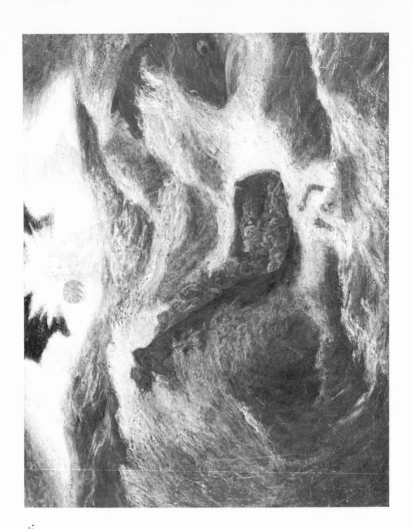

25. A. P. Ryder,
Jonah, 1885.
Oil on canvas;
27¼ × 34⅜ in.

Recognitions of the swimmer

Anthony . . .was shaken to the bottom – indeed there was no bottom, only the unthinkable abyss of human impotence opened under him. . . . Three, maybe four, men gone, swept off and smothered somewhere in the broken wake, was a fact, literal and sharp. At once the misery of wetness and fear, the noise above, like animals crowded in a dangerous pen, became a simpler thing, pitiable. If, a moment ago, Anthony could have wished them all scoured out by the hard sea, buried away and obliterated, now he felt only their wretched humanity, their common helplessness against the inhuman ocean.

James Gould Cozzens, *S. S. San Pedro,* ch. 3

A man adrift on a slim spar
A horizon smaller than the rim of a bottle.
Tented waves rearing lashy dark points
The near whine of froth in circles.
                    God is cold.
Stephen Crane, 'A man adrift on a slim spar'

The world's an orphans' home.

Marianne Moore, 'In Distrust of Merits'

After that moment when the sailor suddenly perceives that he is lost, that his charts have disappeared or become useless, and after that more terrifying moment of shipwreck when his vessel sinks in cross–seas or drives upon a reef, there comes another of those characteristic instants of recognition which inform the modern imagination – that moment when the mariner perceives the sea's complete indifference to what it destroys. It is then that one can no longer refer to the ocean as 'she'. The ocean has irrevocably become 'it', something wholly alien, wholly other. When man recognizes nature's indifference, his isolation is complete. When his ship founders, he has come to disaster – but not always final disaster: for a short time at least he can cling to the wallowing hulk or try for the lifeboat. He still has companions, even though they may soon be companions in death. But when he jumps from the stricken vessel and finds himself in the cold, churning waters, when he feels the iciness of the ocean, then he knows he is completely alone.

85

Stephen Crane, who survived shipwreck off the Florida coast on New Year's Day, 1897, presents this moment of recognition in terms of the way that sea's temperature stuns and disorients the correspondent in his autobiographical short story, 'The Open Boat':

> The January water was icy, and he reflected immediately that it was colder than he expected to find it off the coast of Florida. This appeared to his dazed mind as a fact important enough to be noted at the time. The coldness of the water was sad; it was tragic. This fact was somehow mixed and confused with his opinion of his own situation, so that it seemed almost a proper reason for tears. The water was cold.

The ocean's coldness, a mere physical quality, quickly comes to signify the complete indifference of God and nature to man. In Crane's 'A man adrift on a slim spar', a poem that remained unpublished in his lifetime, God, not the ocean, is cold. Emily Dickinson provides another version of this recognition when she tells the 'little Brig . . . o'ertook by Blast', 'The Ocean's Heart's too smooth – too Blue – / to break for You' (no. 723). Whereas to some, like Dickinson, Melville, and Crane, nature appears appallingly indifferent, to others it merely seems opaque and incomprehensible. As Neruda admits in the opening lines of 'Soliloquio en las olas' ('Soliloquy in the Waves'),

> Sí, pero aquí estoy solo.
> Se levanta
> una ola
> tal vez dice su nombre, no comprendo.

> [Yes, but it's lonely here.
> The wave builds
> and breaks, speaking
> its name, it may be: I understand nothing.
> trans. Ben Belitt]

However, like Melville's Ahab, Crane found himself, not puzzled, but infuriated by such icy indifference, since

> when it occurs to a man that nature does not regard him as important, and that she feels she would not maim the universe by disposing of him, he at first wishes to throw bricks at the

temple, and he hates deeply the fact that there are no bricks and no temples.

As George Monteiro's essential essay on 'The Open Boat' demonstrates, Crane communicates his recognition that there are 'no temples' by invoking a complex gathering of cultural codes that were accepted by most of his contemporary audience. Hymns, sermons, and emblem books taught nineteenth-century Protestants that Christ the pilot was always present in one's lifeboat. Crane's autobiographical short story, therefore, contradicts commonplace Christian interpretations of the emblematic situation of the man in the imperilled vessel.

> Crane's details in 'The Open Boat' were drawn from actual experience, of course, but they are details resonant with meaning, especially when they are viewed against the background of nineteenth-century evangelical Christianity. . . . He matched his personal experiences of shipwreck against the essentialist, allegorical teachings of nineteenth-century Protestantism as he knew them, and he found their optimism decidedly wrong-headed. While the hymns talk of Christianity as the life-boat which in itself provides safety and salvation, Crane's story tells of a dinghy which at the last becomes as dangerous to human life as the sea itself.[17]

Furthermore, as Professor Monteiro demonstrates, the castaway's experience in the waste ocean not only thus disproves the relevance of the Christian scheme of things but it also goes further and wears away at our most basic conceptions of self and causality.[18]

Whereas Crane's 'The Open Boat' uses the situation of the castaway as an implicit criticism and parody of Protestant hymns, the poetry of William Cowper, who himself wrote hymns, arrives at the same modern imaginative landscape by a very different route. Cowper's 'The Castaway', which is probably the best known of all English depictions of the swimmer in the waste ocean, confesses that 'misery still delights to trace/ Its semblance in another's case' and then describes the plight of one swept overboard by raging seas who drowns because help cannot reach him. He then closes the poem by emphasizing his own abandonment and spiritual destruction:

> No voice divine the storm allay'd
> No light propitious shone;

When, snatch'd from all effectual aid,
    We perish'd, each alone:
But I beneath a rougher sea,
And whelm'd in deeper gulphs than he. [ll. 61-6]

Cowper's poem is a turning-point in the iconology of spiritual shipwreck. Before it such shipwreck always represents a divine punishment, test, or lesson, whereas afterwards (perhaps in large part because of this poem's influence) the situation increasingly represents the disappearance of God. What makes 'The Castaway' so difficult to interpret finally is that, although it apparently presents this modern sense of abandonment, the evidence of biography and his other poetry argues that Cowper believed his experience as castaway was God's punishment for his sins.

Even when making apparently straightforward uses of traditional Christian commonplaces, he makes this absence of God an unsettling element in his verse. 'Human Frailty', for example, points out that man inevitably shipwrecks without divine assistance:

Bound on a voyage of awful length
    And dangers little known,
A stranger to superior strength,
    Man vainly trusts his own.

But oars alone can ne'er prevail
    To reach the distant coast,
The breath of heav'n must swell the sail,
    Or all the toil is lost. [ll. 17-24]

When placed in the context of his other poems, such a commonplace statement of man's dependence upon God takes on a particular poignancy, for even here Cowper has no confidence that God will in fact 'swell the sails'. He has stated the conditions of survival, but the conditional nature of the statement reminds us that here, as in so many of his poems, God is mentioned as *not* being present: He is a hoped-for presence, a condition necessary for success, survival, and salvation. Such a description of God is not all that unusual in religious verse and hymnody, but in his most powerful poems Cowper does not seem able to move from a conditional – and absent – deity to a present one who sustains him. 'Temptation', which expresses his hope that he will make safe haven, characteristically closes, not with the certainty that he has reached God or will reach Him, but with the injunction that the difficulties of the voyage might not prevent his search from continuing:

> Tho' tempest-toss'd and half a wreck,
> My saviour thro' the flood I seek;
> Let neither winds nor stormy main
> Force back my shatter'd bark again. [ll. 17-20]

Already envisaging himself as a wreck, he continues his voyage, but the frequently despairing Cowper seems to have little hope that he could close his voyage successfully. Several times, in fact, he expresses the conviction that he is a castaway. Thus, in the verses he wrote on John Newton's safe return from a sea voyage ('To the Reverend Mr. Newton on his Return from Ramsgate'), he tells his friend and Evangelical mentor, who had himself exchanged the life of a slave-ship captain for that of a preacher, that

> Your sea of troubles you have past,
>   And found the peaceful shore;
> I, tempest-toss'd, and wreck'd at last,
>   Come home to port no more. [ll. 13-16]

The poet's sense of being isolated from both man and God led him to see himself in the guise of Robinson Crusoe, and once again, he employs the post-Christian intonation of this figure. In other words, he sees himself, not the way Defoe presented Crusoe – as a man shipwrecked and cast away by God for his spiritual edification – but simply as an example of isolated, abandoned humanity. In Cowper's vision of the voyage of life,

> the wreck'd mariner may strive
>   Some desert shore to gain,
> Secure of life if he survive
>   The fury of the main:
>
> But there, to famine doom'd a prey
>   Finds the mistaken wretch!
> He but escap'd the troubled sea,

To perish on the beach.
['Mortals! Around Your Destin'd Heads', ll. 13-20]

Cowper, who so powerfully presents such vignettes of men perishing in isolation and despair, obviously saw himself living in this situation as the primal castaway. His verses 'On the Death of Sir W. Russell' overtly claim that he is such a hapless survivor of maritime disaster:

See me – ere yet my destin'd course half done
Cast forth a wand'rer on a wild unknown!
See neglected on the world's rude coast,
Each dear companion of my voyage lost! [ll. 15–18]

Similarly, his lines on Alexander Selkirk, the original of Robinson Crusoe, close with the abandoned mariner complaining, 'I must finish my journey alone', and although neither Selkirk nor Crusoe did in fact perish on his respective island, Cowper seemed certain he would do so on his.

The poet's Evangelical sense of sin so convinced him of his own depravity that he came to believe that God had abandoned him, despite his awareness that such conviction was despair, the greatest of sins. His despair thrust Cowper into the modern imaginative landscape in which God has disappeared. The very absence of God in 'The Castaway' makes it a precursor of much later work, for whereas the older Christian uses of the situation, which still appear in Coleridge, Hopkins, and Hugo, always rely on a dual perspective that presents both the abandonment and the presence of God, the later version concentrates solely on the experience of the man shipwrecked and cast away – in other words, on the consequences of God's absence.

Like Crane, Arthur Hugh Clough, the friend of Emerson and Arnold, describes the frightening indifference of the universe which devours man, but he does not have to shipwreck literally to understand this. Gazing at the ocean from the deck of his ship, Clough's protagonist in *Amours de Voyage* perceives man's true situation in this world, and in doing so he employs both the situation of the castaway and one of its equivalents of transformations:

Standing, uplifted, alone on the heaving poop of the vessel,
Looking around on the waste of the rushing incurious billows,

'This is Nature,' I said: 'we are born as it were from her waters,
Over her billows that buffet and beat us, her offspring uncared-for,
Casting one single regard of a painful victorious knowledge,
Into her billows that buffet and beat us we sink and are swallowed.'

[canto 3, sec. 2]

According to Clough, as according to Melville, man exists an
'offspring uncared-for', an orphan, a waif. Like the situation of the
castaway, that of the waif struck men who had lost their religious
belief as a fitting metaphor for the human condition.[19] Throughout
Moby Dick, for example, Ishmael describes the crew of the *Pequod* as
orphans and castaways, gradually making the two as equivalent in the
world of Melville as they are in the world of Dickens. All three
authors would have agreed with Mr Jarndyce's observation in *Bleak
House* that the 'universe makes a rather indifferent parent' (ch. 6).
Each of Dickens's novels has at least half-a-dozen orphans – *Bleak
House* has nine among the main characters – and it is clear that, like
Clough, Melville, and James Thomson, he sees the situation of the
orphan as universally applicable.[20]

Moby Dick provides a fitting emblem of this sense of the world
when Starbuck's boat becomes separated from the *Pequod* one night.
The mate lights a lantern, and then 'stretching it on a waif pole,
handed it to Queequeg as the standard-bearer of this forlorn hope.
. . . There, then, he sat, the sign and symbol of a man without faith,
hopelessly holding up hope in the midst of despair' (ch. 48). This
concern with man shipwrecked, cast away, and orphaned permeates
the imagery of Melville's novel, focusing our attention on the
author's sense of being in the world. At one point Ishmael tells us
that 'our souls are like those orphans whose unwedded mothers die
in bearing them; the secret of our paternity lies in their grave, and
we must there to learn it' (ch. 114). Whether or not we are the
children of God, or of a god, that is the question! The chapter
entitled 'The Castaway', in which the cabin boy, Pip, jumps from the
whale boat in mid-chase, would suggest that whatever our origins,
we are now orphans. Pip, says Ishmael, saw God's foot upon the
loom and was thought mad. Pip, he says, had at last seen the
ambiguous maddening wisdom of the universe and became as
'indifferent as his God'. This same chapter tells how 'from the centre
of the sea, Pip turned his crisp, curling, black head to the sun,
another lonely castaway, though the loftiest and the brightest' (ch.

93), and we receive the impression of an entire world, an entire universe, which has been forgotten by God.

Melville reminds us that just as men have felt the indifference of nature and their situation as orphans, so, too, they realize that in this situation 'the awful lonesomeness is intolerable. The intense concentration of self in the midst of such a heartless immensity, my God! who can tell it?' (ch. 93). *Moby Dick* again and again reveals man struggling to keep himself from being swallowed by what Conrad's *Nostromo* calls 'the immense indifference of things' (pt 3, ch. 10), so that the situation of Pip widens until it encompasses the fates of all on the ill-fated *Pequod*. In this transformation of the castaway's situation into a figure for the human condition, Melville's great novel becomes representative of much art and literature since the late eighteenth century.

Shipwrecked and cast away in the sea of time

Child, you arise and smile to me
Out of the night, out of the sea,
The Nereid of a moment there . . .
O lost and wrecked, how long ago,
Out of the drowning past.

Arthur Symons, 'Stella Maris'

Consider the sea's listless chime:
Time's self it is, made audible, –
The murmur of the earth's own shell.
Secret continuance sublime
Is the sea's end: our sight may pass
No furlong further. Since time was,
This sound hath told the lapse of time.

Dante Gabriel Rossetti, 'The Sea-Limits'

Heroism, endurance, or plain luck can help one survive the oceans of this world, but no one escapes the sea of time. Eventually, in the words of Pablo Neruda's 'Soliloquy in the Waves', 'el tiempo destruyó todos los labios/ con la paciencia/ de la sombra' (time wrecks all lips with the patience of darkness). For those who accept the Christian belief in an afterlife, earthly time appears a trial, a probationary period that readies one for a higher, fuller existence. According to this scheme of things, when one finds oneself at last submerged in the waves of time, one sinks, as Emily Dickinson put it, to mortality's 'Ground Floor . . . Immortality' (no. 1,234). But those who abandon Christianity also necessarily abandon its conception of human time as an ante-room to eternity, and they therefore find themselves in a temporal landscape marked by discontinuity and lack of duration.[21]

Western thought has long employed water analogies to formulate conceptions of time. Either it is conceived as an ocean beneath whose waves one sinks, or else, in an important variant, it is seen as an onrushing river or current whose movement cannot be slowed. Using this second figure, Neruda thus writes of 'el tiempo,/ el transcurrir temible' (time,/ that terrifying flow) and describes in 'A Don Asterio Alarcón conometrista de Valparáiso' ('To Don Asterio Alarcón, Clocksmith of Valparáiso') how

> el relojero,
> entre relojes,
> detenido en el tiempo,
> se suavizó como la nave pura
> contra la eternidad de la corriente.

> [the clockmaker,
> among clocks,
> trapped in time,
> proceeded smoothly, like a clean ship,
> against the eternal current.]

In his essay 'Crabbed Age and Youth' Robert Louis Stevenson similarly compares

> the headlong course of our years to a swift torrent in which
> a man is carried away; now he is dashed against a boulder,
> now he grapples for a moment to a trailing spray; at the end,
> he is hurled out and overwhelmed in a dark and bottomless
> ocean.

In contrast to this ancient metaphor of time as a river, which was a particular favourite of English writers of the 1890s, there is another which conceives it as a devouring ocean. Swinburne, who creates an entire imaginative cosmos out of the notion of being wrecked in the sea of time, emphasizes again and again that all love, all life, all civilization sinks beneath these waters. As the 'Hymn to Proserpine' explains to the old 'Gods dethroned and deceased, cast forth, wiped out in a day' (l. 13) by the coming of Christianity, all things perish in the waters of this ocean:

All delicate days and pleasant, all spirits and sorrows are cast
Far out with the foam of the present that sweeps to the surf of the past:
Where beyond the extreme sea-wall, and between the remote sea-gates,
Waste water washes, and tall ships founder, and deep death waits.

[ll. 47–50]

According to Swinburne, our situation as castaways in the sea of time defines our lives and loves, for like these old gods and their worshippers, we all find ourselves immersed in this ocean.

Many of the poet's presentations of man shipwrecked and cast away in the sea of time appear in the context of works that concern lost love. For him the fact that time destroys all love provides a central or paradigmatic situation that he expands to embrace all human life and activity. As he wrote with self-conscious cynicism to Joseph Knight about his own lyric 'At Parting', he found his emphasis upon the brevity of love far more honest and accurate than the views of other contemporary poets.

I pique myself on its moral tone; in an age when all other
lyrists[sic], from Tennyson to Rossetti, go in (metrically) for
constancy and eternity of attachment and reunion in future
lives, etc., etc., I limit love, honestly and candidly, to 24
hours; and quite enough too in all conscience. [8 July 1875]

Swinburne takes essentially the same view in his early 'Félise', whose epigraph, appropriately, is 'Mais où sont les neiges d'antan?' This dramatic monologue presents essentially the opposite situation to that found in 'The Triumph of Time', which had appeared earlier in the same volume, the 1866 *Poems and Ballads*. In 'Félise' the man abandons the woman, and, rather than remain silent, as does the speaker in 'The Triumph of Time', he explains to her that it is in the nature of things that time wrecks all love and that, once over, such love is drowned forever:

No diver brings up love again
  Dropped once, my beautiful Félise,
  In such cold seas.

Gone deeper than all plummets sound,
  Where in the dim green dayless day
The life of such dead things lies bound
  As the sea feeds on, wreck and stray
  And castaway.

Can I forget? yea, that can I,
  And that can all men; so will you. [ll. 73–82]

Such cynicism is poetically uncharacteristic of Swinburne, no matter how much he displays it in his letters, since his usual practice is to speak from the point of view of the suffering lover – which is to say from within the painful experience of being shipwrecked and cast away.

'The Triumph of Time', one of his finest early poems, opens with the figure of shipwreck, for now, as he is about to part from his unnamed beloved, he realizes that he exists, and will exist henceforth, in the condition of the shipwrecked mariner:

Before our lives divide for ever,
  While time is with us and hands are free,
(Time, swift to fasten and swift to sever
  Hand from hand, as we stand by the sea)
I will say no word that a man might say
Whose whole life's love goes down in a day. [ll. 1–6]

Therefore, all that follows in the poem must be taken as an interior monologue, for the poet has chosen to keep silent and suppress his complaint to the lost beloved. After emphasizing the fact of his loss with a claim that the two of them together could have been as gods and could have made themselves one with the elements, the speaker turns from such broken dreams to confront a desertlike landscape bordering upon the waste ocean. This landscape, we soon realize, serves as the equivalent of the speaker's state of mind and spirit, for both are 'sick of the run and the rain' (l. 60), bleak and burnt. Here, confronting the 'sweet sea, mother of loves and hours' (l. 62), the saddened lover recognizes that

> The loves and hours of the life of a man,
>> They are swift and sad, being born of the sea.
> Hours that rejoice and regret for a span,
>> Born with a man's breath, mortal as he;
> Loves that are lost ere they come to birth,
>> Weeds of the wave, without fruit upon earth. [ll. 73–8]

He then declares that, although he has lost that which he most desires, he will save what he can – and then he immediately realizes how little human beings can preserve at all:

> It is not much that a man can save
>> On the sands of life, in the straits of time,
> Who swims in sight of the great third wave
>> That never a swimmer shall cross or climb.
> Some waif washed up with the strays and the spars
> That ebb-tide shows to the shore and the stars;
> Weed from the water, grass from a grave,
>> A broken blossom, a ruined rhyme. [ll. 81–8]

Man, himself a castaway in the sea of time, can only preserve stray waifs and sea drift, one form of which is poetry.

In 'The Triumph of Time', all of which, we recall, takes place in an unspoken instant of recognition, Swinburne finds a function for poetry and can thus respond affirmatively to the question Gerard Manley Hopkins asks in a very different context – 'is the shipwreck then a harvest . . . ?' (*The Wreck of the Deutschland,* st. 31). Poetry allows Swinburne to transform the sorrows and ravages of time into beauty, and furthermore, it captures – in fact, rescues – certain significant moments from the devouring ocean. For Swinburne as for Rossetti, poetry can enrich these instants of illumination, making them true centres for our lives. Unlike Rossetti, who most characteristically relies upon concentrated forms, such as the sonnet, to create and preserve such significant moments, Swinburne chooses far more diffuse forms that permit him to return to his central poetic idea from different points of the compass. As Jerome J. McGann has pointed out:

> His method of thought turns all sequential processes of
> beginnings, middles, and ends into self-contained circles. This
> is why he characteristically talks about the 'life' of Tristram
> and Iseult in spatial rather than temporal terms: their

essential life never changes, never needs to be sought for and found. . . Stylistically, the result is that his poetry tends not to move in a direction, like a path, but to accumulate additions, like coral. . . . His propensity is toward forms which do not so much move forward as they spin off from a center, accumulating all the while what can be a bewildering variety of figures and images which are constantly interacting with each other.[22]

Whereas Tennyson and Browning write a cumulative poetry that builds to moments of illumination, Swinburne's characteristic poetic form derives from the fact that his poetic ideas develop from a centre or germ, move out from his centre, but are inevitably drawn back to it; and then the process repeats itself over and over, each tracing of the mental path depositing additional layers of meaning and emotion upon the central idea. In 'The Triumph of Time', for instance, the speaker begins by silently telling his beloved (whom he addresses only within the confines of his own mind) that he will not say anything that a man might say on such an occasion of irrevocable loss, but he immediately finds himself forced to think about what they have lost. This dream of what might have been soon brings him back to the fact of loss, he pulls himself up short, and then the process, which dramatizes the obsessive power of his longing, begins again. Such a means of poetic organization simultaneously locks the speaker within the moment of suffering but also allows him to expand it until it encompasses all life and all time. Swinburne's characteristic poetic organization, in other words, is obviously related intimately to his conceptions of time and human life, for although it is ill suited for conveying Tennysonian forms of experience, it permits him to endow certain carefully chosen situations with a central importance and thus turn them into representative moments.

For Swinburne such moments, as we have already seen, often take the form of moments of loss. 'The Triumph of Time' dramatizes the mind of one who experiences the loss of his beloved, and 'Hymn to Proserpine' presents the experience of a Roman of the fourth century A.D. who is losing his gods, the old pagan deities, now that Christianity has become the official religion of the state. After asserting that all gods, men, and things disappear within the sea of time, Swinburne's speaker tells the old Roman deities

Ye are Gods, and behold, ye shall die, and the waves be upon you at last.
In the darkness of time, in the deeps of the years, in the changes of
things,
Ye shall sleep as a slain man sleeps, and the world shall forget
you for kings. [ll. 68–70]

Swinburne thus dramatizes the thoughts and emotions of a person experiencing the shipwreck of an entire culture and its beliefs. Like Browning and Tennyson, he employs dramatic monologues in which historically reconstructed characters serve as Emersonian representative men. Tennyson's Tithonus and Ulysses, however, are, strictly speaking, not historical embodiments of different periods of human culture. Instead, they serve as mythic dramatizations of possible answers to problems troubling Tennyson. Tithonus, the mythic figure who has gained immortality without retaining his youth and vitality, responds, like Swift's Struldbrugs, to the question, what if human beings lived for ever? Ulysses, on the other hand, responds to the question, how should human beings confront death?

Unlike Tennyson, Browning and Swinburne employ, not new versions of well-known mythic figures, but imagined characters who represent a certain historical situation. Browning's Cleon, Karshish, and the bishop ordering his tomb at St Praxed's each captures what he considers the essential ideas and attitudes of a particular lost age, though of course each is also immediately relevant to the poet's readers because he can tell them something of importance about themselves as well. For example, Cleon's intellectual pride, like the bishop's materialism, helps Browning's reader understand both an earlier age's spiritual problems and his own.

In 'Hymn to Proserpine' Swinburne also concerns himself to embody specific historical conditions within a fictional character who thus becomes a representative man. Furthermore, again like Browning, he chooses a figure living in an age of transition from one religion to another. However, when Browning looks at men of late antiquity to learn what they can tell his contemporaries about the needs and difficulties of the human spirit, he conducts his investigations from the vantage-point of a Victorian Protestant. He wishes to demonstrate, for example, what the experience of life in these earlier times can tell his audience of man's essential, defining need for religious faith. Moreover, Browning looks at the transition from the pagan to the Christian world as an essentially good thing, while Swinburne, who had little sympathy with Christianity, does not. As one might expect, 'Hymn to Proserpine' and similar poems identify with the position of the imagined historical character far more than do Browning's analogous works. Whereas Browning's 'Cleon' takes the form of high intellectual satire, as do many of his other poems such as 'Caliban Upon Setebos' and 'The Bishop Orders His Tomb at St Praxed's', Swinburne's poem both makes us understand the pagan's point of view and also suggests that it is one suitable for the nineteenth century. In particular, 'Hymn to Proserpine', which questioned contemporary beliefs in both Christianity and progress, makes us realize that change is not always progress.[23] Christianity came as a form of barbarism to the refined pagans of the fourth century, and the passion with which Swinburne invests his speaker's objections against the new religion makes them seem credible. The poet enforces his historical pessimism by having this representative of a dying age turn prophet and warn that the Christian gods, too, will in their turn find themselves submerged beneath the waves of time.

Using a different poetic strategy in 'By the North Sea', Swinburne argues that time has already wrecked Christianity as it had long ago destroyed the worship of Venus and Proserpine. Whereas 'Hymn to Proserpine' employs a fictional pagan speaker from a vanished age to communicate the experience of crisis and loss, 'By the North Sea' takes the form of a meditation upon a land- and seascape. Swinburne, who is the laureate of the bleak, barren places of the earth, takes Dunwich on the Suffolk coast as an emblem of the way time has already destroyed the faith that had centuries before driven out the pagan gods. In a letter he wrote on 10 January 1876 to his friend Edwin Harrison, he emphasized that this part of the coast had struck him as unique and

> quite new to me except that I read of it in the Odyssey as the shore of Hades. Do you know it? It is unlike any *other* known to me. Fancy a cathedral city, which had its Bishop and members and six great Churches, one a minster, and an immense monastery and hospital for lepers – and now the sea has slowly swallowed all but two shells of ruined masonry, and just twenty cottages, inn and school included. This is Dunwich – literally built on the sand – on and behind a high crumbling sea-bank, looking out to a sea where the nearest

land is Denmark. Great fresh-water lakes sweep away
inland from the very verge of the sea, parted from them only
by pebble-banks and ridge of shingle – a sea without rocks or
cliff, but the worst in England for shipwrecks.

As one can gather from his description of Dunwich, Swinburne
found his imagination compelled by the fact of this once important
religious centre being swallowed by the sea.

When he came to transform his experience of this wasteland into
a poem, he described in detail a desolate, fruitless, exhausted place
that has two deathless lords, 'Death's self, and the sea' (pt 1, st. 3). In
attempting to find language adequate to convey the strange,
inhuman bleakness of Dunwich, he tentatively describes it in terms
of the underworld that Odysseus encountered but then decides that
this landscape is even bleaker and cannot be humanized by such
cultural allusions. This is a landscape 'dispeopled of visions', even
'forlorn of shadows', and entirely without spirits of any sort –
'Ghostless, all its gulfs and creeks and reaches,/ Sky, and shore, and
cloud, and waste, and sea' (pt 3, st. 15). After a characteristically
elaborate parody of the Nicene Creed, whose description of the
Saviour Swinburne applies to time, he depicts vanished religion.

> Church and hospice wrought in faultless fashion,
> > Hall and chancel bounteous and sublime,
> Wide and sweet and glorious as compassion,
> > Filled and thrilled with force of choral chime;
> Filled with spirit of prayer and thrilled with passion,
> > Hailed a God more merciful than Time.
>
> Ah, less mighty, less than Time prevailing,
> > Shrunk, expelled, make nothing at his nod,
> Less than clouds across the sea-line sailing,
> > Lies he, stricken by his master's rod.
> 'Where is man?' the cloister murmurs wailing;
> Back the mute shrine thunders – 'Where is God?'
>
> Here is all the end of all his glory –
> > Dust, and grass, and barren silent stones.
> Dead, like him, one hollow tower and hoary
> > Naked in the sea-wind stands and moans.
>
> > > > > > [pt 6, sts 8–10]

In the succeeding stanzas Swinburne presents a vision of horror, for turning from the desecrated, destroyed buildings that once were built to the everlasting glory of an everlasting Christian God, he draws our attention to the graves that have been uncovered and swallowed by the sea's encroachment upon the land. 'Graves where men made sure to rest' (st. 11) now lie 'displaced, devoured and desecrated' (st. 12), and the bodies of men who thought they would awaken only to the 'archangel's re-creating word' and 'blast of judgment' now 'sink into the waste of waves' (st. 12):

> Tombs, with bare white piteous bones protruded,
>> Shroudless, down the loose collapsing banks,
> Crumble, from their constant place detruded,
>> That the sea devours and gives not thanks.
> Graves where hope and prayer and sorrow brooded
>> Gape and slide and perish, ranks on ranks.

> Rows on rows and line by line they crumble. . . .
> Earth, and man, and all their gods wax humble
>> Here, where Time brings pasture to the sea. [st. 14–15]

The sixth section of the poem, which builds to this grotesque parody of the Last Judgment, thus reveals that time and death conquer all. Man, his graves and his gods sink beneath the literal ocean and beneath the waves of time.

Swinburne, however, does not end the poem on this bleak note. In the final section, which is composed of seven stanzas, he turns away from 'the shadow of this death,/ This place of the sepulchres' (st. 4) to sing a paean to the sun, which for Swinburne represents the powers of poetry and imagination. Finally, accepting time, rejoicing in its changes, the poet closes by rendering thanks for his songs and dreams. Unfortunately, clear and untroubled as the note that Swinburne here sounds is, it cannot dispel the gloom that he has laboured so well to create, and raising his eyes to the sun therefore seems perfunctory and even evasive. Because he has devoted so much energy and so many lines to his personifications of death and time, which became the deities of this wasteland, his introduction of the sun strikes the reader as too abrupt, for either the sun has not room in this pantheon or else, if it does, it should have appeared earlier. One anthology of Swinburne's verse prints 'By the North

101

Sea' and omits the closing section, and while such a procedure distorts what the poet actually wrote, it does make the point that the poem builds towards the close of section six, after which the closing few stanzas seem forced and out of place.

Unlike 'The Dry Salvages' from T. S. Eliot's *The Four Quartets,* which also presents a vision of humanity shipwrecked in a sea of time, Swinburne's 'By the North Sea' does not, finally, have a way to insert a divinity into an apparently godless universe. Eliot, of course, also emphasizes time the destroyer, the wrecker:

> We cannot think of time that is oceanless
> Or of an ocean not littered with wastage
> Or of a future that is not liable
> Like the past, to have no destination. . . .

> There is no end of it, the voiceless wailing,
> No end to the withering of withered flowers
> To the movement of pain that is painless and motionless,
> To the drift of the sea and the drifting wreckage.[24]

Eliot, however, from the beginning of the second section of 'The Dry Salvages' has mentioned that cryptic 'calamitous annunciation' even as he describes his scenes of men shipwrecked in the sea of time. Eventually, we come to perceive that this annunciation is The Annunciation, and that it refers to Christ's appearance in human history; for like Browning, Tennyson, and Hopkins, Eliot finds all human history ordered by the Incarnation. Christ's appearance in human flesh, His earthly career, and His death serve as centres to human time – those true, authentic significant moments upon which Rossetti and Joyce patterned their more limited human ones.[25]

From a poetic point of view, 'The Dry Salvages' succeeds better than does 'By the North Sea' in introducing a deity who can save man from perishing in the waters of time. First of all, this discovery of an immanent God enters the poem, although in cryptic form, not long after the opening, and it does not, therefore, seem a somewhat desperate afterthought. Second, difficult as is the manner of Eliot's presentation, it still refers to those basic tenets of Christianity which make it serve as a cultural code. Even though many in Eliot's audience may not accept Christianity, they can both understand something of its basic notions and recognize that it forms a sincere, serious faith. Swinburne's sun god, in contrast, is too private, too undeveloped, too arbitary to bear the weight placed upon him in 'By the North Sea', however much he may successfully do so in other poems. Of course, one wonders, finally, how much of Eliot's relative success in this matter derives from his willing obscurity? Would a clearer statement of Christian belief have fallen so flat that, like Swinburne, his attempt to introduce a deity into the intellectual landscape dominated by the ocean of time would have immediately revealed its desperation? Indeed, if one does not grant Eliot his High Church Anglicanism, does not his poem, like Swinburne's, succeed largely as a vision of man shipwrecked and cast away in the sea of time?

Variations of Robinson Crusoe

I am no mere sickened leaf on a dead tide. . . . All of us [were] wrecked together in a Chinatown cafe and waiting for the rising tide, another dark whim of the sea. . . . For a moment I saw them, these bloated shapes . . . that marked the long wild curve of our reckless detour into the dark and milky night. Abandoned. As we were abandoned. . . . I fell back and found myself staring up at a gray sky, gray scudding clouds, a thick palpable reality of air in which only the barometer and a few weak signals of distress could survive. An inhuman daytime sky. . . . I was alone, abandoned, left behind. . . . And then my heart was floating in a dark sea, in my stomach the waves were commencing their dark action. . . . I was tossed up spent and half-naked on the invisible shore of our wandering island – old Ariel in sneakers, sprite surviving in bald-headed man of fair complexion . . . I was done with the water, the uncomfortable drift of a destructive ocean, done trying to make myself acceptable to the Old Man of the Sea.

John Hawkes, *Second Skin*

After escaping the surf that has battered and nearly drowned him, Robinson Crusoe manages to drag himself ashore; and looking back at the hostile sea, he is at first carried away by joy at his good luck in escaping the fate of his shipmates. But when he turns his gaze from the sea to examine his new surroundings, he suddenly realizes that he has had, after all, 'a dreadful deliverance; for I was wet, had no clothes to shift me, nor anything else either to eat or drink to comfort me, neither did I see any prospect before me, but that of perishing with hunger, or being devour'd by wild beasts'. Crusoe's first reaction reminds us of Dante's when, in the twentieth line of the *Inferno,* he likens himself to one 'who with labouring breath has escaped from the waters to the shore'. Dante, however, does not find himself perishing in a waste desert, for Vergil, having been sent by Beatrice, soon arrives to save him from the isolation of sin. Crusoe, too, is saved when the ship remains wedged among the rocks that had destroyed it – for his tale, like Dante's, is also one of spiritual education and consequent spiritual deliverance.[26]

An author, a nation, an age all define themselves by what they understand and misunderstand about their predecessors, and almost all nineteenth- and twentieth-century writers who allude to this most famous of castaways completely disregard Defoe's obvious theological emphasis, choosing instead to see Crusoe as an example of man's essential isolation. Hemingway's *For Whom the Bell Tolls* uses the words of John Donne to assert the existence of *communitas,* but far more characteristic of Romantic and post-Romantic literature has been the assertion that life is both metaphysically and humanly islanded.

This interpretation of reality appears with particular clarity in literary allusions to Robinson Crusoe. For instance, the opening lines of Daryl Hine's 'Among Islands' tells how

> We are exiles everywhere we go,
> Stranded upon the veranda, castaways
> In the family living room, like Crusoe,
> Or like Philoctetes, festering,
> Having given away the Herculean bow,
> With nothing to call our own except the wound.

And when Hank, the main character of Twain's *A Connecticut Yankee in King Arthur's Court,* realizes his situation, he concludes that he 'was just another Robinson Crusoe cast away on an uninhabited island, with no society but some more or less tame animals' (ch. 7). Even those who still have faith, like Mrs Gaskell, the author of *North and South,* see *Robinson Crusoe* only as an exemplar of human isolation. When Mrs Gaskell's political novel presents the industrialist Henry Thornton defining the nature of man, he naturally happens upon the image of Crusoe. According to Thornton, who in the earlier part of the novel represents unreconstructed *laissez-faire* capitalism in its harshest form, 'gentleman' is a term that describes the human being only in relation to others,

> but when we speak of him as 'a man,' we consider him . . .
> in relation to himself – to life – to time – to eternity. A casta-
> way, lonely as Robinson Crusoe . . . has his endurance, his
> strength, his faith best described by his being spoken of as 'a
> man'. [ch. 20]

Thus Thornton, who assumes that all men exist in basic isolation as social atoms, can hold that a man's social relations are trivial in comparison to the basic nature of humanity in industrial society. Characteristically, he does not seem frightened by the implications of his image of the human condition. One may add that it is no coincidence that when Georg Lukács comes to describe man in capitalist society, he chooses the same image as the wife of the Victorian minister. For according to his 'Reification and the Consciousness of the Proletariat', the kind of human being who emerges in the industrial age 'must be the individual, egotistic bourgeois isolated aritificially by capitalism . . . [with] an individual isolated consciousness à la Robinson Crusoe.' The degree to which Defoe's character has become the embodiment of human isolation appears most strongly, perhaps, in the fact that when the philosopher Gilbert Ryle comes to attack what he terms the 'official theory' of epistemology since Descartes, he points out how mistakenly it urges the view that 'the mind is its own place and in his inner life each of us lives the life of a ghostly Robinson Crusoe' (*The Concept of Mind,* ch. 1).

Closely related to this characteristically modern reinterpretation of Defoe's story is the image of the island, or more properly, of an island existence. In what we may term its metaphysical form, this image conveys the belief – to use the words of Stevens's 'Sunday Morning' – that we exist in an 'island solitude, unsponsored, free,/ Of that wide water, inescapable.' On the other hand, in its second major form this image emphasizes that every man is an island; or as Matthew Arnold put it:

> Yes! in the sea of life enisled.
> With echoing straits between us thrown,
> Dotting the shoreless watery wild,
> We mortal millions live *alone.*

The islands feel the enclasping flow,
And then their endless bounds they know.
['Switzerland, no. 5. To Marguerite Continued.']

Both versions of the basic image achieve more than the rhetorical force of any good analogy. Both, in fact, are capable of generating an entire imaginative world, an entire metaphysic brought into being by their appearance. Although observing the existence of the image of islanded man is a worthy enough contribution to a study of nineteenth- and twentieth-century iconography, I am far more interested in this image's essential capacity to create an imaginative universe.

One reason, surely, that this literary commonplace can thus function is that it centres on a moment of recognition and is commonly employed to convey the experience of such a moment which marks a break with one's past experience. A new life, however perilous and lonely, begins at the moment of recognition. Sometimes, as in Conrad's *Nostromo,* the recognition is too much to be borne. In that novel, Decoud

> found himself solitary on the beach, like a man in a dream . . .
> [amid] the black wastes of sky and sea around the islet. . . .
> He died from solitude, the enemy known to but few on this
> earth, and whom only the simplest of us are fit to with stand.
> . . . Solitude from mere outward condition of existence
> becomes very swiftly a state of soul. . . . After three days of
> waiting for the sight of some human face, Decoud caught
> himself entertaining a doubt of his own individuality. . . . The
> brilliant Martin Decoud . . . disappeared without a trace,
> swallowed up in the immense indifference of things.
> [pt 3, ch. 10]

Some like Decoud perish; others, like Stevens, Ruskin, and Arnold, try to make an accommodation.

The way nineteenth- and twentieth-century authors have chosen to interpret Defoe's character reveals the great extent to which the situation of the castaway has impressed itself upon the modern imagination. Clearly, there have been many like Poe's Arthur Gordon Pym whose 'visions were of shipwreck and famine . . . of a lifetime dragged out in sorrow and tears, upon some gray and desolate rock, in an ocean unapproachable and unknown' (ch.2).[27]

A twentieth-century writer who has made his poetic accommodation with this sense of being in the world is the contemporary Australian poet A. D. Hope, who rings many changes on the image – or rather *situation* – of islanded man. This recognition of one's existence as a castaway occurs in 'Man Friday', Hope's continuation of *Robinson Crusoe*. According to his version, Crusoe, saved by *his* God, 'Took into exile Friday and the bird':

> Friday, the dark Caribbean man,
> Picture his situation if you can:
> The gentle savage, taught to speak and pray,
> On England's Desert Island cast away,
> No godlike Crusoe issuing from his cave,
> Comes with his thunderstick to slay and save;
> Instead from caves to stone, as thick as trees,
> More dreadful than ten thousand savages, . . .
> The pale-eyed English swarm to joke and stare,
> With endless questions round him crowd and press
> Curious to see and touch his loneliness.

In this new situation 'mere ingenuity', such as had saved Crusoe, is useless, and 'As Crusoe made his clothes, so he no less,/ Must labour to invent his nakedness.' But memories and imagination cannot prevail, and when he and Crusoe visit the shore, Friday follows the prints made by an unshod foot into the surf. When Crusoe comes upon the body later he 'never guessed' that 'Friday had been rescued and gone home.'

Hope himself makes his own human accommodation to Australia,

> a vast parasite robber-state
> Where second-hand Europeans pullulate
> Timidly on the edge of alien shores.

For turning from 'the lush jungle of modern thought', the poet prefers 'the Arabian desert of the human mind', since from 'that waste' springs a 'scarlet' more intense than in supposedly more habitable situations. Hope, as poet, likes his particular island.

The image of the island existence, and its related image of the shipwreck, runs all through Hope's fine poetry, appearing variously in 'Heldensagen', 'Observation Car', 'The Death of the Bird', and, of course, 'The Wandering Islands'. In this last poem Hope develops the poetic commonplace that we are all islands which Matthew Arnold employed with such conspicuous mediocrity. He tells us in the opening lines that

> You cannot build bridges between the wandering islands;
> The Mind has no neighbours, and the unteachable heart
> Announces its armistice time after time, but spends
> Its love to draw them closer and closer apart.

These islands are not on the charts, they wander 'A refuge only for the shipwrecked sailor'. At times two islands – two human beings – come together in an instant of love:

> the castaway hails the castaway,
> But the sounds perish in that earthquake shock.
>
> And then, in the crash of ruined cliffs, the smother
> And swirl of foam, the wandering islands part.
> But all that one mind ever knows of another,
> Or breaks the long isolation of the heart,
>
> Was in that instant. The shipwrecked sailor senses
> His own despair in a retreating face.
> Around him he hears in the huge monotonous voices
> Of wave and wind: 'The Rescue will not take place'.

The grimness of the recognition may momentarily obscure one of the most important qualities of Hope's poetry – his sense of comedy, his sharp wit, his laugh whenever things get too grim to be taken any other way. In fact, what makes Hope's poetry so successful, particularly in his use of this image of islanded human existence, is that it simultaneously creates this imaginative universe and comments upon it ironically. One thing that such a recognition about Hope's verse serves to emphasize is that any one image must be taken in context, for only when we perceive how it functions in its own poetic setting, thus generating a rhetoric, tone, and imaginative world, can we hope to make a truly useful iconology.

Political and social shipwrecks and castaways

We see many instances of cities going down like sinking ships to their destruction. There have been such wrecks in the past and there surely will be others in the future, caused by the wickedness of captains and crews alike. For these are guilty men, whose sin is supreme ignorance of what matters most.

Plato, *Statesman* 302a, trans. J. B. Skemp

Now, just as a ship at sea must have a perpetual watch set, day and night, so also a state, tossed, as it is, on the billows of interstate affairs and in peril of being trapped by plots of every sort.

Plato, *Laws* 758a, trans. A. E. Taylor

Il te ressemble; il est terrible et pacifique.
Il est sous l'infini le niveau magnifique;
Il a le mouvement, il a l'immensité.
Apaisé d'un rayon et d'un souffle agité,
Tantôt c'est l'harmonie et tantôt le cri rauque.
Les monstres sont à l'aise en sa profondeur glauque;
La trombe y germe; il a des gouffres inconnus
D'où ceux qui l'ont bravé ne sont pas revenus;
Sur son énormité le colosse chavire;
Comme toi le despote, il brise le navire.

Victor Hugo, 'Au Peuple'

[It resembles you; it is terrible and pacific.
It is the spirit-level of the infinite;
It has movement, it has immensity.
Calmed by a ray of light and agitated by a breeze,
At one time it is harmony, at another the raucous cry.
Monsters are comfortable in its blind depths;
The waterspout germinates there; it has unknown abysses
From which those who brave them do not return;
The colossus capsizes on its enormity;
Like you a despot, it breaks the ship.

'The People']

In addition to conveying the modern sense of spiritual isolation, the situation of the shipwreck and castaway has often been used to present the political plight of modern man. Just as in spiritual terms the traditional figure of the journey of life has been replaced frequently by the shipwreck, so in political terms the image of the Ship of State, which dates back to Plato,[28] now becomes replaced by the wreck of that ship and the situation of the hapless mariner. Essentially, this political version of the castaway takes two forms, which we may term the liberal and the conservative, right wing and left: whereas the man concerned with the problems of the individual worker sees him cast away in the middle of the hostile ocean of an industrial age, the conservative sees himself being inundated by the impoverished, uncultured, raging masses.

Thus when the hero of William Hale White's *Revolution in Tanner's Lane* continually fails to obtain a job, he wanders in London and thinks of 'the vast waste of the city all around him; its miles of houses; and he has a more vivid sense of abandonment than if he were on a plank in the middle of the Atlantic' (ch. 10). Similarly, Friedrich Engels's *Condition of the Working Classes in England* frequently emphasizes that 'nobody troubles about the poor as they struggle helplessly in the whirlpool of modern industrial life.' The worker 'sinks' into degradation 'owing to the introduction of steam power', and once 'engulfed' by his surroundings, he soon perishes. No matter how hard he works, no matter how virtuously he lives, the worker may perish 'through no fault of his own and despite all his efforts to keep his head above water'. Thus the worker exists in a state of dreadful insecurity, knowing full well 'that employment and food today do not mean employment and food tomorrow. . . . He knows that if he sinks into unemployment it will be difficult, and indeed, often, impossible, to survive.'[29] As Marx, Engels, Carlyle, and countless advocates of the medieval ideal of social order frequently emphasized, the death of feudal relations between master and worker, the decline of cottage industry and the destruction, in England, of yeomanry meant that all human connections between employers and labourers became replaced by the cash nexus. The worker felt himself cast adrift, unsupported, and without connection.

The bourgeois version of this experience of the world is bankruptcy, which figures so importantly in many Victorian novels – Reade's *Hard Cash,* Dickens's *Little Dorrit,* Thackeray's *Vanity Fair,* among so many others. In this last novel, for example, the image appears during the sale of Sedley's effects where some kindly young stockbrokers purchased several dozen silver spoons and 'sent this little spar out of the wreck with their love to good Mrs. Sedley' (ch. 17). As Thackeray points out, the condition of the bankrupt is that of a person desperately trying to keep himself afloat by any means – and his very struggles threaten those who have avoided similar disaster:

> As a general rule, which may make all creditors who are inclined to be severe, pretty comfortable in their minds, no men embarrassed are altogether honest, very likely. They conceal something; they exaggerate chances of good-luck; hide away the real state of affairs; say that things are flourishing when they are hopeless; keep a smiling face (a dreary smile it is) upon the verge of bankruptcy. . . . 'Down with such dishonesty,' says the creditor in triumph, and reviles his sinking enemy. 'You fool, why do you catch at a straw?' calm good sense says to the man that is drowning. 'You villain, why do you shrink from plunging into the irretrievable Gazette?' says prosperity to the poor devil battling in that black gulf.
> [ch. 18]

Similarly, near the close of the novel after Becky has experienced 'the Curzon Street catastrophe' between her husband and Lord Steyne, she slips into poverty and despair, at the last not even taking care of her appearance.

> This abatement and degradation did not take place all at once: it was brought about by degrees, after her calamity, and after many struggles to keep up – as a man who goes over-board hangs on to a spar when any hope is left, and then flings it away and goes down when he finds that struggling is vain.
> [ch. 64]

But even this disaster is not complete, and Becky Sharpe survives to fasten herself to Jos Sedley, destroying him in the process. And Becky, who has played so many roles in the course of this exploration of Vanity Fair, finally presents herself to Dobbin as a helpless 'poor castaway, scorned for being miserable, and insulted because I am alone' (ch. 66). For Mrs Rawdon Cawley, as for so many characters in Victorian fiction, it is economic shipwreck that is the most fearful.

The Black, whether slave or freeman, found himself in a situation similar to that of the industrial proletariat, and one therefore encounters the image of shipwrecks and castaways used to convey the plight of the Black in a hostile society. Thus, Winslow Homer's *Gulf Stream* (Pl. 6) and *After the Hurricane,* like Géricault's *Raft of the 'Medusa'* (Pl. 10), create pictorial analogues to the sense of being in the world presented by Prosper Merimée's 'Tamango'. This tale of rebellion aboard a slave-ship tells how Tamango, 'a well-known warrior and slave-dealer' on the coast of Guinea, is himself captured and made slave after he swims out to Captain Ledoux's ship, ironically named the 'Hope', to obtain the return of his wife whom he had given away in a fit of drunken anger. Whatever other qualities Tamango may have, he remains warrior enough to inspire the others to revolt, and after a particularly savage combat with the captain who had betrayed him, he and his followers take over the ship. But when the conquerors' thirst for vengeance has been satiated, they realize to their horror that little has been achieved which will benefit them: they 'looked up at the ship's sails, which were swollen by the fresh breeze and seemed still to be obeying their oppressors and taking the victors, in spite of their triumph, towards the land of slavery'. Never having seen, much less sailed, in an ocean-going ship, they despair. Tamango tries to turn the ship about, but unskilled as he is, he makes the ship heel over

> so violently that it looked as if she were going to founder.
> Her long yards plunged into the sea; several men were thrown
> off their balance and some fell overboard. Soon the ship
> righted herself and stood proudly against the swell, as if to
> fight once again against destruction. But the wind increased
> its efforts and suddenly, with a deafening crash, the two
> masts fell, snapped off a few feet above the deck which was
> covered with wreckage and a tangled network of ropes.
> [trans. Jean Kimber]

The slave-ship, which immediately becomes a fitting emblem of the Black man's existence in a slave society, continues to bear the Africans towards destruction: even when they destroy their particular oppressors, they cannot destroy the mechanism that supported their oppression. With the crippled ship now drifting helplessly, Tamango convinces his equally ignorant followers to abandon it and attempt to row towards home, but the boats are swamped and almost all are lost. Tamango, however, makes it safely back to the brig with his wife as the drifting vessel becomes the scene of new tortures.

About a score of human beings, crowded together in a narrow space, now tossed about on a stormy sea, now scorched by the burning sun, fought daily over the scanty remains of their provisions. Every piece of biscuit was the object of a fight, and the weaker died, not because the stronger killed him, but because he let him expire.

After a few days only Tamango, who had originally sold his fellows into slavery and had then led the rebellion that seemed to set them free, survives. He is saved, if one can employ that word, by a British frigate, restored to health, and

treated in the same way as the blacks who are found on board a captured slave-trader. They set him free, that is to say they made him work for the government; but he was given threepence a day beside his keep. One day the colonel of the 75th caught sight of this fine figure of a man and made him a drummer in his regimental band. Tamango learned a little English, but hardly ever spoke. On the other hand, he was always drinking rum and tafia. He died in hospital of congestion of the lungs.

So this tale of agony and suffering which began with the heavy irony of a Captain Gentle and his slave-ship *Hope* ends with equally acid irony: Tamango, the slave-dealer, fierce warrior, great chieftain, and leader of revolts, destroys both those he loves and those he hates; and yet he still ends up a castaway, a hopeless, isolated, diminished fragment of his former self, perishing finally not by violence but in hospital, not from rough seas but from rum.

In contrast to these images of the oppressed member of society as shipwrecked and cast away, there is a conservative version that implicitly suggests that the upper classes, the forces of order, are being inundated by the mob. Whereas the left-wing castaway overtly presents the worker or slave in this situation, the right-wing version concentrates instead on presenting the lower orders as a wild, raging sea about to engulf all. The comparison of the representative of order to a castaway thus remains implicit. Perhaps it is slightly unfair to call such imagery necessarily 'conservative' since Carlyle's *French Revolution,* its major source at least in English literature, uses it primarily to indicate that the outraged, oppressed lower classes have become as a natural force, blind, overwhelming, and essentially just.

But when the image of the sea is used again in Carlyle's later works once he has become reactionary, or when it appears in George Eliot's *Felix Holt,* Dickens's *Tale of Two Cities,* or Mrs Gaskell's *North and South* , then it embodies nothing more than fear of the workers.

Participants in the French Revolution, and not nineteenth-century authors, invented this representation of the masses as a raging ocean that sweeps all before it. As Hannah Arendt points out in *On Revolution,* the cataclysm in France introduced an entirely new vocabulary into political language.

> When we think of revolution, we almost automatically still think in terms of this imagery born in those years – in terms of Desmoulins' *torrent revolutionnaire* on whose rushing waves the actors of the revolution were borne and carried away until its undertow sucked them from the surface and they perished together with their foes.[30]

These metaphors of men plunged into raging waters allowed the revolutionaries to link their personal fates to a more general destiny – but only at the major cost of sacrificing their sense of individual freedom.

> The various metaphors in which the revolution is seen not as the work of men but as an irresistible process, metaphors of stream and torrent and current, were still coined by the actors themselves, who, however drunk they might have become with the wine of freedom in the abstract, clearly no longer believed that they were free agents. [p. 105]

Arendt convincingly argues that such a conception of man's relation to the world in which he finds himself arose when the Revolution 'turned from the foundation of freedom to the liberation of man from suffering', for then it removed socially inculcated 'barriers of endurance and liberated, as it were, the devastating forces of misfortune and misery instead' (p 107). Once the masses recognized that a constitution would not end poverty, they turned against the Constituent Assembly as they had turned against the monarchy. The only leaders who could survive were those willing to sacrifice 'artificial', man-made laws

> to the 'natural' laws which the masses obeyed, to the forces by which they were driven, and which indeed were

the forces of nature herself, the force of elemental necessity. When this force was let loose, when everybody had become convinced that only naked need and interest were without hypocrisy, the *malheureux* changed into the *enragés*. . . . Thus, after hypocrisy had been unmasked and suffering had been exposed, it was rage and not virtue that appeared. [p. 106]

One of the more important conservative intonations of this image occurs when the man of culture embodies in it his fear of the masses. As one might expect, the aesthetes and decadents of the late nineteenth century felt themselves buffeted and threatened by the increasingly democratic society that surrounded them. For example, Max Beerbohm characteristically employs this imagery and mocks it in 'Diminuendo', the mock farewell to life he wrote at twenty-four. He tells how after leaving Oxford he 'came to London. Around me seethed swirls, eddies, torrents, violent cross-currents of human activity. What uproar! Surely I could have no part in modern life.' Beerbohm is here echoing the way des Esseintes experienced contemporary French society. In *A Rebours* Huysmans wrote a textbook for the decadence by relating how his protagonist's contempt for humanity led him to withdraw from the world into a Palace of Art. In the novel's opening pages we learn that des Esseintes had from his early years been 'dreaming of a . . . snugly heated ark on dry land in which he might take refuge from the incessant deluge of human stupidity' ('Prologue') which so threatened him. Like the allegorical figure in Tennyson's 'The Palace of Art', des Esseintes builds himself a pleasure dome; and like Tennyson's character he at last finds himself driven back into the sea of his fellow men by his own neuroses, by his own mind: in each case psychological, rather than moral, forces convince the protagonist of the impossibility of surviving in isolation. At the novel's close des Esseintes mournfully considers the state of contemporary culture:

in painting, the result was a deluge of lifeless inanities; in literature, a torrent of hackneyed phrases and conventional ideas – honesty to flatter the shady speculator, integrity to please the swindler who hunted for a dowry for his son while refusing to pay his daughter's, and chastity to satisfy the anti-clerical who . . . was forever haunting the local brothel. [ch. 16]

America, the home of democracy, is of course the source of all these corruptions for the hollow-cheeked, high-strung, anaemic last scion of a once great family. While he rages inwardly at the bourgeois, the door to his study bursts open and des Esseintes catches sight of the moving men. He collapses into a chair as the novel ends with the castaway's recognition:

> 'In two days' time I shall be in Paris,' he told himself. 'Well, it is all over now. Like a tide-race, the waves of human mediocrity are rising to the heavens and will engulf this refuge, for I am opening the flood-gates myself, against my will. Ah! but my courage fails me, and my heart is sick within me! – Lord, take pity on the Christian who doubts, on the unbeliever who would fain believe, on the galley slave of life who puts out to sea alone, in the night, beneath a firmament no longer lit by the consoling beacon-fires of the ancient hope!'

When using the age-old topos of the Ship of State, Carlyle similarly combines perspectives, creating a complex effect, but once again the chief effect is to convey a sense of external forces impinging upon individual men. When Plato and Cicero employ this topos they do so to emphasize the need for hierarchical political organization and obedience to authority in times of crisis. The threat of crisis is always present to a ship, and this is what makes it such an effective image of potential disaster: men rely upon comparatively thin, weak bulwarks to keep away the drowning ocean as they float on the surface of waters that may rise several miles from any bottom. Perched on this surface, like bubbles on a stream, they are at the mercy of all the forces of storm and sea. At the same time that the ship thus provides a fitting image of the insecurity of human life, it also serves as a microcosm and can represent larger sections of human society. Writers about the sea have often taken advantage of the intrinsic capacities of a shipboard narrative to present these broader views. Traven's *Death Ship,* for example, superbly addresses itself to the problem of all workers in an industrial society. Carlyle, of course, is not writing a history about ships, but rather using the ship, and particularly the ship in peril, as an effective analogy. Where he differs from most other authors who make use of such analogies is that he carries them to great lengths, making these topoi part of the texture of his work.

His handling of the image of the Ship of State thus characteristi-cally stresses crisis and imminent disaster; for as he explains once the revolution gets under way and the king has lost power, there is no longer any captain at the wheel; and the

> National Assembly, like a ship water-logged, helmless, lies tumbling . . . and waits where the waves of chance may please to strand it; suspicious, nay on the Left-side, conscious, what submarine Explosion is meanwhile a-charging!

With the titular commander, Louis XVI, now in irons, the former galley slaves and common seamen want to pitch him overboard. Petitions demanding his abdication arrive from Paris and the provinces, and against the power of Danton the legislators, 'with their Legislature water-logged' ('At Dinner', bk V, ch. 5), can do nothing. How can they? Since the Assembly derives 'its authority from the Old, how can *it* have authority when the Old is exploded by insurrection? As floating piece of wreck, certain things, persons, and interests may still cleave to it' ('The Improvised Commune', pt 3, bk I, ch. 1) – and in fact do – but these can hardly steer France away from coming disasters.

Next, the nation becomes 'a kindled Fireship' as

> all hands ran raging, and the flames lashed high over the shrouds and topmast. . . . The Fireship is old France, the old French Form of Life; her crew a Generation of men. Wild are their cries and their ragings there, like spirits tormented in that flame. ['Cause and Effect', pt 3, bk III, ch. 1]

The Reign of Terror arrives putting everything – all men and all ideas – to the test of fire and water: 'Catholicism, Classicism, Sentimentalism, Cannibalism: all *isms* that make up Man in France, are rushing and roaring in that gulf . . .' ('Rushing Down', pt 3, bk V, ch. 1). Institutions, beliefs, allegiances, and finally men are cast into the rushing torrent. The Terror demands more and more lives until, at last, revulsion sets in, and the Assembly, having grown fatigued and disgusted by the guillotining, revolts. Robespierre, 'discerning that it is mutiny', desperately tries to reinforce his authority, for he realizes that

> mutiny is a thing of the fatallest nature in all enterprises whatsoever. . . . But mutiny in a Robespierre Convention, above all, – it is like fire seen sputtering in the ship's powder-room! One death-defiant plunge at it, this moment, and you may still tread it out: hesitate till the next moment, – ship

and ship's captain, crew and cargo are shivered far; the ship's voyage had ended between sea and sky. ['To Finish the Terror', pt 3, bk V. ch. 6]

Though Robespierre does not hesitate, he cannot quell the mutiny – and is destroyed. Now with Robespierre gone, Danton gone, the forces of the Middle and not the tempest of patriots batter the drifting, damaged vessel, for now

there is no Pilot, there is not even a Danton, who could undertake to steer you anywhither, in such a press of weather. The utmost a bewildered Convention can do, is to veer, and trim, and try to keep itself steady; and rush, undrowned, before the wind. Needless to struggle; to fling helm a-lee, and make *'bout ship.'* A bewildered Convention sails not in the teeth of the wind; but is rapidly blown round again. So strong is the wind, we say; and so changed; blowing fresher and fresher, as from the sweet Southwest; your devastating Northeasters, and wild Tornado-gusts of Terror, blown utterly out! ['La Cabarus', pt 3, bk VII, ch. 2]

The winds have changed. The perilous voyage during which so many were lost is nearly over.

But first the much fatigued convention must make safe harbour, passing through new dangers. The people now 'spoiled by long right of insurrection' will not accept the new 'Aristocracy of the Moneybag' ('The Whiff of Grapeshot', pt 3, bk VII ch. 7) which has replaced the old feudal one. Having hurled a royal family and nobility into the deeps, the people do not want to take orders from the captains of industry; having pushed the Church over the side, they do not willingly accept what Ruskin called the Goddess-of-Getting-On. Enraged at the way the new aristocracy of wealth has gained command, the Lepelletier Section arms and marches upon Paris. The soldiers sent to quell these insurgents go over to the people, and once more chaos threatens the Ship of State.

Our poor Convention, after such voyaging, just entering the harbour . . . has *struck on the bar;* – and labours there frightfully, with breakers roaring round it, Forty-thousand of them, like to wash it, and its Sièyes Cargo and whole future of France into the deep! Yet one last time it struggles, ready to perish. [ibid.]

The convention chooses 'Citizen Buonaparte, unemployed artillery officer, who took Toulon', as commandant of military forces and he takes the wheel in this new crisis. The Ship of State, caught once again in danger, struggles to survive. 'It is an imminence of shipwreck, for the whole world to gaze at. Frightfully she labours, that poor ship, within cable-length of port. . . . However, she has a man at the helm.' Four October 1795: a roar of artillery, some two hundred men of Lepelletier dead, and the last tempest dissipates itself.

> The miraculous Convention Ship has got to land; – and is there, shall we figuratively say, changed as Epic Ships are wont, into a kind of *Sea Nymph,* never to sail more; to roam the waste azure, a Miracle in History! [ibid.]

After enduring great dangers the 'Convention Ship' thus arrives in port. Many of its crew have perished, others will never recover from the voyage, but the voyage, for all its pain and peril, had to be made; it was essential, for otherwise France and her people would have perished from the quackery and 'gigamanty' of the Old Regime. Even though new quackery and 'gigamanty' will attempt to replace the old, the perilous journey was worth its toll in lives. The spectators of this voyage, who have been making their own way through Carlyle's history, have learned that falsehood and oppression inevitably lead to shipwreck and death. But from this sight of shipwrecks and near-shipwreck comes cause for hope.

The one thing that immediately strikes the reader of *The French Revolution* is the way Carlyle can immerse him in crisis after crisis, continually conveying a feeling of the *power* of events. Carlyle's adept manipulation of the metaphor of ships and shipwrecks plays an important role in his success. For example, he uses the topos of the Ship of State, not as an analogy to support an argument, but as a means of conveying what it feels like to be caught and carried along by forces that threaten total destruction. Even when apparently employing this topos to make us realize how chaos threatens the structure of government, Carlyle in fact always brings the threats home to the reader – *he* is made to take his place on the Fireship, on the drifting vessel. Perhaps this is one inevitable result of elaborating upon such metaphors: it comes alive and makes us feel that the events are happening to us and not to those *others.* At any rate, Carlyle's use of the paradigm of the Ship of State, like his handling of the individual shipwrecked mariner, emphasizes man alone, abandoned, at the mercy of massive forces beyond his control.

Closely related to these images of political and cultural crisis are Richard Hughes's depictions of what happens when a society based upon the machine finds that the machines have broken down. *In Hazard,* his superb novel about a freighter caught in a hurricane, shows the perils of becoming completely dependent upon machines. Battered by the storm, the *Archimedes* finds itself 'totally dead'.

> Everything about her worked by steam or by electricity – so little, on a modern ship, is left to man-power. There being no steam there was also no electricity. She was dark everywhere, but for the pin-points of a few electric torches and oil lamps. Water still poured down her gaping fore-hatch – but the pumps were perforce idle. The wireless apparatus, being dependent on main electricity, was dumb. Her propeller was still; her rudder immovable. She was dead, as a log is dead, rolling in the sea; she was not a ship any more. She was full of men, of course; but there was no work for them to do, because ships, having once discarded man's strength, cannot fall back on that strength in an emergency. [ch. 4]

In the days of wooden sailing ships, a vessel, no matter how battered, had a better chance of survival once the worst was over. Men worked the pumps and would have kept working them; and though a storm might carry away the masts, the carpenter could jury-rig something that would enable the ship to limp home. The modern steam ship, in contrast, becomes a 'mere lifeless log' once its machines have failed. Hughes's novel, which is first and foremost a sea story, none the less tells a parable that encompasses all of modern society, all civilization based on the machine.

Before closing this brief examination of the social and political uses of this imagery, we should glance at its relation to the modern experience of the city. Since the beginning of the nineteenth century there have been many like the hero of White's industrial novel who have felt the modern city as a waste ocean. Thus, whereas Camus perceives Oran as desert, and Balzac sees Paris similarly, others look upon the cities in which they find themselves as threatening oceans. Like White, Shelley described London as a dangerous ocean that wrecks and makes castaways of men. As he wrote in his 'Letter to Maria Gisborne',

You are now
In London, that great sea, whose ebb and flow
At once is deaf and loud, and on the shore
Vomits its wrecks, and still howls for more. [ll. 192–5]

The hero of Charles Kingsley's *Alton Locke* similarly experiences the 'dark, noisy, thunderous' London life as 'a troubled sea that cannot rest, casting up mire and dirt.' In the last decade of the nineteenth century William Sharp similarly wrote in 'A Paris Nocturne' of

the sea of the city
With all its shoals and its terrors,
Its perilous straits and its breakers.

Clearly, the scale of the modern city, its population so much greater than that of village or town, and its assertion of the cash nexus as the essential human relation, made many feel as though they were about to be submerged by a hostile element.

The advantages of the castaway

Those whom an excess of prosperity has rendered sluggish may justly be called unfortunate; a dead calm holds them fast, as it were, on a motionless sea. . . . All excesses are injurious, but immoderate prosperity is the most dangerous of all. It affects the brain. . . . What is the duty of the good man? To offer himself to Fate. . . . He must be wave-tossed and steer his craft through troubled waters, he must maintain his course in the face of Fortune. Much that is hard and rough will befall him, but he will himself soften it and smooth it down. Gold is tried by fire, brave men by misfortune.

Seneca, *On Providence. Why any Misfortunes Befall Good Men When a Providence Exists,* trans. Moses Hadas

From this the poem springs: that we live in a place
That is not our own and, much more, not ourselves
And hard it is in spite of blazoned days.

Wallace Stevens, 'Notes Toward a Supreme Fiction'

but he had a beautiful daughter
and the young sailor
distracted him
as the wreckage rocked
in the swell.

Rosemarie Waldrop, 'No Horizon'

Whether appearing in a political or metaphysical context, the iconography of shipwreck conveys the experience of crisis and frequently of final disaster as well. None the less, that complete despair which colours James Thomson's *City of Dreadful Night* is rare. In explaining why he writes so darkly of the human condition, he finds himself forced to admit in his 'Proem' that he does so only because 'a cold rage seizes one . . ./ To show the bitter old and wrinkled truth/ Stripped of all vesture that beguiles' and 'because it gives some sense of power and passion/ In helpless impotence to try to fashion/ Our woe in living words.' In contrast, many who use the figure of man shipwrecked and cast away try, often desperately, to find some advantage, however limited, to their recognitions. For example, near the close of Bernard Malamud's *The Fixer*, Yakov Bok, who has been imprisoned unjustly in Tsarist Russia for ritual murder of a Christian child, thinks:

> So I learned a little . . . but what good will it do me? Will it open the prison doors? . . . Will it free me a little once I am free? Or have I only learned to know what my condition is – that the ocean is salty as you are drowning, and though you knew it you are drowned? Still, it was better than not knowing. A man had to learn, it was his nature. [ch. 4, pt 4]

Yakov Bok's insight, then, provides some consolation, though only of the bleakest, bitterest kind: man, the animal who can understand, at least is able to know the truth, even if it is about his destruction.

Similarly, in *Servitude et grandeur militaires (The Military Condition)*, Alfred de Vigny, like Tennyson, asks

> In the universal shipwreck of belief what flotsam is there to which noble hands may still cling? Save for the love of comfort and ephemeral luxury, not a vestige shows on the surface of the deep. It is as if egotism had submerged all;

even those who, seeking to save souls, plunge courageously
into the waters feel themselves on the point of being engulfed.

Adopting a very different solution from that of Tennyson, de Vigny
tells how he

> described in the midst of these dark waters one apparently
> solid and immobile point. . . . I drew near to it and looked all
> around it and above and below it, and I laid my hand on it
> and found it strong enough to bear a man up in the midst of
> the storm.

What, then, is this life-raft fit for the nineteenth-century deluge?

> It is no new creed, no newly invented cult, no vague concept;
> it is a sentiment born in us, independent of time, place, and
> even religion. . . . This faith, which I think we all still possess,
> and which reigns supreme in the army, is called HONOUR,
> [ch. 10, trans. Marguerite Barnett]

Apparently unable to believe that man in the nineteenth century can
still found a life on Christian belief, de Vigny accepts that honour is
an idea innate to man. While such a decision strikes one as curiously
naive and even desperate, it does serve as a kind of proto-
existentialism in which each human being must create himself.

Although he calls his life-raft 'heroism' rather than 'honour',
Norman Mailer arrives at a very similar solution to the problem of
man's shipwrecked condition. *Of a Fire on the Moon,* Mailer's search
for heroism in a technological world, explains that in the twentieth
century one can no longer ignore man's dangerous relationship to
nature and society.

> In the Nineteenth Century, they had ignored Kierkegaard. A
> middle-class White man, living on the rise of Nineteenth
> Century technology was able to feel his society as an eminence
> from which he could make expeditions, if he wished, into the
> depths. He would know all the while that his security was still
> up on the surface, a ship – if you will – to which he was
> attached by a line. In the Twentieth Century, the White man
> had suddenly learned what the Black man might have told
> him – that there was no ship unless it was a slave ship. There
> was no security. Everybody was underwater, and even the
> good sons of the middle class could panic in those depths, for

if there was no surface, there was no guide. Anyone could lose his soul. That recognition offered a sensation best described as bottomless. [pt 1, ch. 5, ii]

Mailer begins his examination of the first moon landing with the death of Hemingway eight years before, since for him

Hemingway constituted the walls of the fort: Hemingway had given the power to believe you could still shout down the corridor of the hospital, live next to the breath of the beast, accept your portion of dread each day. Now the greatest living romantic was dead.

Mailer's great fear is that 'technology would fill the pause' (pt 1, ch. 1, i), driving out life and imagination and heroism. He therefore seeks to experience the events that make up the moon voyage so that he can enable us to re-experience them, at each step of the way probing for possibilities of heroism. Twice he leads us through the launch, flight, landing and return. The first time we perceive these events from outside, from the vantage-point of the reporter, noting size and expense, and the climax here comes when, borrowing Mailer's sensibilities, we experience the Lift-Off, discovering the twentieth-century sublime in technology, in the sheer quantity of a man-made thing, in the noise and thunder that shakes every nerve, muscle, and bone. Mailer's second time through these events takes the form of a voyage of understanding. It moves towards the climactic drama of 'The Ride Down', making us understand – and experience – the last four minutes of the moon landing when men at computer consoles, men coupled to technology, make heroic decisions, as Mailer discovers that Hemingway's brand of heroism is not the only form, that perhaps the heroism of the apparently unromantic young men in white short-sleeved shirts and crew-cut hair is ultimately more relevant and more life-giving. At any rate, it exists – and right in the bosom of the machine itself. Mailer finally, we recognize, turns out to be much closer to Whitman than his description of our shipwrecked condition might at first permit one to realize. Like Whitman's large-hearted captain, he too would hold up a chalkboard bearing the message – 'Do not despair.'

To the life-rafts of honour and heroism, Virginia Woolf's Clarissa Dalloway adds that of service to others. Peter Walsh, another character in *Mrs Dalloway,* thinks that she was one of the most thorough-going sceptics he had ever met, and possibly . . . she said to herself, As we are a doomed race, chained to a sinking ship (her favourite reading as a girl was Huxley and Tyndall, and they were fond of these nautical metaphors), as the whole thing is a bad joke, let us, at any rate, do our part; mitigate the sufferings of our fellow-prisoners.

In closing this study's cursory examination of the way the past two centuries have employed the situation and metaphor of shipwreck, I would like to look at three very different men to see some cause, however slight, for consolation in man's situation as one shipwrecked and cast away – Thomas Carlyle, Jose Ortega y Gasset, and Jean-Paul Sartre. Each believes the human condition is epitomized by that instant after shipwreck when man is hurled into the cold, alien sea; and each emphasizes this instant not as cause to despair, but as cause to act, to choose, to create oneself.

In the Carlylean version of this perilous situation, the castaway chokes, coughs up the stinging cold water, and, flailing his arms, discovers to his surprise, nay, to his joy, that he can keep his head above water – by struggling against this fearful element, he can make it support him. It is difficult; 'it is like swimming with a millstone round your neck' (p. 198), he tells Emerson, but it is not impossible. Thus the major discovery enunciated in *Past and Present*: work will save the man who finds himself immersed in the waste ocean of life:

> All work is as the swimmer's: a waste ocean threatens to devour him; if he front it not bravely, it will keep its word. By incessant wise defiance of it, lusty rebuke and buffet of it, behold how loyally it supports him, bears him as its conqueror along. 'It is so', says Goethe, 'with all things that man undertakes in this world.' ['Labour', bk III, ch. 11]

Goethe says so, true, but with a very different emphasis, with a markedly different sense of the world. His swimmers, to begin with, are hardly Carlylean castaways, abandoned in mid-ocean. In Carlyle's own translation of *Wilhelm Meister's Travels,* the Overseer of the young in Goethe's educational Utopia tells Wilhelm:

> We look upon our scholars as so many swimmers, who, in the element which threatened to swallow them, feel with astonishment that they are lighter, that it bears and carries them forward: and so is with everything that man undertakes. [ch. 14]

125

Goethe's description of education and human activity conveys little of the sense of crisis and danger, and none of the sense of isolation, we feel in Carlyle. The context of Goethe's similitude makes it apparent that the education of the young boys which Wilhelm has come to observe is a common effort: all head co-operatively in the same direction, the older helping younger. When these young boys find themselves in the situation of the swimmer, they feel little danger because there is always someone near to give assistance. But when Carlyle uses this situation to convey his sense of being in the world, he shows us a swimmer who struggles alone, far from help in the midst of an ocean that has already dragged many to watery deaths. Carlyle, who described himself to Emerson as a 'Castaway' (p. 457), frequently returns to this paradigm in public and private writings throughout his life. Quite characteristically, he described the style of *Sartor Resartus* to Sterling in terms of the castaway: 'This is not Art, I know well. It is Robinson Crusoe, and not the Master of Woolwich, building a ship.'[31] In other words, the Carlylean style and method which convey Teufelsdröckh's 'mad pilgrimings' must conform to the experience of the castaway, producing not a finely balanced work – some stately ship of literature – but a raft, a lifeboat rigged during an emergency.

Sartre, like Carlyle, conceived – better, feels – human life in terms of the situation of the man shipwrecked and cast away; and though he rarely uses this figure overtly to express his sense of being in the world, it informs his descriptions of it. In *Existentialism* he presents us, for instance, with man abandoned, with the swimming castaway, when he emphasizes that 'everything is permissible if God doesn't exist, and as a result man is forlorn, because neither within him nor without does he find anything to cling to.' Man has no 'fixed and given human nature' which would simultaneously limit, define, and support him in his alien surroundings. Thus, man is condemned to be free. 'Condemned, because he did not create himself, yet in other respects he is free; because once thrown into the world, he is responsible for everything he does.'[32]

Sartre expands upon this mode of being in the world in *Being and Nothingness* where he once again presents man as man overboard, as Robinson Crusoe. Emphasizing man's responsibility and freedom, now in relation to the 'for-itself', his term for consciousness, he asserts it is precisely thus that the for-itself apprehends itself in anguish; that is, as a being which is neither the foundation of its own being nor of the Other's being nor of the in-itselfs which form the world, but a being which is compelled to decide the meaning of being – within it and everywhere outside of it. The one who realizes in anguish his condition as *being* thrown into a responsibility which extends to his very abandonment has no longer any remorse or regret or excuse; he is no longer anything but a freedom. [pt 4, ch. 1, iii]

Sartre, like Carlyle and Ortega y Gasset, tries to convince us that this perilous situation is not only inevitable but preferable:

I am responsible for everything, in fact, except for my own responsibility, for I am not the foundation of my own being. Therefore everything takes place as if I were compelled to be responsible. I am *abandoned* in the world, not in the sense that I might remain abandoned and passive in a hostile universe like a board floating on the water, rather in the sense that I find myself suddenly alone and without help. [pt 4, ch. 1, iii]

One can, of course, refuse to move one's arms. One can sink beneath the waves. But one cannot refuse to make a choice, for 'to make myself passive in the world, to refuse to act upon things and upon Others is still to choose myself, and suicide is one mode among others of being-in-the-world' (pt 4, ch. 1, iii). Granted this situation, the fact that one must choose, Sartre, like Carlyle, offers us the grimly complimentary opportunity to bestir ourselves and keep our heads above the waste ocean.

Like Sartre, Ortega y Gasset both sees man's abandoned situation as inevitable and finds cause in it for consolation. Indeed, far more than either Carlyle or Sartre, the Spanish philosopher looks cheerfully upon our condition as men shipwrecked and cast away. According to 'The Self and the Other', since the human condition 'is essential uncertainty' and since 'no human acquisition is stable',

This thing we call 'civilization' – all these physical and moral comforts, all these conveniences, all these shelters, all these virtues and disciplines which have become habit now, on, which we count, and which in effect constitute a repertory or system of securities which man has made for himself like a raft

127

in the initial shipwreck which living always is – all these securities are insecure securities which in the twinkling of an eye, at the least carelessness, escape from man's hands and vanish like phantoms. [trans. Willard R. Trask]

And then man drowns. The present peril, says Ortega y Gasset, writing in 1939, is that having lost our sense of risk, we have also lost our sense of responsibility which is our means of preserving ourselves amid great danger; since we are unaware of the peril, we do not try for solutions – we do not try to fit out lifeboats or learn to swim. When shipwreck comes, as it must, we find ourselves taken by surprise. This dangerous complacency is the result of a 'progressivist' theory of history which assumes that humanity necessarily improves, becoming ever more secure and comfortable. Not only does the idea of 'humanity' – itself 'an abstract, irresponsible, non existent entity' – tend to hide from us our rather terrifying freedom but the equally misleading notion of progress anaesthetizes us as well. The progressivist view of things makes human history lose all 'sinew of drama', reducing it 'to a peaceful tourist trip, organized by some transcendent "Cook's"'. Travelling thus securely toward its fulfillment, the civilization in which we are embarked would be like that Phaecian ship in Homer which sailed straight to port without a pilot.' Unfortunately, such pipe dreams, which assure us that we do not have to exert ourselves since some force of history will bring us to the millennium, do nothing to ready us for the shipwreck that both individual men and civilizations have always encountered eventually. To believe in such conceptions of humanity is to hold that man is a fixed essence, that he is what he is – and hence bears no responsibility. Whatever its short-term advantages, such security is dearly purchased.

It is dearly bought because for it one must give one's responsibility, that which makes one human. In describing that 'unique drama, which constitutes the very condition of man', Ortega y Gasset like other existentialists, seems instinctively to describe man in terms of the castaway. According to him, man finds himself 'a prisoner of the world' surrounded by things that terrify, attract, and engage him, but unlike the animal, who shares these basic conditions, he can detach himself from his surroundings, turn his back on them, concern himself with himself. Man's mind provides that extra dimension which enables him to survive.

It is clear, then, that man does not exercise his thought

because he finds it amusing, but because, obliged as he is to live submerged in the world and to force his way among things, he finds himself under the necessity of organizing his activities . . . which is what an animal does not do.

Man's thinking allows him to construct a raft in his continual and essential emergency – or, rather, man's thinking is that raft itself. To save ourselves in the crisis of modern times Ortega y Gasset suggests that we should do what each individual does in his own life: 'simply suspend action, withdraw into ourselves, review our idea of the circumstances, and work out a strategy.'

This movement into the self which thus enables the individual man to prosper is repeated necessarily on a broader scale by entire civilizations. We find 'three different moments . . . repeated cyclically throughout the course of human history'. First, 'Man feels himself lost, shipwrecked upon things; this is *alteracion* [alteration, otherness, or state-of-tumult].' Second, man retires into himself to consider things and his possible command of them; this is the contemplative life. Third, man again 'submerges himself in the world', acting according to a preconceived plan; this is the active life. Thus, unlike Nietzsche, who railed that man's quest for knowledge was speeding him towards shipwreck, the Spanish philosopher sees this shipwrecked existence as necessary and inevitable – and, as such, perhaps no longer so terrifying as it had seemed before.

'In Search of Goethe from within', an essay written for the centenary of the poet's death, takes this characterization of human life even further, claiming, in fact, that cultural shipwreck is itself good for man. Pointing to the twentieth-century crisis of knowledge, of universities, of culture in general, he argues that a gulf separates us from our past and holds further that however terrifying the isolated situation in which we find ourselves may seem at first, it is a good thing, for it makes us strip down and rid ourselves of clutter:

Life is, in itself and forever, shipwreck. To be shipwrecked is not to drown. The poor human being, feeling himself sinking into the abyss, moves his arms to keep afloat. This movement of the arms which is his reaction against his own destruction, is culture – a swimming stroke. . . . But ten centuries of cultural continuity brings with it – among many advantages – the great disadvantage that man believes himself safe, loses the feeling of shipwreck, and his culture proceeds to burden itself with parasitic and lymphatic matter. Some discontinuity must therefore intervene, in order that man may renew his feeling of peril, the substance of his life. All his life-saving equipment must fail, then his arms will once again move redeemingly. [trans. Willard R. Trask]

One of the great advantages to us that appears in the crisis of our particular culture is that by making us live without the old supports, it forces us to see that *essentially* man always lives in crisis. This recognition prevents us from treating ourselves as essence, as fully created beings, forcing us to choose, to be responsible, to be – once more – men.

Thus, with Ortega y Gasset, as with Carlyle and Sartre, the instant of shipwreck conveys a fearful recognition of freedom. This recognition, this consciousness of shipwreck, remains at the centre of their thought, but though they, like so many others since the eighteenth century, find the metaphor of shipwreck more relevant than that of life's journey, they do not find this cause to despair. Rather, they believe, once man recognizes his true situation, 'then', in the words of Ortega y Gasset, 'his arms will once again move redeemingly'.

CHAPTER THREE

RELATED PARADIGMS

Each of the topics, tropes, and themes that will be discussed in this chapter relates differently to our reference paradigm, the shipwreck on the journey of life, and each has something of interest to tell us about modern iconology. The Deluge, a literal event recorded in the Old Testament, exemplifies a supposed fact that the Judaic and Christian traditions have endowed with paradigmatic significance. According to the Book of Genesis, God sent His flood to punish man for his evil, and therefore the Deluge serves as the biblical equivalent to the notion of the shipwreck as punishment. In both situations, God sends water to engulf the guilty. At the same time that Genesis provides a culturally paradigmatic instance of the Lord's punishing guilty human beings by using the forces of nature to do so, it also offers a corollary one of His preserving the faithful. Since the Middle Ages the ark that saved Noah and his family has been taken by believers as a divinely intended type of the Christian church, or Christ Mystical: it indicates, say the exegetes, that God placed in history an example of the principle that one is saved only by joining with others in the Church of Christ, a church which, like the ark itself, finds itself besieged by destructive forces from without but which God ultimately preserves and employs to lead man to new life. The accepted meanings of ark and Deluge, however, become subverted in the nineteenth century, as many begin to question the nature of divine justice. Since the Deluge stands as such an explicit instance of divine vengeance, its subversion requires a particularly explicit questioning of Christianity. Considered from the point of view of the shipwreck paradigm, then, the Deluge, in many of its nineteenth-century artistic and literary manifestations, represents the post-Christian subversion of an unambiguous biblical event traditionally taken as paradigmatic.

The figure of Odysseus, in contrast, exemplifies ironic and subversive intonations of a secular literary or mythic personage. One of the prime facts about this cunning, much-travelled, much-suffering man who has descended to us from the ancient, pre-Christian past is that he is the man who would return home. Therefore, the Homeric hero has many similarities to St Augustine's figure of man voyaging to his heavenly home, for both Odysseus and *homo viator* must return to their points of origin to become themselves fully.

Like the Deluge, the rainbow receives a specific paradigmatic value from Genesis, which relates that the Lord Himself declared that it would always be a covenant-sign, the emblem of His promise to man. Unlike the Deluge itself, which can never occur literally again, the rainbow placed in the heavens by God appears both in biblical and in contemporary history. It therefore provides problems and possibilities for the artist who would employ it. The rainbow also provides the iconologist with an opportunity to distinguish the different ways that images, situations, and figures function in pictorial and literary arts.

The Deluge transformed

In the six hundredth year of Noah's life, in the second month, the seventeenth day of the month, the same day were all the fountains of the great deep broken up, and the windows of heaven were opened.

And the rain was upon the earth forty days and forty nights. . . .

And the flood was forty days upon the earth; and the waters increased, and bare up the ark, and it was lifted above the earth.

And the waters prevailed, and were increased greatly upon the earth; and the ark went upon the face of the waters.

And the waters prevailed exceedingly upon the earth; and all the high hills, that were under the whole heaven, were covered.

Fifteen cubits upward did the waters prevail; and the mountains were covered.

And all flesh died that moved upon the earth, both of fowl, and of cattle, and of beast, and of every creeping thing that creepeth upon the earth, and every man:

All in whose nostrils was the breath of life, of all that was in dry land, died.

And every living substance was destroyed which was upon the face of the ground, both man, and cattle, and the creeping things, and the fowl of the heaven; and they were destroyed from the earth: and Noah only remained alive, and they that were with him in the ark.

And the waters prevailed upon the earth an hundred and fifty days.

Genesis, ch. 8

Like God's drowning the Egyptian host in the Red Sea, the Deluge offers a definite, unmistakable instance of divine punishment, and the ark that preserved Noah and his family offers a similarly unmistakable instance of divine protection. This connection between preserving the good and destroying the evil provides a structure that recurs frequently in biblical history. As Patrick Fairbairn, the great nineteenth-century student of hermeneutics, explains in *The Typology of Scripture,*

> This principle of salvation with destruction, which found such a striking exemplification in the deluge, has been continually appearing anew in the history of God's dealings among men. It appeared, for example, at the period of Israel's redemption from Egypt, when a way of escape was opened for the people of God by the overthrow of Pharaoh and his host; and again at the era of the return from Babylon, when the destruction of the enemy and the oppressor broke asunder the bands with which the children of the covenant were held captive. But it is in New Testament times, and in connection with the work of Christ, that the higher manifestation of the principle appears. . . . In Christ, however, the very foundations of evil from the first were struck at, and nothing is left for a second beginning to the cause of iniquity. ['Noah and the Deluge']

The Genesis narrative of the Flood, which thus contains one of the central principles of history, also functions typologically in several ways. First of all, this instance of divine punishment serves as a type of later ones. Indeed, according to John Keble, who was one of the founders of the Oxford Movement, 'Even if our Lord had not told us. . . we should scarce have failed to perceive how nearly we are concerned in this fearful picture. The history of the world before the Flood is but too nearly a type and shadow of our own history, and our own condition in God's sight' ('As it was in the days of Noah', *Sermons,* vol. 4). Keble of course takes the title of his sermon from Luke 17: 26–7, which provides scriptural sanction for thus taking the Deluge typologically:

> And as it was in the days of Noah, so shall it be also in the days of the Son of man. They did eat, they drank, they married wives, until the day that Noah entered into the ark, and the flood came and destroyed them all.

With such biblical sanction or authentication for typological readings, exegetes easily found other prefigurative elements in the Genesis story. Fairbairn, for example, explained that Noah himself 'was the type, but no more than the type, of Him who was to come – in whom the righteousness of God should be perfected' ('The New World and its Inheritors'). In addition, the ark, that obvious vessel of salvation, serves as a type of the Church of Christ. Therefore, says J. C. Ryle, the great Evangelical Anglican Bishop of Liverpool, in his commentary on Luke 17: 26–37, 'We must come out from the world and be separate. ... We must flee to the ark like Noah' *(Expository Thoughts on the Gospels)*.

The first Epistle of St Peter 3: 21 also taught Christians to take the Deluge as a type of Baptism, and High Church Anglicans, such as Isaac Williams, often emphasize this particular typological reading, but by far the most common eighteenth- and nineteenth-century one is that the ark is a type of the Church of Christ. As Thomas Scott's immensely popular Bible commentary, which was found in many English and American Protestant homes, joyfully exclaims:

> Happy they, who are part of Christ's family, and safe with him in the ark! They may look forward without dismay, and rejoice in the assurance, that they shall triumph, when a deluge of fire shall encircle the visible creation. But, unless we dare to be singular, and renounce the favour, and venture the scorn and hatred of the world: unless we are willing to exercise self-denial and diligence; we can find no admission into this ark. And, even in the ark, while in this world, we shall need faith and patience, and have much to try them. [commentary on Genesis 5: 17–24]

Furthermore, as Bible commentators explain, since the Church of Christ is the mystical body of Him, or Christ Mystical, the ark serves doubly as such a divinely intended prefiguration – first as a type of the Church and second as a type of Christ Himself. Both these ideas appear as commonplaces of Evangelical hymnody. For example, 'On the Commencement of Hostilities in America', one of John Newton's *Olney Hymns,* opens:

> The gath'ring clouds, with aspect dark,
>   A rising storm presage;
> Oh! to be hid within the ark,
>   And shelter'd from its rage!

In contrast, other of Newton's influential hymns use this figure as a means of poetic resolution. 'The Hiding-Place' thus begins with the speaker pointing to 'the gloomy gath'ring cloud,/ Hanging o'er a sinful land' and warns that 'Times of trouble' are upon us. Immediately, however, this hymn reassures the believer that no matter how bad the earthly situation becomes, 'they who love his name' have nothing at all to fear. The hymn closes by having Christ Himself use this figure of the ark to comfort those he loves:

> You have only to repose
> On my wisdom, love, and care;
> When my wrath consumed my foes,
> Mercy shall my children spare;
> While *they* perish in the flood,
> You that bear my holy mark,
> Sprinkled with atoning blood,
> Shall be safe within the ark.

This pattern of introducing an initial unquiet and insecurity which is then resolved by the appearance of the ark appears in yet another of Newton's hymns, 'Rest for Weary Souls', in which the speaker first describes his weakness, sinfulness, and consequent spiritual misery. The third of four stanzas then introduces the type of the ark:

> In the ark the weary dove
> Found a welcome resting-place;
> Thus my spirit longs to prove
> Rest in Christ, the ark of grace:
> Tempest-toss'd I long have been,
> And the flood increases fast;
> Open, Lord, and take me in
> Till the storm be overpast.

The concluding stanza, which resolves the conflict posed by the hymn, moves ahead to that time the believer finds himself secure in Christ, and, rejoicing in the 'wondrous change' he experiences when His Saviour soothes his 'troubled mind', he addresses his former fellow sufferers and invites them to join him in the ark:

You that weary are like me,
Hearken to the gospel call;
To the ark for refuge flee,
Jesus will receive you all

The ark, which is a type of both Christ and His Church, long offered Christians a paradigm, therefore, of the way that God could preserve them from the Deluge of this world, and the Deluge, in turn, offered a figure for a wide range of fearful things and events one wished to escape – divine punishment, one's own sinfulness, an oppressive world, and so on.

As John Ruskin reminded his Victorian readers in the chapter on 'Torcello' in *The Stones of Venice,* 'in the minds of all early Christians the Church itself was most frequently symbolised under the image of a ship, of which the bishop was the pilot.' Ruskin, who is engaged in explaining how Venice had its beginnings on those outlying islands settled by refugees from the mainland, next instructs his reader to 'consider the force which this symbol would assume in the imaginations of men' to whom the spiritual Church had become an ark of refuge in the midst of a destruction hardly less terrible than that

> from which the eight souls were saved of old, a destruction in
> which the wrath of man had become as broad as the earth and
> as merciless as the sea, and who saw the actual and literal
> edifice of the Church raised up, itself like an ark in the midst
> of the waters.

Therefore, says Ruskin, who tries to convince his contemporaries that Venice stands as a type and warning for Victorian England, if one wishes to 'learn in what spirit it was that the dominion of Venice was begun, and in what strength she went forth conquering and to conquer', one should not seek in her arsenals, armies, and palaces. Rather, one must climb to where the Bishop of Torcello used, centuries before, to sit,

> and then, looking as the pilot did of old along the marble ribs
> of the goodly temple-ship, let him repeople its veined deck
> with the shadows of its dead mariners, and strive to feel in
> himself the strength of heart that was kindled within them.

Their reliance on God, their faith, says Ruskin, make the Venetians great – and when they fell away from that faith, they left their ark and were destroyed. If England, he warns in the very first paragraph of *The Stones of Venice,* neglects to learn from the example of its predecessors, his nation and his people 'may be led through prouder eminence to less pitied destruction.'

Unfortunately, even at the time that Ruskin was writing *The Stones of Venice,* he was beginning that long, painful process which resulted, finally, in his abandonment of his childhood faith. The man, in other words, who had so emphasized that societies could only survive by making the worship of God their ark, found, soon enough, that he could find no God, and no ark. Before acquiring a much qualified belief more than a decade later, he joined that company of 'melancholy Brothers' whom James Thomson described in *The City of Dreadful Night* 'battling in black floods without an ark' (sec. 14).

Such 'melancholy Brothers', who find themselves in the condition of castaways, represent one of the two major transformations the Deluge-figure receives – the disappearance of the ark. Throughout the nineteenth and twentieth centuries, those who, like Wordsworth, retain their Christian belief employ the scriptural type in its old sense. In *The Excursion,* for example, the poet has one of his characters assert that at the baptismal font the child is

> received
> Into the second ark, Christ's church, with trust
> That he, from wrath redeemed, therein shall float
> Over the billows of this troublesome world
> To the fair land of everlasting life. [bk 5, ll. 281–5]

For those who do not believe, however, there is no ark, and they find themselves alone while the waters rise.

Byron thus contemplates the history of Napoleon in the fourth canto of *Childe Harold's Pilgrimage* and sees 'An universal Deluge, which appears/ Without an ark for wretched Man's abode,/ And ebbs but to reflow!' (ll. 826–8). Byron implores 'Renew thy rainbow, God!' (l. 828), but he has no faith that He will renew His covenant with man, and in Byron all the rainbows are illusive and delusive. The rainbow that comes after the storm in *Don Juan* thus brings no safety and salvation for the shipwrecked men. In fact, it stands as a paradigm of capricious flux and not any eternal Christian covenant; and appropriately when a white bird appears, it is no dove of peace, hope, and grace, but potential food for the starving men:

And had it been the dove from Noah's ark,
  Returning there from her successful search,
Which in their way that moment chanced to fall,
They would have eat her, olive-branch and all. [canto 2, st. 95]

In the Byronic conception of things, nature smiles while men perish; and men, not surprisingly, grant no credence to covenants of grace and arks of salvation.

The other major transformation of the Deluge, which takes the form of questioning its justness and morality, is even more radical. By the late eighteenth and early nineteenth century, even this most definite, most unmistakable example of divine punishment of guilty man had become problematic and ambiguous. Benjamin West's wash drawing of *The Waters Subsiding After the Deluge (c.* 1791, Boston Museum of Fine Arts) introduces us to the common Romantic and post-Romantic vision of this event. In the immediate foreground the heaped bodies of men, women, and children command our attention; and looking past them, we perceive the ark come to rest on high ground beneath an overarching rainbow. The artist's thrusting forward the bodies of the slain, who in death bear no trace of any evil nature or action, creates a powerful image of the aftermath of the Deluge in which its meaning becomes intensely problematic. The very presence of the rainbow, a commonplace type of Christ and the new covenant of grace, makes the entire scene appear ironic.

Francis Danby's magnificent and terrifying *Deluge* (1837–40, Tate Gallery, Pl. 14) makes the problematic nature of this event even more obvious, for rather than allowing us to stand emotionally outside the events and judge the supposedly guilty who perish, the canvas forces us to sympathize with these victims of fate. Danby's representation of the Flood thus subverts its traditional religious meaning in two ways. First of all, making a recognition that became increasingly common in the Victorian period, Danby places major pictorial emphasis upon the fact that the innocent are killed. As the protagonist of J. A. Froude's *The Nemesis of Faith* (1849), who explains his loss of belief, points out: 'The sucking children of the unchosen were not saved in Noah's flood.' The painter also shows us terrified, dying children, thus making us doubt the ethical nature of such an event and the God who prompted it. In fact, moral revulsion against the cruelty of both such instances of divine punishment in history and the doctrine of eternal damnation played a major role in the mid-nineteenth-century crisis of belief. As Josef L. Altholz argues in 'The Warfare of Conscience with Theology',

> The issue on which the intensity of Victorian religion first began to turn inward on itself was not an external challenge of science or criticism, but a felt conflict between the morality which evangelicals have cultivated and the theological doctrines which they taught.[1]

Whether or not leading nineteenth-century artists consciously took part in such a spiritual conflict, their works present the Flood fom the vantage-point of one who has ethical objections to the usual interpretation of it as an instance of just punishment.

Danby, for example, not only makes the common point that God destroyed innocent children but he also subverts Christian conceptions of the Flood by emphasizing the selflessness and even heroism of the victims. We thus find none of the savagery one might expect when maddened men and animals strive desperately to save themselves. No mothers loose their hold on loved ones to secure their own safety; no fathers hurl children from higher ground to save their own lives. Instead, we have a somewhat sentimentalized vision of all too sympathetic suffering human beings trying wherever possible to save one another.[2]

In this emphasis the painting differs markedly from most earlier representations of the Deluge and the Last Judgment, such as those by the Northern Renaissance painters, which stress the sinfulness of the sufferers. To be sure, there were painters of the Renaissance and after who sympathetically depicted the victims of the Flood; and since preachers in word and paint often emphasized that those God punished in the Deluge were not entirely evil, it was therefore quite orthodox to show these victims acting with some nobility. The artist was on sure theological ground when he tried to make the spectator identify with these earlier objects of divine wrath because such identification made their punishment immediately relevant. Poussin's *Winter* in the Louvre cycle of *The Four Seasons* (1660–4, Pl.15) exemplifies such a generally sympathetic view of the Flood by a pre-Romantic painter who was clearly a devout believer. At the centre of the canvas a man prays, too late, to the raging heavens as his boat capsizes, while at the right a father passes his child down to the safety of a boat. Although Poussin's figures do not act heroically, they do not do anything markedly unheroic or bestial either; and,

141

indeed, were it not for the presence of the ark, which appears in the left distance, and the fact that the other three pictures in this series depict Old Testament subjects, his version of the Flood could be interpreted as any inundation and not the archetypal one.

The same generally sympathetic attitude colours Leandro Bassano's much more crowded representation of *The Flood* (*c.* 1600, Museo de Arte Ponce, Puerto Rico, Pl. 16), for the victims are portrayed taking care of children and animals, and in the distance there is a particularly moving group in which a woman standing on a roof prays with outstretched arms to heaven. Again, there is nothing either heroic or sentimental about Bassano's conception of the actions of those soon to perish in the Flood; and the fact that many of the figures, including the old man in the foreground, are shown still trying to save their worldly goods reveals that the painter places the traditional interpretation upon these biblical events. Similarly, the way most of the people in Bassano's painting seem almost unaware of the others surrounding them shows that he does not emphasize an ennobling fellow-feeling among the suffers in the manner of Danby.

In contrast, Danby's *Deluge* (Pl. 14) seems to have escaped its conventional meaning, for clearly it portrays more of a slaughter of the innocents than a punishment of the guilty. Danby's dying men, women, children, and animals force us, whatever preconceptions (or paradigm allegiances) we bring to the painting, to sympathize with them. And to sympathize with those the Lord punishes is to become one of the Devil's party.

Similarly, as the eye moves across Turner's *Deluge* (1813, Tate Gallery, Pl. 17), one encounters images of men and women helping one another. We are carried from the kneeling Magdalen-like figure in the lower left corner to the group immediately beside and behind her in which a man upholds a nude woman to whom a young boy is clinging. Next to this trio a leaning man tries to lift a woman from the water, while farther towards the centre we encounter the dramatic action of a parent trying to hold an infant from the waters. This emphasis upon saving children, which seems a characteristic of Romantic versions of the Deluge, appears in several other places in Turner's picture; and although helplessness and desperation colour his work far more than they do Danby's our final impression is of suffering innocents.

Gustave Doré's famous Bible illustrations (1865) make it even clearer that a savage nature destroys innocent beings. Doré, who (as

Ruskin pointed out) loved to depict sensational violence, devotes three plates to the Flood, each more destructive of traditional readings than the last. In *The World Destroyed by Water* (Pl. 18), we come upon many examples of panic as the seventy or so figures desperately attempt to escape the rising waters, but again there is none of the viciousness and cruelty one expects in scenes of panic. Indeed, a sense of community and humanity characterizes the acts of these people. In the foreground, for instance, a father heroically tries to hold wife and child above the waters, while above him two parents strain to push their infants to higher points of safety. In the centre of the plate the arm of a drowning parent rises from the water and holds up a child to grant it a few more moments of life. Similarly, in the pyramid of men and animals on higher ground which dominates the major portion of the illustration, love, fellowship, and community prevail: innocent children are pushed to the heights, and supposedly guilty human beings sacrifice themselves to save innocents.

In *The Deluge* Doré brings us closer to the end as only a few remain on a small bit of rock while the drowning waters close in, but once again the same heroism and dying innocence prevail. When the artist presents his interpretation of *The Dove Sent Forth from the Ark,* the last plate in this series, we observe the white bird at the centre of the picture as it flies through a valley of corpses. This voyage through a nightmare landscape of death makes the bird seem not a messenger of hope and grace, but a predatory avenging creature. In other words, in Danby, Doré, and Turner the subject takes on a new, particularly bitter meaning. The need to present visual images of divine punishment makes that punishment seem cruel and unusual indeed until, finally, one wonders if God had anything to do with it. The nineteenth-century imagination here destroys the traditional Christian significance of the Deluge in these works, twisting it and transforming it into something blasphemous, for the need to use one's sympathetic imagination, feeling and perceiving as if one were inside the scene itself, has betrayed some artists into creating subversive images and encouraged others to do so. I assume that Turner, a sceptic, quite consciously subverted the usual significances of the subject, and the same could be true of Doré, but Danby's general artistic approach, more than any conscious programme, is probably responsible for the transformation of the Deluge he creates.

At any rate, these artists' instinctive portrayals of the suffering inhabitants of earth result in images, not of men who suffer justly, but of those who suffer and do not understand why – and neither do we, the spectators of these events. We encounter images not of a universe in which God rules, but one in which nature runs rampant. We move, in other words, from the universe of the Bible and Evangelical hymnody to that of Melville. As his Ishmael tells us in *Moby Dick,*

> Foolish mortals, Noah's flood is not yet subsided: two thirds of the fair world it yet covers. . . . The sea dashes even the mightiest whales against the rocks, and leaves them there side by side with the split wrecks of ships. No mercy, no power but its own controls it. Panting and snorting like a mad battle steed that has lost its rider, the masterless ocean overruns the globe. [ch. 58]

Anyone who shares this vision of nature and this vision of the Deluge is unlikely to take the Flood as an instance, a paradigm, of just punishment.

Versions of Odysseus

> The man, for wisdom's various arts renown'd,
> Long exercis'd in woes, oh muse! resound;
> Who, when his arms had wrought the destin'd fall
> Of sacred Troy, and raz'd her heav'n-built wall,
> Wand'ring from clime to clime, observant stray'd,
> Their manners noted, and their states survey'd.
> On stormy seas unnumber'd toils he bore.

> Alexander Pope's translation of the opening lines of
> *The Odyssey*

A great wave drove down from above him
with a horrible rush, and spun the raft in a circle,
and he was thrown clear far from the raft and let the steering oar
slip from his hands. A terrible gust of stormwinds whirling
together and blowing snapped the mast tree off in the middle,
and the sail and the upper deck were thrown far and fell in the water.
He himself was ducked for a long time, nor was he able
to come up quickly from under the great rush of the water. . . .
so the raft's long timbers were scattered, but now Odysseus
sat astride one beam, like a man riding on horseback.

> Richard Lattimore's translation of passages from book 5

Effortlessly
Odysseus in one motion strung the bow.
Then slid his right hand down the cord and plucked it,
so the taut gut vibrating hummed and sang
a swallow's note.

In the hushed hall it smote the suitors
and all their faces changed. The Zeus thundered
overhead, one loud crack for a sign. . . .
He dropped his eyes and nodded, and the prince
Telémakhos, true son of King Odysseus,
belted his sword on, clapped hand to his spear,
and with a clink and glitter of keen bronze
stood by his chair, in the forefront near his father.

'You yellow dogs, you thought I'd never make it
home from the land of Troy. You took my house to plunder,
twisted my maids to serve your beds. You dared
bid for my wife while I was still alive.
Contempt was all you had for the gods who rule wide heaven,
contempt for what men say of you hereafter.
Your last hour has come. You die in blood.'

Robert Fitzgerald's translation of passages from books 21 and 22

Like the figure of Robinson Crusoe, that of Odysseus has served as a basic paradigm or structure capable of conveying attitudes very different from those originally associated with this archetypal survivor. The intonations of Odysseus, however, present us with far more complex matters of literary and cultural history than do the comparatively simple variations of Defoe's castaway. The creative misinterpretations of Robinson Crusoe take the form of removing the divine perspective from the narrative. Removing Defoe's God transforms his narrative of punishment, trial, and spiritual education which lead a prodigal son back to his father into a figure of human and metaphysical isolation. No such simple change in one element characterizes recent intonations of *The Odyssey;* and furthermore, unlike the English castaway, Odysseus is an extraordinarily complex figure who descends to us surrounded by complex and often contradictory traditions.[3] The modern variations of Crusoe and his situation clearly begin with Defoe's novel – an easily identifiable work which has a single text fixed in all its essentials. In contrast, Odysseus comes down to us from classical times in two different versions: whereas the wise, pious, courageous, much-suffering hero of the Homeric poems stands as a defining example of what is greatest in humanity, he appears in Vergil as the archetypal trickster and betrayer. The ambiguities of this figure are not simply a matter of whether he appears as Odysseus or Ulysses – not, that is, merely a matter of Greek or Roman traditions – since Sophocles' *Philoctetes* already presents him as a dishonourable cheater willing to blame his superiors for his acts. Similarly, Plato, who variously presents Odysseus as both a good and an evil man, describes him as false and wily in the *Lesser Hippias*. It is this darker Odysseus who appears in Vergil and Dante and to whom Hugo refers in the opening lines of 'Après avoir lu les lettres à l'inconnue': 'Cela ne change pas beaucoup, la turpitude./ Ulysse peut tromper Polyphème.'

Since ancient times men have manipulated *The Odyssey* to convey their own conceptions of human existence. Odysseus is, above all, the *man who would return home,* and his longing for Ithaka has long been taken as a figure of every man's desires for spiritual bliss. In the ninth book of *The Odyssey* the hero defines himself in relation to his homeland when he tells Alkinoös

My home is on the peaked sea-mark of Ithaka
under Mount Neion's wind-blown robe of leaves . . .
I shall not see on earth a place more dear,
though I have been detained long by Kalypso
loveliest among goddesses, who held me
in her smooth caves, to be her heart's delight
as Kirkê of Aiaia, the enchantress,
desired me, and detained me in her hall.
But in my heart I never gave consent.
Where shall a man find sweetness to surpass
his own home and his parents? In far lands
he shall not, though he find a house of gold. [trans. Robert Fitzgerald]

This desire to return to that place where a man may be truly himself and truly at home has long been taken to be a defining and even archetypal human characteristic. Since late classical times commentators like Porphyry have allegorized *The Odyssey,* turning its hero into a figure for the soul of Everyman.[4] As Plotinus argues in the sixth tractate ('On Beauty') of the first Ennead, we should flee the snares of material beauty and seek to reach the beloved Fatherland.

> How are we to gain the open sea? For Odysseus is surely a parable to us when he commands the flight from the sorceries of Circe or Calypso – not content to linger for all the pleasure offered to his eyes and all the delight of sense filling his days.
> [trans. Stephen MacKenna]

The ancient tendency to perceive the Homeric poems as a treasure hoard of analogies that possess universally applicable significance has often thus led commentators to treat the poem as a series of emblems. Frequently, creative misinterpretation seems the guiding rule when poets and polemicists alike interpret the great hero for their own ends. For example, when Boccaccio defends poetry in the *Genealogia deorum gentilium* against the charge that its beauties perniciously lead men from virtue, he makes a traditional, if somewhat bizarre, reference to the episode with the Sirens, arguing that 'Ulysses, noble soul, spurned the sound, not of songs read in the closet, but the dulcet music of the Sirens, whom he passed by for fear of harm at their hands' (ch. 14, trans. C. S. Osgood). This episode, in other words, is supposed to show us the way the wise man resists the temptations of false beauty and art – as in a sense it does. But having truncated the original episode by removing the major element of the hero's insatiable curiosity, Boccaccio produces a quite un-Homeric Odysseus.

Clearly, some of the post-Homeric versions of Odysseus present a less than heroic figure simply because they remove him from his original context and surround him with alien ideologies. *The Odyssey,* which draws a picture of a man possessing almost all human virtue, portrays the much suffering, brave wanderer as not only steadfast and courageous but also actively heroic. Odysseus, who is a great athlete and a great warrior, is also intellectually curious, cunning, and eloquent. At the same time, he is pious, for even in times and places of great scarcity he sacrifices to the Gods. He is also masterful, and in book 18 he warns the suitor Amphinomos, hoping to save him, but Athena clouds the fated man's mind and Odysseus' mercy is of no avail. Later, after he has destroyed the suitors, he tells Eurykleia, his old nurse,

> No crowing aloud, old woman.
> To glory over slain men is no piety.

> Destiny and the gods' will vanquished these,
> and their own hardness. [bk 22]

None the less, although Homer is careful to emphasize that Odysseus knows the proper role and limitations of human beings, he does present his hero as a daring, deceptive man who comes close to being a Faustian figure. In the famous scene in the thirteenth book, when he dissembles with the disguised Athena, the goddess comments upon his powers of deception with admiration impossible for Vergil and Dante:

> Whoever gets around you must be sharp
> and guileful as a snake; even a god
> might bow to you in ways of dissimulation.
> You! You chameleon!
> Bottomless bag of tricks!
> Here in your own country
> would you not give your stratagems a rest
> or stop spellbinding for an instant?
> You play a part as if it were your own tough skin.
>   [trans. Robert Fitzgerald]

In the English Renaissance, when men regarded the Faustian quester with horrified fascination, George Chapman's translation (1614–15) appropriately has Athena address Odysseus as 'insatiate/ in over-reaches!' Chapman, however, goes beyond the original text, for Homer makes it clear that, while his hero might come dangerously close to such prideful trespass, his actions do remain within proper limits. Indeed, Homer provides Odysseus with divine approbation since Athena joys in his deceptions:

> Two of a kind, we are,
> contrivers, both. Of all men now alive
> you are the best in plots and story telling.
> My own fame is for wisdom among the gods –
> deceptions, too. [trans. Robert Fitzgerald]

Vergil, who did much to disseminate the darker version of Odysseus as the betrayer, clearly could not find such qualities either amusing or admirable. Such 'godlike' cunning did not seem godlike to him because he had an un-Homeric view of both the gods and morality. Moreover, since such cunning created the wooden horse that led directly to the destruction of Troy, Vergil has a particular reason for detesting Odysseus' deviousness. In the age of Augustus, Homeric virtues become impious viciousness.

Odysseus, skilled in words, has occasionally also been used as a figure for the poet. Since classical times authors have described writing a poem in terms of the sea voyage, and therefore the paradigmatic ocean wanderings of the hero naturally are available for such analogies. Equally important, Odysseus who knows the proper respect due to bards – he excuses Phemios from the general slaughter – is himself something of a poet. He is not only a teller of tall tales and a creator of false identities that enable him to survive, he is also a truthful bard who preserves the deeds of the past. As Alkinoös tells him,

> You speak with art, but your intent is honest.
> The Argive troubles, and your own troubles,
> you told as a poet would, a man who knows the world.
> [bk 11, trans. Robert Fitzgerald]

George Chapman's translation expands upon this praise with characteristic exuberance, thus making Odysseus into a complete poet, for according to this Renaissance version his royal host lavishes this more detailed praise on him:

> You move our eies
> With forme, our minds with matter, and our eares
> With elegant oration, such as beares
> A musicke in the orderd historie
> It layes before us. Not Demodocus
> With sweeter strains hath usde to sing to us
> All the Greeke sorrowes, wept out in your owne.

In thus turning Odysseus into a classical poet and rhetorician, Chapman may be following an ancient tradition, for as far back as Plato's *Phaedrus* the hero is credited with composing a manual of oratory during his leisure before Troy.

Since Odysseus would seem to have much in common with Ishmael, Cain, the Wandering Jew, and other common Romantic and post-Romantic images of the artist-poet, one is surprised not to find him employed more frequently in this way. Ruskin, it is true, does argue that in *Ulysses Deriding Polyphemus* (1829) Turner created an image of his relation to the English art public.

He had been himself shut up by one-eyed people, in a cave 'darkened by laurels' (getting no good, but only evil, from all the fame of the great of long ago) – he had seen his companions eaten in the cave by the one-eyed people – (many a painter of good promise had fallen by Turner's side in those early toils of his); at last, when his own time had like to have come, he thrust the rugged pine-trunk – all ablaze – (rough nature, and the light of it) – into the faces of the one-eyed people, left them tearing their hair in the cloud-banks – got out of the cave in a humble way, under a sheep's belly – (helped by the lowliness and gentleness of nature, as well as by her rugged-ness and flame) – and got away to the open sea as the dawn broke over the Enchanted Islands. [*The Turner Bequest*, item 508]

Ruskin, who does not hold that the artist intended his picture to communicate such experiences, is of course merely employing the Odyssean confrontation with a blind one-eyed monster as a satiric analogy with which to lambast the British public.

One of the rare uses of the Homeric figure as an image of the poet appears, perhaps expectedly, in Wallace Stevens, who frequently envisages the modern creator as a heroic quester. In both 'The Sail of Ulysses' and its briefer version, 'Presence of an External Master of Knowledge', Stevens presents the soliloquy of this *'Symbol of the seeker, crossing by night/ The giant sea'* (italics in original) in which his hero claims

> A freedom at last from the mystical,
> The beginnings of a final order,
> The order of a man's right to be
> As he is, the discipline of his scope
> Observed as an absolute, himself. . . .
> There is no map of paradise.

Heroically living and questing without the comforts of religious belief, this symbol of the seeker, as Stevens terms him, knows that his only source of truth must be 'the sibyl of the self . . . whose diamond . . . is poverty' ('The Sail of Ulysses'). Such confident presentations of the poet as voyaging hero are rare in Romantic and post-Romantic art and literature.

In fact, modern intonations of the Odysseus story, like those of the Pisgah sight, tend to emphasize irony and failure. In 'Ithaka'

C. P. Cavafy urges that, since all goals are illusory, we must gain our
rewards from the journey itself:

> Have Ithaka always in your mind.
> Your arrival there is what you are destined for.
> But do not in the least hurry the journey.
> Better that it last for years,
> So that when you reach the island and are old,
> rich with all you have gained on the way,
> not expecting Ithaka to give you wealth.
> Ithaka gave you the splendid journey.
> Without her you would not have set out.
> She hasn't anything else to give you.
>   [trans. Edmund Keeley and Philip Sherrard]

In contrast to Cavafy, who explicitly takes the voyage of Odysseus as
an image of human life, A. D. Hope in 'The End of a Journey' focuses
specifically upon the hero's return home. Odysseus' arrival in Ithaka
turns out to be not, as Homer has it, a return to the hero's full nature
as father, son, husband, householder, and king, but rather an
encounter with disillusionment and emptiness, for he is now but an
'old man sleeping with his housekeeper'.

> He prayed but knew Athene would not come.
> The gods at last had left him, and the day
> Darkened about him. Then from far away
> And long ago, he seemed once more to be
>
> Roped to a mast and through the breaker's roar
> Sweet voices mocked him on his reeling deck:
> 'Son of Laertes, what delusive song
> Turned your swift keel and brought you to this wreck,
> In age and disenchantment to prolong
> Stale years and chew the cud of ancient wrong,
> A castaway upon so cruel a shore?'

The appearance of the word 'castaway' in this final line of the poem
brings about, or crystallizes, the recognition to which we – and the
now-failed hero – have been led. Whereas Cavafy views the
possibility of a triumphant return in much the same manner as

Hope, his concentration upon the experiences of the voyage makes his poem far more optimistic. His poem, which is meant to console men for the fact that there are no true Ithakas, tries to come to terms with things as they are, while Hope, who savagely reinterprets the ancient narrative itself, concentrates upon the moment of failure.

Such attractions to failure and the failed constitute a major use of the Odysseus narrative during the past century and a half. Thus, in the *Pisan Cantos* Ezra Pound employs Elpenor, Odysseus' failed comrade, as narrator and hence as figure of the poet, while in *The Suitors,* Gustave Moreau's main interest is in the defeated and dying. Similarly, although critics disagree about the importance of the Homeric analogies in Joyce's *Ulysses*, the one clear example of such allusion seems to be the ironic use of Odysseus' encounter with Telemachus to emphasize that Bloom does not find his spiritual son, nor Stephen his father.[5]

These reinterpretations of *The Odyssey* suggest that well-known narratives do not serve as mere repositories of allusion and analogy for later authors, but rather that, like techniques such as point of view, these narratives themselves constitute a medium. In other words, these tales are as much a part of the artist's and the poet's means of conveying ideas and emotions as are colour, outline, and language. Artists like Moreau and poets like Hope and Cavafy convey their meanings by reshaping a pre-existent story.

Tennyson's 'Ulysses' and 'Enoch Arden' exemplify two different modes of thus employing the original Odyssean narrative and its accretions. 'Ulysses', one of the Laureate's best-known poems, takes the form of a dramatic monologue delivered by the ageing hero, who, bored with 'an aged wife' and savage people, purposes to 'sail beyond the sunset, and the baths/ Of all the western stars, until I die.' For most of its critical history the poem has been interpreted as a rather straightforward expression of the idea that one must persevere with courage regardless of the difficulties. Such an interpretation places greatest emphasis upon the poem's famous closing lines in which Odysseus exhorts his mariners

> that which we are, we are;
> One equal temper of heroic hearts,
> Made weak by time and fate, but strong in will
> To strive, to seek, to find, and not to yield.

This reading gains support from the poet's own statement that 'The poem was written after Arthur Hallam's death, and it gives the feeling about the need of going forward and braving the struggle of life perhaps more simply than anything in *In Memoriam*.'[6]

Despite such strong external testimony to the apparent validity of such a reading of the poem, several critics within the last quarter-century have argued that 'Ulysses' must be read as a dramatic monologue in which the speaker does not necessarily have Tennyson's approval. Pointing to the scorn that Ulysses seems to direct at his wife, son, and subjects, E. J. Chiasson argues that he unconsciously reveals an essential arrogance and irresponsibility quite in keeping with the poem's Dantean and Byronic sources but which are quite out of harmony with Tennysonian belief.[7] The argument that 'Ulysses' was prompted by the death of Hallam does not in itself necessarily argue for the traditional interpretation since other poems, such as 'Tithonus' and 'The Lotos Eaters', which had similar origins, have speakers who clearly do not voice their author's own ideas. In fact, since the poet was trying to gain some emotional and aesthetic distance from the overwhelming fact of Hallam's death in these poems, he approaches his own beliefs only in the most indirect fashion. Perhaps it might be best to say that he is working these ideas out and often testing the validity or weakness of those that might have some appeal but to which he is in no way committed. According to such an argument, Tennyson, who admittedly drew upon Dante's Ulysses in *Inferno* 26: 90–142, might be experimentally imagining what it would be like to pursue his own quest without regard for the cost to others. 'Ulysses', then, despite its supposedly Victorian optimism, would be read as embodying ethical attitudes like those espoused by the speakers in 'The Lotos Eaters' and 'The Palace of Art' (in the first part of the latter poem).

However appealing such a reading was in the 1950s when all critics seemed enthralled with literary irony, it does not finally find a means of discounting the poet's own statements about 'Ulysses'. It does, however, point to some apparent inconsistencies in the poem. A third possible reading, which sees it as a deathbed statement, receives support from the fact that the speaker is addressing

My mariners,
Souls that have toiled, and wrought, and thought with me –

That ever with a frolic welcome took
The thunder and the sunshine, and opposed
Free hearts, free foreheads.

Since the hero returned home alone and all his fellow mariners are dead, it is possible that Ulysses is here expressing a courageous willingness to voyage into the last unexplored land. His invitation – 'Come, my friends,/ 'Tis not too late to seek a newer world' – and much of the poem is quite in keeping with such an interpretation, which has the value of recognizing both the biographical genesis and the apparent inconsistencies Chiasson perceives. Of course, the major argument against reading 'Ulysses' as a more positive version of something like Browning's 'The Bishop Orders His Tomb' is that Hallam Tennyson, though not the poet himself, claimed that the mariners who are addressed in the poem are those of Ulysses' later voyages – and hence not dead. None the less, unlike many of the statements in the *Memorials,* this one does not have the poet's own authority; and moreover, Tennyson has clearly departed far from the Dantean narrative in which the voyagers, who are not old, do not survive their first voyage. At any rate, whatever the reading one adopts, one perceives that Tennyson has characteristically attempted to use the ancient narrative and its medieval intonations to convey modern, personal themes.

'Enoch Arden', a very different poem because it is not a dramatic monologue, draws upon the narrative structures of both *The Odyssey* and *Robinson Crusoe.* Tennyson's story of a castaway's self-sacrifice also draws upon several nineteenth-century verse narratives (which include Thomas Woolner's 'The Fisherman's Story' and George Crabbe's 'The Parting Hour') in portraying the world of a man shipwrecked and castaway. Enoch, 'a rough sailor's lad/ Made orphan by a winter shipwreck' (ll. 14–15), himself three times saves other men from watery deaths. After seven happy years of marriage to Annie Lee, financial distress drives him to go as the boatswain on a China trader. He is marooned on an island and after more than a decade of awaiting his return, Annie accepts the offer of marriage from their mutual friend Philip. Ironically, she finally accepts his fervent offers of his hand only after she has misinterpreted an ambiguous dream. As she desperately seeks for a sign from the Bible, Annie

Suddenly put her finger on the text,
'Under the palm-tree'. That was nothing to her:
No meaning there: she closed the Book and slept:
When lo! her Enoch sitting on a height,
Under a palm-tree, over him the Sun:
'He is gone,' she thought, 'he is happy, he is singing
Hosanna in the highest: yonder shines
The Sun of Righteousness, and these be palms
Whereof the happy people strowing cried
"Hosanna in the highest!" ' Here she woke
Resolved, sent for him, and said wildly to him [Philip]
'There is no reason why we should not wed.' [ll. 493–504]

Like Leodogrand in the 'Coming of Arthur', Annie makes a decision about a crucial marriage after having an ambiguous dream. As it turns out, she misreads her visionary experience, because the unhappy Enoch is stranded on a tropical paradise, his 'beauteous hateful isle' (l. 613). He finally returns to find that his Penelope, who has been living in poverty and not riches, has accepted her suitor; and since he does not wish to destroy the happiness of his friend, wife, and family, he resolves to continue his castaway existence. Knowing that he is about to die,

Enoch bore his weakness cheerfully.
For sure no gladlier does the stranded wreck
See through the gray skirts of a lifting squall
The boat that bears the hope of life approach
To save the life despair'd of, than he saw
Death dawning on him, and the close of all. [ll. 823–8]

He dies at last,

Crying with a loud voice 'A sail! A sail!
I am saved;' and so fell back and spoke no more. [ll. 906–7]

By this point Tennyson's narrative of a shipwrecked and castaway existence has included so many ironies that one begins to wonder if this last hope of rescue may not prove so deluded as his earlier ones. In fact, this bleak tale so continually inverts the patterns of *Robinson Crusoe* and *The Odyssey,* both of which it follows quite closely, that one is left, finally, not with an image of heroic endurance but one of inexplicable suffering and isolation. Like many of the equally bleak narratives in Crabbe's *Village* and Wordsworth's *Excursion,* 'Enoch Arden' requires that one import a Christian perspective to provide the tale with meaning. Otherwise, it tends to seem a parable of a meaninglessly heroic, yet islanded and suffering, existence. Tennyson does mention Enoch's own consolatory faith, and we know that Tennyson himself believed firmly in Christianity, but his poem – like Hopkins's 'The Loss of the Eurydice' – seems to convey ideas and attitudes unintended by its author. Placing it in the historical context of similar work by Crabbe and Wordsworth suggests that this sentimental tale of sacrifice has a religious meaning; placing it in the context of its other literary forebears, *The Odyssey* and *Robinson Crusoe,* suggests a very different meaning. As we have observed, the presence of the modern shipwreck situation in literature and art over the past two centuries has meant that an author can move his readers from an imaginative cosmos in which God is present to one in which He is absent. Even when the artist and writer are believers, this alternative universe – whether believing or unbelieving – hovers beneath the desired one. Occasionally, as in 'Enoch Arden', it is difficult to ascertain in which one we are supposed to find ourselves.

Rainbows: problematic images of problematic nature

> When the rainbow arching high
> Looks from the zenith round the sky,
> Lit with exquisite tints seven
> Caught from angels' wings in heaven,
> Double, and higher than his wont,
> The wrought rim of heaven's font, –
> Then may I upwards gaze and see
> The deepening intensity
> Of the air-blended diadem . . .
> Ending in sweet uncertainty
> 'Twixt real hue and phantasy.

Gerard Manley Hopkins, 'Il Mystico', ll. 107–15, 121–2

The Leeds City Art Gallery contains a landscape by Atkinson Grimshaw (Pl. 19) that is especially intriguing to anyone interested in iconology. In particular, Grimshaw's oil painting reveals much about the difficulties nineteenth-century artists and writers faced when they attempted to transform facts of nature into paradigmatic images, tropes, or situations. This representation of a mountain stream with rainbow has little to differentiate it visually from other carefully observed nineteenth-century representations of nature in its rougher aspect. Utilizing the sharp declivities of rock-walled valleys on both sides of his canvas, the painter carries our eye into a picture space that has a remarkably conservative – that is, remarkably Claudean or Wilsonian – organization for a work of the latter half of the nineteenth century. Hillsides replace the Claudean (or Turnerian) tree, but the same motifs divide the picture into foreground, middle distance, and distance, while the traditional winding stream serves to unite these spatial zones. Within this rocky world a single shepherd and his small flock provide the only life and the only sense of scale; and this figure's back, perhaps significantly, is turned away from the beautiful rainbow that reaches down from the sky to touch the earth not far from where he stands. This rainbow serves as an important compositional element, creating the second half of an ellipse, the first part of which is formed by the steep hillside on the right. Grimshaw's painting differs from most nineteenth-century portrayals of the rainbow, which most often depict it above either a flat, open plain or a woodland scene, but like them it uses one of nature's more lovely optical phenomena to provide a striking visual motif. It does not, however, seem to have anything that distinguishes it iconographically from other pictures of the rainbow, such as Constable's *Hampstead Heath with a Rainbow* (1836, Tate Gallery) or Turner's *Buttermere Lake* (1798, Tate Gallery). One is thus somewhat jarred to discover that Grimshaw has chosen to call his work *The Seal of the Covenant,* thereby claiming a religious significance for the scene before us which it does not seem to warrant. In other words, the verbal context this title provides for the visual image does not match our experience of it.

The Seal of the Covenant is not unique among nineteenth-century works of art and literature in the problematic uses it makes of this traditional landscape motif. J. T. Linnell's *The Rainbow* (1863, Pl. 20), now in the Forbes Magazine Collection, similarly directs the spectator to perceive an ordinary English landscape existing within the context of biblical events. Less unusual in its setting than *The Seal of the Covenant,* Linnell's now sadly deteriorated painting includes its rainbow as part of a pastoral scene framed by a woodland setting;

and here it seems to betray the obvious influence of the famous Rubens *Landscape with a Rainbow* (1635–8, Wallace Collection, London) and its many heirs, which include Paul Sandby's *The Rainbow* (after 1802, Nottingham). Our problem with this picture comes not from its title but from the scriptural text that Linnell placed on his frame as an epigraph: 'And it shall come to pass, when I bring a cloud over the earth, that the bow shall be seen in the clouds' (Genesis 9: 14). Although one does not react so strongly to this painting as to Grimshaw's, perhaps, the suggestion that this English scene embodies God's covenant with man is none the less disturbing because again one encounters an obvious separation of word and image. One doubts either these painters' control over their materials or their sincerity, so that one is driven to inquire how essential are that title and that text from Genesis to the pictures themselves. In other words, these rainbow landscapes lead us to the question, can a painting of nature exist independently of the verbal statements about that nature which the artist himself appends to it? Or, to rephrase that problem in terms more acceptable to the twentieth century, *must* a painting of nature exist independently of verbal statements about it?

That these paintings by Grimshaw and Linnell lead directly to such crucial questions tells us much about the situation of landscape painting in the nineteenth century. To claim religious significance for the rainbow is to make definite assertions about man, God, and nature. Furthermore, to make such a claim in work of visual art is to make an assertion about both that art and the audience for whom it is intended. Our reactions to these rainbow landscapes make clear that we do not grant all these claims. Let us look at some of these claims to see why they make these rainbow landscapes so problematic.

There was certainly ample precedent for thus endowing the rainbow with sacred meaning, and therefore the difficulties we encounter with these paintings by Linnell and Grimshaw do not arise in any eccentric personal symbolism, such as one comes upon in the works of Blake and Friedrich. A long tradition had made the rainbow a commonplace symbol of peace, hope, and grace not only in scriptural exegetics but also in pictorial and literary iconography as well. The source of this iconographical tradition is Genesis, which explicitly makes this optical phenomenon a divinely instituted covenant-sign:

And God said, This is the token of the covenant which I
make between me and you and every living creature that is
with you, for perpetual generations:

I do set my bow in the cloud, and it shall be for a token of
the covenant between me and the earth.

And it shall come to pass, when I bring a cloud over the
earth, that the bow shall be seen in the cloud:

And I will remember my covenant, which is between me
and you and every living creature of all flesh; and the waters
shall no more become a flood to destroy all flesh.

And the bow shall be in the cloud; and I will look upon it,
that I may remember the everlasting covenant between God
and every living creature that is upon the earth.

And God said unto Noah, This is the token of the
covenant, which I have established between me and all flesh
that is upon the earth. [Genesis 9: 12–17]

According to the Bible, then, the Lord Himself specifically made the
natural phenomenon of the rainbow to function as a sign. In St
Augustine's *De doctrina christiana,* his treatise on the correct manner
for reading scripture, he explained that God made two books – the
Bible and the book of the world. But only in the Bible do natural
objects have symbolical or allegorical significance, for it is only
within the context of a divinely inspired narrative or other discourse
that natural facts can possess a further, or (as St Augustine would put
it) spiritual, meaning. However, as this passage from Genesis makes
quite clear, the rainbow possesses a unique status: in its natural
context, as an event that occurs after any rainstorm when the light
conditions are adequate, it functions linguistically and symbolically
as a divinely instituted sign. The rainbow, in other words, is a prime
example of a natural object or event interpreted as part of an
allegorical, sacramental universe. One problem that artists and
writers in the nineteenth century had to face, then, was that although
many men no longer accepted such a vision of reality, the Bible
made it abundantly clear that the rainbow should be understood in
this manner.

As Patrick Fairbairn, a popular interpreter of the Bible, explained to
his audience in *The Typology of Scripture,* 'The fitness of the rainbow . . . to
serve as a sign of the covenant made with Noah, is all that could be
desired', because there is an 'exact correspondence between the

natural phenomenon it represents, and the moral use to which it is applied.' Such a divine promise means, not that God will never again visit His judgment upon guilty men, but that He will never again do so to the extent that He will destroy the world. In the moral as in the natural sphere, says Fairbairn, storms will occur, but no second Deluge will follow since God's mercy will always thus 'rejoice against judgment'. The most important significance of the rainbow is as an emblem, a promise, of grace:

> How appropriate an emblem of that grace which should always show itself ready to return after wrath! Grace still sparing and preserving, even when storms of judgment have been bursting forth upon the guilty! And as the rainbow throws its radiant arch over the expanse between heaven and earth, uniting the two together again as with a wreath of beauty, after they have been engaged in an elemental war, what a fitting image does it present to the thoughtful eye of the essential harmony that still undoubtedly is its symbolic import, as the sign peculiarly connected with the covenant of Noah; it holds out, by means of its very form and nature, as assurance of God's mercy, as engaged to keep perpetually in check the floods of deserved wrath, and continue to the world the manifestation of His grace and goodness. ['The New World and its Inheritors']

For the Christian the most important manifestation of God's grace and goodness was, of course, Christ; and long exegetical tradition held that the rainbow served not only to record God's covenant with Noah but also as a type of the second, or new, covenant, brought by Christ. As Thomas Scott's popular Bible commentary pointed out, it is 'the new covenant, with its blessings and securities, which in all these events was prefigured.'

The audience in Victorian England, where this tradition seems to have retained vitality longer than anywhere else, learned this interpretation of the rainbow not only from preachers and scriptural expositors but also from a revered tradition of devotional poetry. The London Religious Tract Society included several such traditional readings of the heavenly arch in its *English Sacred Poetry of the Olden Time* (1864). Henry Vaughan's 'The Rainbow', for example, relates how gratefully the poet catches sight of this

> Bright pledge of peace and sunshine, the sure tie
> Of the Lord's hand, the object of His eye!
> When I behold thee, though my light be dim,
> Distant, and low, I can in thine see Him
> Who looks upon thee from His glorious throne,
> And minds the covenant betwixt all and One.

Vaughan's poem is of particular interest to us because he thus reacts to the rainbow as a divinely instituted covenant-sign when coming upon the rainbow in a natural, not a biblical, setting. He does not, in other words, merely interpret the scene of the rainbow's first appearance in Genesis but rather interprets the scene with the rainbow in which he, Henry Vaughan, a man of the seventeenth century, finds himself; and for this reason his poem is a direct verbal analogue to the paintings of Linnell and Grimshaw. In contrast, *Paradise Lost,* which many nineteenth-century Evangelicals read as a doctrinal tract, explains the significance of the Bible scene. When Adam asks Michael the meaning of the 'color'd streaks in Heaven', his angelic teacher instructs him that they have been placed there to remind the sons of Adam that

> Such grace shall one just Man find in his sight,
> That he relents, not to blot out mankind,
> And makes a covenant never to destroy
> The earth again by flood, nor rain to drown the world
> With man therein or beast; but when he brings
> Over the earth a cloud, with therein set
> His triple-color'd bow, whereon to look
> And call to mind his Covenant. [bk XI, ll. 890–7]

Both Noah and the rainbow itself were types of the Christian dispensation, and the covenants to which both Milton and Vaughan refer are the new as well as the old, for the one just man is that second, greater man, Christ. George Gascoigne's 'Good Morrow', which also appeared in the Tract Society volume, explicitly relates the grace signified by the rainbow to his Saviour:

> The rainbow bending in the sky,
>   Bedecked with sundry hues,
> Is like the seat of God on high,

And seems to tell this new:
That as thereby He promised
To drown the world no more,
So, by the blood which Christ hath shed,
He will our health restore.

The Rev. L. B. White, editor of *Sacred Poetry in the Olden Time,* assists our study of this image by referring his reader to Thomas Campbell's 'To the Rainbow', which rejoices that God never 'lets the type grow pale with age/ That first spoke peace to man.' Like Milton, Vaughan, and Gascoigne, this nineteenth-century poet accepts a sacred meaning of this optical occurrence in the heavens. One cannot tell whether by 'type' Campbell means that the rainbow prefigures Christ or is merely a symbol of His mercies, but his interpretation of the rainbow in traditional Christian terms is evident.

Although such readings of the rainbow are not common among Victorian English poets, one finds a few examples, and one finds them in just the poets one might expect – Newman, Keble, and Hopkins. For example, in his early lines on 'My Lady Nature and Her Daughters', Newman appears to allude to the notion of the rainbow as a sign of divine grace, and he far more explicitly develops this notion in his sonnet 'Hope'. Explaining that ever since 'the stern baptism' of the Flood, we are no longer the children of 'a guilty sire', he admits that the Deluge did not wash us clean enough to return to Eden.

But thoughts were stirr'd of Him who was to come,
Whose rainbow hues so streak'd the o'ershadowing gloom,
That faith could e'en that desolate scene admire.

Now that Christ has 'come and gone' from earth, we await, says Newman, the 'second substance of the deluge type,/ When our slight ark shall cross a molten surge' at the Last Judgment, and after judgment we shall enter 'Eden's long-lost gate'. Here the rainbow is clearly Christ Himself, as it is in John Keble's 'Quinquagesima Sunday', which asserts that the rainbow, like Christ Himself, exemplifies God's merciful accommodation to man:

The Son of Man in radiance beam'd
Too bright for us to scan,

> But we may face the rays that stream'd
> From the mild Son of Man.

As he further explains, 'God by his bow' writes in the sky that 'every grace is love.' John Ruskin draws upon much the same exegetical tradition when he explains in the last volume of *Modern Painters* that 'the bow, or colour of the cloud, signifies always mercy, the sparing of life.' The sunlight, symbol of God's righteousness, is, like that righteousness itself, too intense for man to contemplate directly, and so God mercifully 'divided, and softened [this sunlight] into colour . . . Thus divided, the sunlight is the type of the wisdom of God, becoming sanctification and redemption.'[8] Clearly, Ruskin, like Newman and Keble, conceived the world in a manner more characteristic of the Middle Ages than of the reign of Victoria. All three – Evangelical, High Churchman, and Roman Catholic – accept that the glorious optical phenomenon of the rainbow is a divine messenger, a perpetually reappearing sign of the old and new covenants. All three, in other words, were able to *read* natural phenomena as if such phenomena contained a language of divinely instituted symbols.

Gerard Manley Hopkins was another major Victorian author who shared this attitude towards nature. As one can see from the closing lines of 'The Caged Skylark', Hopkins was able to make traditional interpretations of the rainbow part of his characteristically complex theological wit. Likening man's spirit to a caged bird, Hopkins concludes,

> Man's spirit will be flesh-bound when found at best,
> But uncumbered: meadow-down is not distressed
> For a rainbow footing it nor he for his bónes rísen.

The poet's play upon 'distressed' well prepares us to recognize not only the rainbow's lack of earthly weight but also the way God frees man from the 'stress' of his terrestrial, fallen existence. The rainbow in this poem, unlike the others at which we have looked, appears within an analogy, but it none the less seems clear that Hopkins employs it for all its traditional significances – and that he accepts them.

Since the traditional religious symbolism of the rainbow plays such an effective part in these various poems, one wonders why it should appear so problematic in the paintings by Linnell and Grimshaw. One might assume that this is a simple matter of symbolism functioning differently in painting and poetry, but we do not in fact encounter the same difficulties when we view nineteenth-century representations of Noah's sacrifice, such as that by Daniel Maclise (1847, Leeds City Art Gallery, Pl. 21) or the popular Bible illustrations by Gustav Jäger. Such portrayals of the scriptural narrative of course had a long pictorial as well as literary tradition attached to them. For instance, Cesare Ripa's *Iconologia* (1603) includes such a scene of Noah and the rainbow in its emblem of grace. The figure of the woman who represents this spiritual gift holds an olive branch signifying 'the peace the pardoned sinner gets through grace', while the *fatto,* or background portion of the emblem, depicts Noah and his family kneeling in prayer beneath a rainbow as heavenly light streams down upon them.[9] The existence of such a traditional reading of the rainbow as emblem of Christian grace is not a decisive factor here, since the poetic heritage suggests the same tradition pertains to rainbows in landscape as well.

The basic difference, however, is that *Noah's Sacrifice* (Pl. 21) is a work of sacred history while *The Seal of the Covenant* (Pl. 19) and *The Rainbow* (Pl. 20) are landscapes. The complicating factor arises from the fact that these landscapes make further claims to sacred history which their images for some reason will not support. The presence of the same image in two different genres, in two very different contexts, has important effects upon our reactions to it. First of all, by illustrating scriptural narrative, Maclise and Jäger effectively insulate the painting's symbolism. Thus, when they depict the details and setting of Noah's sacrifice, they provided us with a representation of a well-known scene that has a received meaning. Therefore, any scriptural references appended to their pictures simply aid the clear identification of subject. Such depiction of a traditional scene whose meaning is easily comprehended also serves to forestall any difficult questions about the artist's belief and sincerity. Although there is nothing in *Noah's Sacrifice* to indicate whether Maclise believed in the literal truth of biblical narrative, such matters of faith do not enter into our reaction to the picture since we have no doubts that it clearly and unambiguously offers an image of an event related in Genesis. The oldest and most basic rule of interpretation is that when one finds something puzzling or enigmatic, it is taken as a signal to search for a more complex system of meaning. Such is the rule of St Augustine and such, if we examine it, is also the rule of modern exegesis – whether the subject be the Bible, literature, painting, or other humanistic studies. But by providing a coherent biblical context for the rainbow, these illustrations of Noah's sacrifice prevent the appearance of anything that might puzzle us and thus prompt us to look further. The information provided by these pictures, in other words, appears sufficient, and hence we do not feel impelled to search for new questions or new answers. Perhaps paradoxically, Maclise's painting, like the illustration of Jäger, insulates itself from the world of the spectator because it follows the biblical text so closely.

These two pictures insulate the symbolism of the rainbow specifically because they restrict themselves to depicting a single event that took place in the ancient past: Noah, we realize, will never again offer his sacrifice to God beneath the appearance of the world's first rainbow. The paintings by Linnell and Grimshaw, in contrast, are both historical and predictive. They are historical because they ostensibly portray the artists' own encounters with the phenomenon of the rainbow in an English landscape, and they are predictive because they claim that these and all other rainbows, now and in the future, bear sacred significance. Whereas Maclise's painting makes no assertion about any sacramental significance of any rainbows we might see, those by Grimshaw and Linnell claim that an everyday event remains within the context of biblical history and must be read according to the codes it supplies.

Since the arts have always been praised for their universality, one might perhaps wonder why the more generalized claim of these artists resulted in such problematic, such ineffective, art. The answer seems obvious: our own experience of landscape will not permit us to accept their particular claims about the universal spiritual significance of the rainbow. Like most obvious answers, this one is deceptively simple, for what is at issue here is a complicated mixture of changed attitudes towards art, nature, and faith. To begin with, Linnell's *The Rainbow* and Grimshaw's *The Seal of the Covenant* force the spectator to confront the nature of his religious belief. The extreme claims they make for the sacramental aspect of the universe collide directly with Victorian and modern doubts about both the divine origins of the Bible and the presence of divinity in nature.

Whereas to Newman and Keble, who both believe that a still immanent God fills nature with types and symbols, and the sudden appearance of the rainbow is a wonderful indication of His love for man, to many other nineteenth-century poets the rapid *disappearance* of this heavenly bow is what matters. Thus, in both Shelley's 'When the Lamp is Shattered' and his 'Hymn to Intellectual Beauty' he sees the rainbow as an emblem of transience, and even the devout Wordsworth in the 'Immortality Ode' takes the fact that the 'Rainbow comes and goes' to be a sign of our earthly state. Similarly, in Tennyson's *Becket* the rainbow will not stay but disappears as quickly as it came.

Like Byron, Shelley mocks the conventional notions of rainbow and covenant. Rather than deflating them in a comic poem, as Byron does in the second canto of *Don Juan,* he makes use of them in the blasphemous parody of *Queen Mab:*

> Yes! I have seen God's worshippers unsheathe
> The sword of His revenge, when grace descended,
> Confirming all unnatural impulses,
> To sanctify their desolating deeds;
> And frantic priests waved the ill-omened cross
> O'er the unhappy earth: then shone the sun
> On showers of gore from the upflashing steel
> Of safe assassination, and all crime
> Made stingless by the Spirits of the Lord,
> And blood-red rainbows canopied the land. [pt 7, ll. 225–34]

Granted, these shrill lines furnish an extreme example of a nineteenth-century poet rejecting the Christian belief that founds the traditional symbolic import of the rainbow. None the less, they do suggest how difficult it would be for later authors to employ the rainbow literally as a divinely intended emblem of grace.

Shelley's parodic inversion of the traditional significance of this symbol, like Doré's and Turner's representations of the Deluge, reveals that ethical objections played an important role in nineteenth-century loss of belief. Equally crucial, of course, were the many intellectual objections fostered by geology, biology, and comparative philology since by casting doubt upon the veracity of the Scriptures, these necessarily made it difficult to take the rainbow as a divinely instituted covenant-sign. Furthermore, the discoveries of Newton, as Keats felt, 'destroyed all the poetry of the rainbow by reducing it to the prismatic colours'.[10] Although the poets of the previous century had been moved to wonder by the divine order Newton's *Optics* had revealed, by the time the first Romantic generation arrived this sense of wonder had dissipated; the poets mourned the loss of mystery.

> Do not all charms fly
> At the mere touch of cold philosophy?
> There was an awful rainbow once in heaven:
> We know her woof, her texture; she is given
> In the dull catalogue of common things.
> Philosophy will clip an Angel's wings,
> Conquer all mysteries by rule and line,
> Empty and haunted air and gnomèd mine –
> Unweave a rainbow. [*Lamia,* pt 2, ll. 229–37]

By the time that Grimshaw and Linnell painted their pictures, it was a commonplace that natural science had taken the joy and wonder from the rainbow. As Ruskin, who so frequently tried to bridge a scientific and religious conception of nature, admitted, 'I much question whether any one who knows optics, however religious he may be, can feel in equal degree the pleasure or reverence which an unlettered peasant may feel at the sight of a rainbow' ('The Moral Landscape', *Modern Painters,* vol. 3).[11]

These changing attitudes toward god and nature made it very difficult for most nineteenth-century writers to take the rainbow literally as God's seal of the covenant. Unlike Byron and Shelley, few Victorian poets were likely to take such pleasure in directly confuting or mocking the religious tradition upon which this symbolism had been based. Instead they exercise other options: first of all, they can, like Tennyson, Browning, and many other nineteenth-century authors, simply employ the rainbow at times as a beautiful optical phenomenon. Second, they can find some literary device to insulate it from questions of belief; and third, they can make use of the rainbow precisely because it is problematic, thus employing it as a paradigm of man's experience of having to make sense of an often puzzling world.

By insulating or bracketing the symbol, authors can draw upon its traditional associations and yet not make any commitment. There are many different methods of thus bracketing the rainbow and similar symbols with religious or other problematic associations. First, the writer can make an allusion, or have a character do so, in such a way as to employ the traditional meanings for some purpose, such as delineating character, without himself admitting to any particular belief. For instance, in *The Ring and the Book* Guido tells us much about himself when he laments that Pompilia did not come to him 'rainbowed about with riches' (bk 11, l. 2, 130), for to him grace, luck, and wealth are all pretty much the same; and he is incapable of comprehending the meaning of grace, much less of covenant or moral law. This effective allusion, which thus tells us a great deal about Guido, tells us little about what Browning himself believes. An additional reason for this insulating effect is that Browning here characteristically places his allusion in the mouth of a character. A second form of bracketing the rainbow appears when writers employ it as an analogy. In Hopkins's 'The Caged Skylark', at which we have already looked, the poet, who almost certainly believed in the traditional interpretation of the rainbow himself, yet insulates his image to make it more rhetorically effective. In this manner he forestalls any adverse reaction on the part of his reader. In contrast, Tennyson's 'The Two Voices' exemplifies a poem that draws upon the rainbow as emblem of hope and grace without having to admit literal belief in it. At the close of his debate with the voice of doubt, the speaker victoriously asserts that it had failed to 'wreck' his 'mortal ark' (l. 390) and as a reward for this spiritual triumph he finds himself able to hear the voice of hope.

> From out my sullen heart a power
> Broke, like a rainbow from the shower,
>
> To feel, although no tongue can prove,
> That every cloud, that spreads above
> And veileth love, itself is love. [ll. 443–7]

Significantly, only after this battle has been won can he walk forth amid nature's bounty, becoming however briefly a Wordsworthian: for he must bring his vision and faith to nature before it can offer him anything of value. Tennyson here draws upon all the traditional meanings of the rainbow as emblem of hope and grace, and he connects it to the Deluge. But he uses the traditional significances of the rainbow, as he uses the image from nature itself, as a simile and not as a fact, not as something in which he literally believes.

Placing the rainbow within fantasy, allegory, or visionary experience offers yet another way of bracketing this symbol. George MacDonald's 'The Golden Key', one of the most beautiful of all nineteenth-century fantasies, well exemplifies how effectively such traditional imagery can function within the closed world of the imaginative vision. Using the form of the fairy tale, this fantasy provides us with an allegory of human life which is at once mysterious, easy to understand, and deeply moving. After the two children Tangle and Mossy grow into adulthood, age, and die, they return to earth. But having found the mysterious door's key, which is imagination and belief, they pass through it into the rainbow:

> Tangle went up. Mossy followed. The door closed behind them. They climbed out of the earth; and, still climbing, rose above it. They were in the rainbow. Far abroad, over ocean and land, they could see through its transparent walls the earth beneath their feet. Stairs beside stairs wound up together, and beautiful beings of all ages climbed along with them.
>
> They knew that they were going up to the country whence the shadows fall.

Clearly, in MacDonald's delicate allegory the rainbow is Christ and a Jacob's ladder that connects heaven and earth, eternity and time. MacDonald, a clergyman who gave up his parish because of problems of belief, here found an accessible and yet deeply personal means of drawing upon the Christian tradition.

Browning's 'Christmas Eve' exemplifies another effective use of this image within a vision. In this poem Browning's speaker has taken shelter from the rain in an Evangelical chapel, and he finds himself so annoyed by the narrow sectarian zeal of the preacher and his congregation that he returns to the rainy night. He thereupon catches sight of 'a moon-rainbow, vast and perfect,/ From heaven to earth extending' (sec. 6), and he rejoices that

> This sight was shown me, there and then, –
> Me, one out of a world of men,
> Singled forth. . . .
> With upturned eyes, I felt my brain
> Glutted with the glory, blazing
> Throughout its whole mass, over and under
> Until at length it burst asunder

And out of it bodily there streamed
The too-much glory. [sec. 7]

At first convinced that God has vouchsafed this vision of the rainbow to him as a reward for his broader, more charitable faith, he becomes terrified when, catching sight of Christ – 'He himself with his human air' – he realizes that his Saviour has turned His back on him and is walking away. Begging forgiveness, he catches hold of Christ's robe and is carried to several scenes each of which teaches him to respect belief. Suddenly he awakens again in the chapel, discovering that he has apparently not left it in body but has been dreaming. Thus Browning triply brackets his rainbow: he places it within the experience of a character who relates a vision that turns out to have been a mere dream – or was it? However ironic was his first understanding of the rainbow, the speaker was yet essentially correct since it did come to him, by whatever means, as a form of grace and it did succeed in changing his life.

Such use of rainbows in fairy tales, visions, and fantasies became a Victorian convention – a way of asserting the miraculous and wonderful in nature without having to believe literally that it was really there. Mrs S. C. Hall's 'Midsummer Eve: A Fairy Tale of Love' (1849) thus rewards the selfless devotion of her woodcutter with a vision of a rainbow, which promises hope and joy.[12] Another means of similarly employing the rainbow appears in the poems of Gerald Massey, a minor Victorian author who was almost addicted to this symbol. Showing the strong impress of eighteenth-century verse, his 'Lines to My Wife' and 'The Ballad of Babe Christabel' make it part of personification allegories, while many of his other works use elaborate allusion to the scriptural narrative on which traditional interpretation of the rainbow was based.

All these various devices isolate the symbol within a linguistic structure, thus forestalling any questions of belief. A third major use of the rainbow appears in the poems of Tennyson where he employs it precisely because of its problematic nature. For example, 'The Coming of Arthur', which proceeds by means of a series of conversion experiences that authenticate the young monarch as true king, fittingly uses the rainbow to convey the complex, personal way people attain to belief. In answer to Bellicent's query about Arthur's authenticity, Merlin replies in 'riddling triplets of old time':

Rain, rain, and sun! a rainbow in the sky!
A young man will be wiser by and by;
An old man's wit may wander ere he die.
Rain, Rain, and sun! a rainbow on the lea!
And truth is this to me, and that to thee:
And truth or clothed or naked let it be.
Rain, sun, and rain! and the free blossom blows;
Sun, rain, and sun! and where is he who knows?
From the great deep to the great deep he goes. [ll. 402–10]

About this riddling reply Tennyson himself commented that 'Truth appears in different guise to divers persons. The one fact is that man comes from the great deep and returns to it.'[13] And one may add that in the presence of the great facts of birth and death, Tennyson sees all else as ridden through by doubt and comprehensible only by acts of belief, acts of faith. Tennyson himself can decide that nature red in tooth and claw is yet suffused with a God of love, a God Who will assist us to a higher evolution of spirit and being. The rainbow, problematic and yet beautiful, well expresses his own attitudes towards nature.

He was able to achieve an optimistic poem in *In Memoriam,* which dramatizes his own experience of faith, doubt, and authentication of belief, but he presents the opposite side of the coin in the *Idylls,* which shows a society falling apart because men have such essential difficulties in having and keeping faith. So, too, in his other poems he presents the rainbow as potentially deluding. In 'The Voyage of Maeldune', for example, the ship passes over the city under the sea, and some of the mariners are destroyed by its vision of beauty and promise:

Over that undersea isle, where the water is clearer than air:
Down we looked: what a garden! O bliss, what a Paradise there!
Towers of a happier time, low down in a rainbow deep
Silent palaces, quiet fields of eternal sleep!
And three of the gentlest and best of my people, what'er I could say,
Plunged head down in the sea, and the Paradise trembled away.

[ll. 77–82]

These lines, like Merlin's riddle, perhaps present just as dark a vision of things as does Shelley's *Queen Mab*, but there is a major difference: whereas Shelley sees malignant men harming other men, and Byron sees an indifferent nature devouring helpless men, Tennyson sees a sphinx-like, dangerous, but ultimately far more mysterious, external world. He fights neither the Romantic battle to see the earth as a garment of God nor that other Romantic battle to deny such a claim, for he is more concerned to suggest and dramatize man's experience of a puzzling, potentially destructive, and yet frequently beautiful nature. This nature may yet be a garment of God, but if so it is one that veils as much as it reveals of the divine form. If it is an accommodation to postlapsarian man's limited senses, it is one that confuses as much as it informs, which mocks as much as it consoles and offers hope. Nature, like God, has become something wholly Other, and faith must help us see the rainbow. In other words, for Tennyson the rainbow must become as much a visionary as a visual phenomenon, because we must perceive its meaning and relevance with the eye of faith. It is not surprising, therefore, that he composed no Victorian equivalent to Wordsworth's 'My heart leaps up', because for him it is not the experience of natural fact, of nature itself, which counts.

But in a rainbow landscape, such as those of Grimshaw and Linnell, it is precisely that visual experience of nature which counts and which so commands our attention. Changing attitudes towards the relation of man, God, and nature forced Victorian poets to resort to various formal verbal devices that effectively bracket the symbol of the rainbow. Such verbal devices were not available to the painter, and their visual analogues are considerably less effective. The crucial point here is that a verbal description of a rainbow can easily be contained, insulated, or bracketed because it remains a linguistic statement about a visual object, while a pictorial representation of a rainbow is simply too obtrusive. Furthermore, whereas the drive toward realism in poetry leads to emphasis upon subjective, phenomenological experience of nature, in painting it leads in the contrary direction. As Kermit S. Champa has pointed out,

> Realism, or the commitment to defining pictorial effects directly visible in nature, . . . inevitably emphasizes the visual importance of the image itself and isolates it from whatever literary values it may hope to convey. Realism ruptures the balance between formal and literary intention that stands as the highest ideal in Western painting from Giotto to Delacroix.

Professor Champa goes on to remark that it was landscape painting that 'demonstrated more successfully than any other branch of painting a growing independence of subject matter from the literary issues of traditional Western imagery.'[14] Such independence, we may observe, particularly characterizes many rainbow landscapes. In fact, the large majority of such pictures painted in the eighteenth and nineteenth centuries simply turn their back on the traditional iconography of this image, allowing the spectator to bring his own associations, if any, to the scenes they present. Ford Madox Brown's *Walton-on-the-Naze* (1860, Birmingham City Art Galleries), Claude Monet's *Jetty at Le Havre* (*c*. 1868, Marlborough Galleries, N.Y.), Turner's *Buttermere Lake* (1798, Tate Gallery), and many other paintings and watercolours exemplify the use of the rainbow merely as a visual motif.[15] Such pictures of the rainbow of course do not originate in the nineteenth century or even in the eighteenth, since it has apparently long been the essence of the landscape painting to assert the independent existence of nature. The landscape with a double rainbow by Allaert van Everdingen (1621?–75) at Minneapolis, like the famous Rubens landscape in the Wallace Collection, exemplifies such tendencies.

Therefore, when Grimshaw and Linnell assert that their rainbows bear a sacred meaning, they are going not only against intellectual and spiritual currents of the nineteenth century but also against what had come to be dominant expectations about landscape art. These are not the only Victorian artists to make such unfashionable and even anachronistic uses of the rainbow. John Everett Millais and William Holman Hunt, two founding members of the Pre-Raphaelite Brotherhood, also do so, and the reasons for their greater success tells us some interesting things about how one could employ such potentially problematic symbolism in the visual arts. But before we look at their pictures, we would do well to examine Jacob van Ruisdael's *Jewish Cemetery* (*c*. 1660, Detroit), in which the Christian symbolism is quite clear. In the centre foreground of the painting Ruisdael has placed a tomb upon which light falls, making it one of the most obvious features in the canvas. Looking back into the picture space, we then come upon the rainbow, which provides an obvious visual as well as theological contrast to this whited sepulchre. It seems clear that the artist opposes the Old Dispensation to the New, the law of death to that of life, the way of Moses to that of Christ. What Ruisdael's *Jewish Cemetery* suggests is that for an artist to indicate that this rainbow bears a religious significance, he must deploy at least one other obvious symbolical element. In other words, a picture must contain at least two different signals or bits of information which can direct us to read it in symbolic terms. Such is precisely the method of Millais's *The Blind Girl* (1854–6, Birmingham City Art Galleries, Pl. 22), in which the butterfly, traditional emblem of the soul, indicates to the spectator that he is to take the rainbow symbolically as well. The young girl sits with her back to the rainbow, oblivious of the beauties that have captivated the artist, while the younger child, who is her companion and guide, looks back at the glorious sight behind them. Millais thus asserts that in the better world to come, Christ will raise the blind girl with new and better vision – an action that will be an antitype or fulfilment of His earlier restoration of sight to the blind recorded in the Gospels. Again, only the presence of the second image of the butterfly persuades us that the painter intends us to read the rainbow as a sign of the Christian dispensation.

William Holman Hunt far less successfully uses a similar con-catenation of religious symbols in his first version of *The Scapegoat* (1854, Manchester City Art Gallery). In this remarkably poor picture the goat, who stands as a type of Christ, is juxtaposed to the rainbow, another prefiguration of Christ and His dispensation.[16] What is particularly interesting here is that we know the artist in fact encountered a rainbow on his first sight of Osdoom, the Dead Sea setting of the picture. The painter's decision to use a white, rather than a black, animal for the final version of *The Scapegoat* (1854-6, Lady Lever Art Gallery, Port Sunlight) may have furnished one reason for his decision to abandon the rainbow. Another, more important, was that, thus contrasted, the symbols do not function very coherently: whereas the rainbow in Millais's painting promises hope and salvation to the blind girl, in Hunt's picture it seems to do so to the goat. Since the point of the picture is to record the horrifying sufferings of Christ as they were prefigured in an Old Testament ritual, such an implication had to be removed. In fact, even if we read the rainbow as a promise to the spectator, it still interferes with the chief intention of the painting.

This iconological principle, that the picture must contain a second pictorial symbol to signal that we are to take the rainbow symbolically, appears in somewhat different form in the works of the American contemporaries of Hunt and Millais. Drawing upon a political and religious tradition that dates back to the seventeenth-century Puritan settlers, American landscape painters frequently conceive of the American landscape as a new Eden or Promised Land of Canaan.[17] Within this context the rainbow therefore becomes an emblem of Manifest Destiny or God's new covenant with the United States. Such an interpretation of the motif appears necessary for its appearance in Frederic E. Church's *Rainy Season in the Tropics* (1886, J. W. Mittendorf Coll.) and his *Niagara* (1857, Corcoran Gallery of Art, Washington, D.C.). Paintings of Niagara Falls, which for many artists was an emblem of the United States, present us with another problem since rainbows, after all, are a constant feature of this natural landmark. Samuel F. B. Morse's *Niagara Falls from Table Rock* (1835, Boston Museum of Fine Arts) and George Inness's *Niagara Falls* (1893, Hirshorn Coll.) make use of the same motif apparently with the same symbolical intention, just as does the latter artist's *Delaware Water Gap* (1861, Metropolitan Museum of Art, N.Y.). None the less, this apparently conventional interpretation of the American land creates problems, for what are we to make of Inness's *Etretat, Normandy* (1877, Campanile Gallery, Chicago), a rainbow landscape where such a religio-political tradition doesn't apply? Because of its peculiar circumstances, American landscape painting asserted its independence of traditional pictorial symbolism far more slowly than did that of contemporary England.

Without this kind of nationalistic tradition to provide a defining context, the rainbow motif in English and American painting became increasingly difficult to employ without uncontrolled ambiguities. Occasionally one comes upon an idiosyncratic religious symbolism, such as Helmut Börsch-Supan finds in the rainbow landscapes of Caspar David Friedrich, but most nineteenth-century artists painted the rainbow, as they painted other natural phenomena, as something upon which human beings could no longer impose their own meanings.[18] Only rarely do we encounter works of visual art which make use of this problematic imagery and symbolism precisely because it is problematic. Significantly, the few pictures that incorporate the rainbow motif in this manner juxtapose it to the idea of shipwreck – in essence thereby making secular commentary upon the originally paradigmatic connection of the Noachian Flood and the rainbow that God placed in the heavens after the patriarch's sacrifice to Him.

Francis Danby's last painting, recently rediscovered after being lost for many years exemplifies such a juxtaposition of rainbow and sea disaster. The artist sent his untitled work to the 1860 Royal Academy exhibition with an unidentified epigraph:

> When even on the brink of wild despair,
> The famish'd mariner still firmly looks to thee,
> And plies with fainting hand and broken oar;
> While o'er the shatter'd ship thy arc is spann'd,
> Though all alas! seems lost, still there is HOPE.

There is hope, yes, but is it delusive? A contemporary review in the *Art-Journal* commented that 'Mr. Danby leaves the title to the taste of the visitor, who, rather than resolve it into "a shipwreck," will determine it as "Hope"; for amid the turmoil of the elements, a rainbow appears in the sky.'[19] Such an optimistic reading of Danby's last work seems clearly disproved by the recent discovery by David Rodgers, who identified the long-lost picture, that the wrecked vessel bore the name *Hope*.[20] As Rodgers points out, the painting is therefore likely to be an analogue to Friedrich's lost *The Wreck of the 'Hope'*, and one may add that the contrast of the rainbow and the doomed vessel *Hope* functions to emphasize both how harsh nature is to man and also how little one can believe supposedly divine promises impressed upon her. Had the artist given some indication that the rainbow symbolizes hope of salvation and the ship earthly hope, one might have been able to argue that he was contrasting true versus false hope, that of salvation versus earthly safety, but, in fact, nothing in the painting or epigraph encourages the spectator to take the picture thus as an analogue to Thoreau's Christian interpretation of the shipwreck on Cape Cod. Like the rainbows in Byron and Turner, this one seems to embody a fallacy of hope.

Turner, painter of many shipwrecks and many rainbows, opposes the two motifs in *The Wreck Buoy* (1849, Walker Art Gallery, Liverpool, Pl. 23). In this picture the juxtaposition of the two ideas functions as it does in Danby's later painting of the destruction of the *Hope*. As the *Art Journal* review made clear, when one looks at a shipwreck with a rainbow, one first reacts to the disaster itself – it dominates the canvas – and only later does one qualify it by the presence of the rainbow. Turner's painting makes us proceed in the opposite direction, as it were, since we first catch sight of the rainbow, a potential emblem of grace and hope. Only then do we move from this most commanding element of the picture's composition and colour to the wreck buoy in the foreground, perceiving this marker placed to warn ships away from sunken hulks that might destroy them. In Turner's painting, then, the rainbow as emblem of hope is qualified and rendered ambiguous by juxtaposition to the idea of disaster. The artist, in other words, seems to be directing us to guard ourselves against all kinds of fallacious hopes, whether spiritual or secular. He therefore makes this picture, like so many others in the series connected to his poem 'The Fallacies of Hope', into a kind of wreck buoy that can warn others against the dangers of illusion.[21] In his version of the rainbow's first appearance to man – *Light and Colour (Goethe's Theory): The Morning after the Deluge Moses Writing the Book of Genesis* (1843, Tate Gallery) – he also qualifies the traditional symbolism of this natural phenomenon. His epigraph tells us that when the sun appeared after the 'ark stood firm on Ararat', it brought with it

> in prismatic guise
> Hope's harbinger, ephemeral as the summer fly
> Which rises, flits, expands and dies.

Turner, who spans the Romantic and early Victorian years both spiritually and chronologically, finally believes that to see nature's rainbow as an emblem of hope is itself one of the great Fallacies of Hope: it is to believe, as Grimshaw and Linnell apparently did, that God marked nature with signs for the sake of man; it is to believe that man finds in nature meanings that he himself has hidden there – and finds them to be true. Like Tennyson and Browning, Turner realizes that the 'thoughtful eye' demanded by Fairbairn no longer can see in this optical phenomenon an unambiguous covenant-sign. Like these poets, he transforms the rainbow into a powerful symbol of man's problematic relation to problematic nature.

A postscript to rainbows

Since, like unicorns, rainbows have become an extraordinarily popular decorative motif in American popular culture of the late 1970s and early 1980s, one cannot stop the tale here. One encounters rainbows on wall-hangings, posters, teapots, key chains, jewellery, writing paper, tote bags, mobiles, woven fabrics, and virtually anything else upon which the colours can be applied. Thom Klika, 'the Rainbow Man' from Woodstock, N.Y., has done much to popularize the motif in paintings, books, and decorative arts, and in his work it appears more as a general image of nature's beauty and man's hope. Occasionally, as in the objects either created or simply distributed by the Abbey Press, which is owned by the Benedictine St Meinrad Archabbey, the rainbow receives its traditional Christian significance, but such is generally rare.

The contemporary American painter John Shroeder, on the other hand, employs the rainbow to make his characteristically ironic, sceptical commentaries on traditional religious solutions to the problem of pain and evil, and he emphasizes precisely this motif's problematic, ambiguous nature. Many of his works, which he describes as 'metaphysical cartoons', are peopled with strange and delightful combinations of characters from the Bible, classical myth, and contemporary and earlier American culture. For example, in *Country Dance with Sky Clowns* (1977, private coll.) the angelic visitants appear as flying circus entertainers; and in the recent *The Same old Thing* (1980, Joan Barrows, Carter Coll.), a representation of the Fall, the guardian angels, who have not done a particularly effective job, appear as Keystone Cops. Many of Shroeder's paintings embody the structure of the situation of crisis in which helpless human beings find themselves surrounded and threatened by powerful forces, usually invaders, which promise to destroy them. His *Parable of the Rainbow Dancers* (1975, private coll., Pl. 24) presents Adam and Eve, who have been wandering around Eden well before the Fall, finding themselves surrounded by pirates from outer space. As the artist explained in a description of this work written for one of its exhibitions, 'Job's Comforters, Eliphas, Bildad, and Zophar, touring the Garden of Eden as God's guests, see the Space Pirates menacing Adam and Eve', and horrified, they anxiously inquire of the Lord 'the great question', how can He allow such things to happen? Why, when we do no wrong, does He permit suffering to fall upon us and not upon evil-doers who deserve it? Instead of answering this question directly, however, God

sprouts from the palm of his hand the Parable of the Rainbow Dancers. Suffering, the parable asserts, is of no consequence. God allows us to suffer undeservedly because, in the long view, it doesn't matter, it isn't worth his worrying about. Good and Bad, virtuous and wicked, Innocents and Space Pirates, we shall all alike in our perfected forms be dancers of rainbows, and the memory of our earthly sorrows will be but as mist in the hot sun.

Such might be a devoutly Christian reading of the rainbow, the problem of evil, and the nature of man's eventual place in the universe. Shroeder, however, completes his description of *The Parable of the Rainbow Dancers* by indicating that God, somehow, has not been very candid with poor Eliphas, Bildad, and Zophar – much less with Adam and Eve: 'As the Duke of Wellington remarked to a man who approached him saying "Mr. Smith, I believe," "If you can believe that, you can believe anything!"' Rainbows in Shroeder's imaginative world here turn out to be not just potentially misleading and ambiguous but intentionally so.

CHAPTER FOUR

ICONOLOGY AND TECHNIQUE

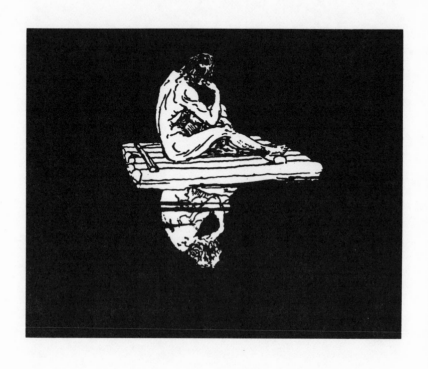

Paradigm, point of view, and narrative distance in verbal and visual arts

Every literary description is a *view*. It would be said that the speaker, before describing, stands at the window, not so much to see, but to establish what he sees by its very frame: the window frame creates the scene. To describe is thus to place the empty frame which the realistic author always carries with him (more important than his easel) before a collection or continuum of objects which cannot be put into words without this obsessive operation (which could be laughable as a 'gag'); in order to speak about it, the writer, through this initial rite, first transforms the 'real' into a depicted (framed) object; having done this, he can take down this object, *remove* it from his picture: in short: de-depict it (to depict is to unroll the carpet of the codes, to refer not from a language to a referent but from one code to another). Thus, realism (badly named, at any rate often badly interpreted) consists not in copying the real but in copying a (depicted) copy of the real.

Roland Barthes, S/Z, sec. 23, trans. Richard Miller

Whereas the Christian intonation of the shipwreck and similar paradigms implies – indeed requires – the presence of a concerned, judging God, the very point of Romantic and post-Romantic ones is that they occur in His absence. From this absence follow two implications important to the student of iconology. First, whereas the traditional Christian uses of these situations of crisis portray the victim of disaster as a perceived object, the post-Christian ones present him as a perceiving subject (or consciousness). Second, each form of the situation is associated with both a particular point of view and a characteristic narrative distance. For example, in the Christian intonation of the shipwreck the narrator aligns himself with God (or a divine nature) and looks from a distance at those others who are experiencing this crisis, but in the post-Christian form the narrator relates the experience from within.

The fact that a particular narrative position and distance appear associated with each form of this paradigm is of interest to the iconologist because it suggests that paradigms are crucially related to other aspects of literary technique, theme, and form and that individual paradigms, as elements within a work, cannot be simply or mechanically interchanged: changing, exchanging, or transforming any one element requires an adjustment in at least some of the others as well. The relation of the paradigm to the work of visual and verbal art is therefore never merely additive.

The contrast between Christian and post-Christian intonations of the shipwreck paradigm appears in the fourth book of *Childe Harold's Pilgrimage* where Byron employs both of them. When Childe Harold speaks as a moralist, he makes an elaborate use of the essentially Christian form, and he removes himself both physically and emotionally from those he would have the waters destroy:

> Roll on, thou deep and dark blue Ocean – roll!
>   Ten thousand fleets sweep over thee in vain;
>   Man marks the earth with ruin – his control
>   Stops with the shore; – upon the watery plain
>   The wrecks are all thy deed, nor doth remain
>   A shadow of man's ravage, save his own,
>   When, for a moment, like a drop of rain,
>   He sinks into thy depths with bubbling groan –
> Without a grave – unknelled, uncoffined, and unknown. . . .
>
>   Thou dost arise
>   And shake him from thee; the vile strength he wields
>   For Earth's destructions though dost all despise
>   Spurning him from thy bosom to the skies –
>   And send'st him, shivering in thy playful spray
>   And howling, to his Gods, where haply lies
>   His petty hope in some near port or bay,
> And dashest him again to Earth: – there let him lay.
>   [canto 4, st. 179–80]

Thus, like another deity, the speaker would send a Deluge to cleanse the earth of men who corrupt and abuse nature. His description of man's acts and qualities as 'vile' and 'petty' implicitly removes him from those other human beings upon whom he calls down the forces of the sea. Summoning the ocean's energies, on the other hand, places the speaker close to the centre of power and morality. Such attempts to remove oneself from other men and assume the position and perquisites of a judging deity continue to the present day. They become increasingly difficult, however, for two reasons, one religious and one aesthetic. Such a stance becomes thus problematic once the religious attitude that provided its basis began to weaken; and in addition, the demands of Romantic and post-Romantic art to present the experience of things from within often creates major rhetorical difficulties for the author who wishes to distance himself from the experience.

To Byron's traditional use of the situation of crisis we may compare his Romantic intonation of it earlier in the same canto. Standing amid the ruins of Rome, the Childe tells us he has thought about his own past.

> Till I had bodied forth the heated mind
> Forms from the floating wreck which Ruin leaves behind;
>
> And from the planks, far shattered o'er the rocks,
>   Built me a little bark of hope, once more
>   To battle with the Ocean and the shocks
>   Of the loud breakers, and the ceaseless roar
>   Which rushes on the solitary shore
>   Where all lies foundered that was ever dear:
>   But could I gather from the wave-worn store
>   Enough for my rude boat, where should I steer?
> There woos no home, nor hope, nor life, save what is here.
>   [canto 4, st. 104–5]

Here in the common Romantic version of this situation, Byron presents his speaker as a spiritual castaway, one who cannot force himself to rig a lifeboat, because even if he were successful, he would have nowhere to go – he has no destination, he does not know if any exists, and even if he suspected one does exist, he has no idea how to go about finding it. What immediately strikes one about this second passage from *Childe Harold's Pilgrimage* is that it is less seen than experienced. The shipwreck metaphor has become a means of conveying a certain experience of crisis, of loss, and not, as in the more traditional passage, a device to convey a moral judgment. Once God disappears – whether he has ceased to exist or has just inexplicably hidden himself – the moral centre of the shipwreck and similar paradigms moves inward, into the experience, into the situation itself, for there is no longer any other intellectually acceptable vantage-point.

The use of the shipwreck as punishment or test hardly ceases entirely with the onset of Romanticism, but there are not many major authors like Gerard Manley Hopkins who believe firmly enough to use the commonplace in the traditional Christian manner. 'The Loss of the Eurydice', which does so, opens with the poet emphasizing the presence of God, Who was neither indifferent to this terrible disaster of a training vessel nor absent from the world when it occurred.

> The Eurydice – it concerned thee, O Lord:
> Three hundred souls, O alas! on board,
>   Some asleep unawakened, all un-
> warned, eleven fathoms fallen
> Where she foundered! [ll. 1–5]

The poet explains that since the sunken ship carried neither money nor merchandise, it did not sink as punishment for mercantile greed – the explanation cited by Turner and Falconer. Although Hopkins states that the ship did not 'pride her, freighted fully, on/ Bounden bales or a hoard of bullion' (ll. 9–10), he none the less manages to accuse the ship of pride:

> Too proud, too proud, what a press she bore!
> Royal, and all her royals wore.
> Sharp with her, shorten sail!
> Too late; lost; gone with the gale. [ll. 33–6]

This witty play on 'proud' yet hardly seems adequate to explain why these many young men perished or what lesson their death bears for us.

After remarking upon the innocence of the drowned men, the heroism of Captain Hare, and the beauty of one unidentified corpse, Hopkins quietly relinquishes his initial concern to explain why this shipwreck happened. Instead, he treats the victims as emblems, and we can observe the crucial shift in method when he comments that the handsome drowned sailor

> was but one like thousands more,
> Day and night I deplore
> My own people and born own nation,
> Fast foundering own generation. [ll. 85–8]

Hopkins deplores England, his own nation, because it is Protestant, having fallen away from Roman Catholicism, which he takes to be the true faith, centuries before. Like Dante, he uses the metaphor of shipwreck to threaten a people he believes due for divine punishment. Indeed, once Hopkins announces that England is a Protestant nation, he becomes so troubled by sixteenth-century destruction of shrines that he almost forgets this nineteenth-century shipwreck. Rather than answer his initial question, he simply bypasses it.

The poet's unsureness in handling the shipwreck as fact and metaphor in this poem appears most obviously when he describes the crew, in 'Unchrist, all rolled in ruin' (l. 96); for although one can admire the complex ambiguities here, the impression one receives none the less is that matters have got out of Hopkins's control. The young men, as Protestants, are already 'in ruin', though it must be primarily spiritual ruin that he intends here; it is also true that the young Protestants, who are 'in Unchrist', have met the ruin of physical death in this shipwreck, but one does not know if being Protestant is itself sufficient moral cause for their deaths. Thus, by moving unsurely between a literal explanation of why these three hundred identifiable people died and a use of them as emblems, Hopkins seems to evade an overt statement that Protestants die because they are Protestants and that therefore the shipwreck was just punishment; and yet his argument seems to demand this necessary conclusion.

Hopkins's failure to solve the rhetorical problems caused by narrative distances makes 'The Loss of the Eurydice' a failed poem, for after the reader has been led to sympathize with the drowned men and boys, he finds himself jarred when the poet pulls back and makes them guilty victims.[1] In contrast, Lautréamont's *Les Chants de Maldoror,* which strives to shock the reader, capitalizes upon the jarring effect created by this traditional intonation of the shipwreck situation in post-Romantic and post-Christian literature. His long fugue on the theme of sea disaster opens with a grim parody of the Romantic prospect poem, for rather than attain to a vision of the Promised

Land or imaginative grace, Maldoror enjoys a vision of destruction – the destruction of others:

> I sat on a rock near the sea. A ship had just put out from shore a full sail: an imperceptible dot had appeared on the horizon and was gradually approaching, growing rapidly, pushed on by the squall. The storm was going to begin its onslaughts and already the sky was darkening, turning into a blackness almost as hideous as a man's heart. [trans. Alexis Lykiard]

Full of his hatred for other human beings, Maldoror places himself in a physical position to observe their destruction, and what makes this description of maritime disaster so shocking is that it remains an experience for Maldoror which has no conventional moral meaning. In other words, Maldoror places himself at the physical but not the moral vantage-point of an avenging God, so that the effect resembles a Northern Renaissance painting of the Last Judgment in which the artist depicts the blessed enjoying the suffering of the damned but removes God and the angels.

Beginning at a distance from the stricken vessel, Maldoror guides us through the stages of its destruction and at each makes us aware of the suffering of those on board only to emphasize his distance from them:

> The vessel, which was a great warship, had dropped all her anchors to avoid being swept on to the rocks along the coast. The wind whistled furiously from all four points of the compass, and made mincemeat of the sails. Claps of thunder crashed amid the lightning but could not outdo the sound of wailing to be heard from the foundationless house – a floating sepulchre. . . . The pumps were quite unable to expel the vast quantities of salt water which smashed foaming over the deck like mountains.
>
> The distressed ship fires off her alarm gun but slowly, majestically, founders.
>
> He who has not seen a vessel founder in the midst of a hurricane, sporadic lightning, deepest darkness – while those aboard are overcome by the despair with which you are familiar – knows not life's mischances. Finally from the ship a universal shriek of sheer woe bursts forth, while the sea redoubles its redoubtable attacks....

The distressed ship fires off her alarm gun but slowly, majestically, founders.

All day long they have had the pumps in action. Futile efforts. And to cap this gracious spectacle, night has fallen, dense, implacable. Each man tells himself that once in the water he will no longer be able to breathe. . . .

The distressed ship fires off the alarm but slowly, majestically, founders.

Having watched the ship go down, this histrionic descendant of Byron's Manfred and Maturin's Melmoth exclaims: 'O heaven! how can one live after tasting so many delights! It has been my lot to witness the death-throes of several of my fellow men.' The would-be connoisseur of pain tries hard to experience what is happening to these others and so he relishes the sounds that come to him across the waves: 'Heard now . . . would be the bawling of some old woman mad by fear; now, the solitary yelps of a suckling infant. . . . By an effort of will I drew nearer to them.' In his mad attempt to feel and thus enjoy the sufferings of others, the narrator parodies Romantic notions of imaginative sympathy. He thus tells us that when listening to the groans of the dying, he would 'jab a sharp iron point into my cheek, secretly thinking: "They suffer still more!" Thus, at least I had grounds for comparison.' The fact that Maldoror has separated himself from other human beings appears with clarity in this inflicting pain upon himself to gain some idea of their mental sufferings. This scene, in other words, mocks those theories of moral sympathy proposed by Hume, Smith, Burke, and others.[2] These philosophers, who assume that man's innate moral sense imaginatively thrusts him into the emotional situation of other men, argue that such a capacity for sympathy or fellow-feeling is the basis of moral decision. According to them, one does not do evil unto others because one feels how they would be affected. One does not have to strain to experience what another feels since any normal man or woman does so automatically. But Lautréamont, who clearly has no such belief in the innate goodness of man, makes his character attempt desperately to experience the fates of others. Maldoror must do so because he looks at them as though they were laboratory specimens behind a pane of glass – removed, unconnected, alien.

Lautréamont's protagonist sees himself as other than human; and indeed, he dispassionately uses his musket to murder a survivor who has almost reached the shore, thus making himself the murdering lieutenant of murdering nature. Maldoror, in other words, is in large part a case study of a man without what the philosophers who provided the foundations of Romanticism took to be a defining human faculty. If *Tristram Shandy* is simultaneously a parody of Locke's ideas and a mock case study of what happens if one does not live according to them, then one might say that *Les Chants de Maldoror* is a similar double parody of the moral philosophers who responded to Locke.[3]

One must be careful, however, not to oversimplify Lautréamont's surrealistic, decadent playing upon the perspectival conventions of the shipwreck paradigm since his work so concerns itself with parody and grim inversion. In the passage at which we have looked, for example, he mocks not only theories of the moral imagination but also the Romantic prospect poem, both pre- and post-Romantic shipwrecks, and the Gothic situation of survivors beset by robbers on the beach. At the same time, the narrator's continuous revisions of the event while it is supposedly taking place (such as his later mention of infants and old women aboard a warship) suggest that this often strained representation of disaster is entirely imagined and not experienced by Maldoror. Similarly, his obvious projection of self-hatred and yearning for death upon these imagined victims further complicates the significance of the shipwreck section of *Les Chants de Maldoror.* None the less, one thing is clear: Lautréamont seeks his primary effect by playing upon the traditional Christian association of the shipwreck with a divine point of view removed from the disaster.

With a heavy-handed irony appropriate to the strident tone of the book, the protagonist who would watch others perish by shipwreck finds himself increasingly implicated in this situation himself. Quite early in *Les Chants.* Maldoror asks his fictive gravedigger, 'Why do you weep? . . . Remember this well: we are aboard this dismasted vessel in order to suffer. It is a credit to man that God had judged him capable of overcoming his deepest sufferings.' The narrator thus finds himself within the shipwreck, with all men, to suffer some inexplicable test of endurance. He also likens himself to a ship's prow lifted by an enormous wave; and later when he tries to convey his exhaustion, he happens upon an elaborate simile that seems derived from Géricault's *Raft of the 'Medusa'* (Pl. 10):

When the storm, with the palm of its hand, has thrust a

vessel vertically to the bottom of the sea; if, on that raft, only one man out of the entire crew remains, broken by weariness and every kind of privation; if the billow belabours him like flotsam for hours longer than the life of man; and if a frigate later ploughing through these desolate latitudes of staved keels sights the unfortunate whose wasted carcass bobs upon the ocean, and brings him the help that is almost too belated I believe this shipwrecked fellow would understand still better the degree to which the drowsiness of my senses was carried.

Lautréamont has made extravagance such a virtue that it is difficult to know how seriously he finally wishes us to understand Maldoror to be himself a castaway, but the evidence of the text suggests that, like so many other decadents, the one who would enjoy the sight of others shipwrecked found himself a victim.

Once the relation between paradigm and narrative point of view and distance is recognized, this relation becomes a convention, and as such it becomes a code available to any author who wishes to make use of it. A poet like Hopkins who employs the shipwreck as divine punishment must find ways to solve the rhetorical difficulties created by breaking this convention. Lautréamont, on the other hand, depends precisely upon breaking it to achieve his ends, which are not merely to shock the reader but by doing so to make him look at life, art, and morality in new ways. Thomas Carlyle, who combines the pre- and post-Romantic intonations of the paradigm, exemplifies yet another option available to the nineteenth-century writer. Moving between two perspectives, he is able to convey both the meaning and the experience of an event, something he conceives essential to his self-appointed task as secular prophet.

In the opening pages of *The French Revolution* we thus come upon poor Louis XV, the do-nothing king, 'swimming passively . . . towards issues which he partly saw.' Without vision, without conviction, he finds himself trying to make 'incoherence into coherence', and he cannot. 'Blindest fortune has cast *him* on the top of it: he swims there; can as little sway it as the drift-log sways the wind-tossed moon-stirred Atlantic' (pt 1, bk I, ch. 4). Then there is D'Orleans, who, defending the prerogatives of the Convention against his brother Louis XVI, 'has *cut* his Court-moorings, shall we say? And now will sail and drift, fast enough, towards chaos?' (pt 1, bk III, ch. 6). Unlike D'Orleans, Loménie-Brienne, the finance minister who replaced Necker, clearly perceives his danger. Desperately seeking a plan, any plan, to keep the national finances from going under, he asks the intellectuals of France to furnish him with one.

> What could a poor minister do? . . . A sinking pilot will fling out all things, his very biscuit-bags, lead, log, compass and quadrant, before flinging out *himself.* It is on this principle, of sinking, and the incipient delirium of despair, that we explain likewise the almost miraculous 'invitation to thinkers.' Invitation to Chaos to be so kind as build, out of its tumultuous drift-wood, an Ark of Escape for him! [pt 1, III, ch. 8]

The invitation to thinkers leads to the return of the Estates General as France continues to float towards freedom, towards chaos, towards the deluge that will drown many good men and many, like Loménie-Brienne himself, who are not of much value.

These examples reveal how complex is Carlyle's use of this metaphor in *The French Revolution.* Considered as an individual, Louis XVI is seen to be a decent, essentially good man who is shipwrecked through little or no fault of his own. Like his father, he looks heavenward and earthward and can find no guidance; he drifts and is destroyed by forces beyond his control. Considered, however, as king and as representative of a functionless aristocracy, a class that in Carlyle's view is a living lie, then Louis is seen to shipwreck as punishment. Appropriate to a work that combines history, epic, mock-epic, and sermon, the perspectives from which we view men and events continually change, thus controlling the way we react to these paradigms. Thus, when we see Louis and Marie Antoinette close at hand, we sympathize with them, whereas when we look at them from a distance, from outside their vantage-point, as it were, we judge them. As Carlyle moves us away from his characters, he also places us at the moral and philosophical centre of his cosmos, so that when we perceive the plight of these people, we evaluate them not by their standards and needs but by what Carlyle takes to be eternal ones; and in larger terms we understand their destruction to be just, even deserved.

In the traditional Christian uses of the situation of crisis, the author and the reader alike view the disaster from the vantage-point of divine law; in Romantic and post-Romantic ones, they view (or experience) the destroying waters from within the sinking vessel, for the existence of divine law is itself in doubt. Carlyle's complex and ironic use of this paradigm in *The French Revolution* arises from the fact that although he concentrates on the situation of shipwreck from within, he is ultimately able to believe in a transcendental order of the kind that enables or requires us to judge the mariner from without. None the less, despite the essential morality of Carlyle's source of eternal order, it cannot serve as a judging God because it is both impersonal and largely unknown. The result of this complex interplay of perspectives is that however much some of the characters may deserve the disaster they encounter, at some point in the narrative we are made to feel this shipwreck is something for which they are not responsible. Sympathy prevails.

Although the writer is free to choose between portraying the shipwreck and similar paradigms from inside – that is, from on board the vessel – or from a more distant vantage-point, the painter must depict this situation from without. Since narrative distance is itself a convention, or meaningful code, which the author uses to convey his judgments, the painter's portrayal of events from 'outside' makes this code essentially unavailable to him. Although still photography and cinematography have presented air, ship, train, and automobile disasters from within the situation, painterly representations have not. Géricault, for instance, does not portray the raft of the *Medusa* from within the confines of that perilous assemblage of planks, for to create such a representation would be to produce the image as seen by those on the raft and not the image of those on the raft themselves. Painting, in other words, is condemned to take such an external view; or rather one should state that painting in a realistic style must adopt such a vantage-point, since, as Boris Uspensky has shown, ancient and medieval art occasionally adopted an interior point of view.

In 'Structural Isomorphism of Verbal and Visual Art', the Russian semiotician claims that 'some of the most ancient pictorial forms ... definitely point to the internal position of the artist', and he offers as examples Assyrian landscape reliefs dating from the eighth century B.C. in which

> the hills and trees on both sides of the river are pictured as if they lay flat. On the one side of the river the tops of the hills and trees point upwards, while on the other side they are directed downwards.

Similarly, in various parts of the ancient world the usual representation of a fortress depicts the towers lying flat and pointing 'from the center to the periphery of the picture, upwards, downwards and sidewards. It is clear that this picture could only be made when the artist mentally located himself in the center of the space represented.'[4]

According to Uspensky, a second example of this artistic phenomenon appears in medieval art, in which an internal light source in the picture's centre casts a shadow in the foreground, since this 'internal light corresponds to the internal position of the observer (artist) inside the picture' (p. 12). A third evidence of interior vantage-point in visual arts appears in perspectival modes:

> The classical linear perspective presents the image as it is perceived externally (from the outside, i.e. from a fixed point of view–EXTERNAL as regards the reality to be represented). . . . On the other hand, the so-called inverse perspective (*die umgekehrte Perspektive*) characteristic of ancient and medieval art is based on not an external, but an internal position of the artist. A typical feature of the inverse perspective is the reduction in the size of the objects represented which does not correspond to their remoteness from the spectator (as in linear perspective), but, on the contrary, to their nearness to him, i.e., the figures in the background are larger than those in the foreground. The phenomenon may be interpreted in such a way that in this system the reduction in sizes is not presented from OUR point of view (i.e., from the point of view of the observer who assumes an external position as regards the picture), but from the point of view of our vis-à-vis – an abstract internal observer who is thought to be located in the interior of the picture. [pp. 12–13]

Uspensky's discussions of internal perspectives, positioning, and light sources demonstrate that such are not only possible in the visual arts but entirely dominated them for hundreds and even thousands of years. Realistic styles of painting, however, do not permit the use of such techniques of internalization.

Even though the nineteenth-century painter in a realistic style could not, like the contemporary poet, move into the situation of the disaster, he could move closer to the event, thus making it dominate his image and endowing it with immediacy. This use of a vantage-point close to the victims appears, for instance, in Joseph Franque's

Scene During the Eruption of Vesuvius (*c.* 1827, Philadelphia Museum of Art) in which the four victims entirely fill the canvas. Géricault, who gradually evolved his conception of *The Raft of the 'Medusa'* (Pl. 10), chose much the same method of implicating the spectator in the situation of crisis. As Eitner has pointed out, the artist first placed the raft farther away from the spectator and facing him. He then

> re-oriented the figures on the Raft, turning them away from
> the spectator toward a point in the depth of the picture. At the
> same time, he moved the Raft so close to the foreground as to
> make the viewer feel transported onto its planks and to involve
> him in its drama as a participant rather than a detached
> observer.[5]

Géricault's influence made such close-up views of imperilled mariners and the ship in danger popular in Romantic painting. For example, Delacroix, who paints few explicit shipwrecks, employs such a vantage-point in *Dante and Virgil* (1822, Louvre), *Christ on the Sea of Galilee* (1854, Walters Art Gallery, Baltimore), and *The Shipwreck of Don Juan* (1840, Louvre), and one encounters it in the works of Ryder, Homer, Stanfield, Turner, and many others.

Géricault, however, did not rely solely upon a close vantage-point to encourage the spectator's empathy with the endangered victims of sea disaster. In an intermediate version of the picture, which Eitner calls *Hailing an Approaching Rowing-boat,* he first made the decisive changes of employing a close vantage-point and also opposing the position of the nearby victims to the distant one of their rescuers. As Eitner has shown, 'The effect of the scene now hinges on the juxtaposition of near and far elements' (p. 26). The closeness of the raft leads the spectator to identify with those on board, and his eye is led by their actions to the small boat approaching. Géricault intensified this crucial juxtaposition in the final version, in which the men on the raft experience, not hope, but disappointment:

> His final enlargement of the figures was intended not only to
> give them the impressiveness – or 'sublimity', to use
> Delacroix's word – which a superhuman scale can confer, it
> was also to serve an expressive function essential to the
> meaning of the picture. Without representing the vastness of
> the ocean directly, Géricault sought to dramatize the isolation
> of the men on the Raft and the strain of their effort, by
> withdrawing beyond hope the rescue, toward which they

frantically strive. He activated the distance, making it appear as a plunging recession, rather than a horizontal expanse, and intensified the illusion of space by means of radical foreshortenings. The enormous foreground figures push the horizon back; the few inches of canvas which separate the signalling men from the speck which signifies the *Argus* demand to be read as miles. It was clearly Géricault's purpose to draw the beholder into a close, empathetic participation with the action of his picture, and to make him feel the drama of the scene with his muscles as much as with his eyes. [p. 31]

To make the spectator participate vicariously in the scene taking place upon the raft, Géricault thus had to join a major image observed from nearby with one observed at a distance.

Turner, a master at manipulating codes and conventions, makes a particularly effective contrast between distant and near views in *The Slave Ship* (Pl. 5). When Ruskin, who once owned the picture, described it in the chapter 'Of Water, as Painted by Turner' in the first volume of *Modern Painters,* he correctly placed major emphasis upon the way Turner created an image of shipwreck as punishment. After an elaborate purple passage that describes the various colours and forms of the heaving waters, he turns to that part of the ocean surrounding the slave-ship:

Purple and blue, the lurid shadows of the hollow breakers are cast upon the mist of night, which gathers cold and low, advancing like the shadow of death upon the guilty ship as it labours amidst the lightning of the sea, its thin masts written upon the sky in lines of blood, girded with condemnation in that fearful hue which signs the sky with horror, and mixes its flaming flood with the sunlight, and, cast far along the desolate heave of the sepulchral waves, incarnadines the multitudinous sea.

As Ruskin's closing allusion to *Macbeth* indicates, Turner's painting in part represents nature about to punish guilty human beings. The full title of the picture is *Slavers Overthrowing the Dead and Dying – Typho[o]n Coming On,* and in the left distance the beholder observes the guilty vessel about to meet its deserved end, while in the right and centre foreground he encounters thrust upon him slaves being devoured by the sea and its creatures. Although Turner's painting presents images of fanciful ocean predators, his image of Gothic horror is not the product of his imagination. In fact, he was portraying what had become sound business practice: since insurance on slave-cargoes covered only those drowned at sea and not slaves who perished from brutality, disease, and the dreadful conditions on board, profit-minded captains cast the dead and dying into the ocean. As John McCoubrey has demonstrated, the artist painted his picture specifically for an anti-slavery campaign, and one may add that he has succeeded in creating a particularly effective image of these horrors.[6] Works as different as Heinrick Heine's 'Das Sklaven-schiff', Robert Hayden's 'Middle Passage', and Norman Mailer's *Of a Fire on the Moon* have elaborated upon the situation and paradigm of the slave-ship, but few, if any, have done so more powerfully than this painting. The closing lines of Turner's epigraph – 'Hope, Hope, fallacious Hope!/Where is thy market now?' – further suggest that he was attacking not only the specific horrors of the slave-trade but also the situation of all men in a society whose basic bond had become the cash nexus.[7]

Like Carlyle's *French Revolution, The Slave Ship* thus opposes vantage-points to communicate both sympathy and judgment. Whereas Carlyle's work makes us experience the plight of those he yet sees justly destroyed in the Revolution, Turner's painting, in contrast, makes us sympathize with the victims of those about to receive deserved retribution. Since this opposition of near and far images in this way demonstrates for the viewer the essential justice of the ship's destruction, one effect of using this Romantic (or 'close up') vantage-point is to make *The Slave Ship* iconologically quite traditional. But the very closeness of the dying slaves to the spectator creates a second effect, which is the recognition that the nature which will justly punish the ship is the same nature that is already unjustly devouring the ship's innocent victims.

To Turner's combination of distances which complicate his painting, one may compare Albert Pinkham Ryder's *Jonah* (1885, National Coll. of the Fine Arts, Washington, D.C., Pl. 25), a work that may well derive from *The Slave Ship*. Like his English predecessor, Ryder places his castaway, here Jonah himself, in the foreground to the right of centre, and as in Turner's picture a frightful inhabitant of the deep approaches from the right distance and will soon engulf the swimmer. Ryder positions his ship, which is not a guilty vessel, quite close to the castaway, and together with the approaching giant fish and surrounding waves it bends to a powerful rhythm that surrounds the fleeing Jonah. At the top centre of the painting appears God, Who controls the fierce energies of the ocean with calm power. By including this image of the Lord, the artist provides the spectator with not a visual, but an intellectual, vantage-point within the picture space. Like Turner, the American painter places his castaway close to us so we can feel ourselves implicated in his situation; but by including a representation of God overseeing this imperilled swimmer, he forces us to realize that this is not an image of abandonment or isolation.[8]

Some brief observations on paradigms and literary structure

The grouping of codes, as they enter into the work, into the movement of the reading, constitute a braid (*text, fabric, braid:* the same thing); each thread, each code, is a voice; these braided – or braiding – voices from the writing: when it is alone, the voice does no labor, transforms nothing: it *expresses*; but as soon as the hand intervenes to gather and intertwine the inert threads, there is labor, there is transformation.

Roland Barthes, *S/Z,* trans. Richard Miller

The complex relation of the paradigm to point of view in the arts also appears when one examines its relation to other elements of literary form, such as plot, characterization, and plot resolution. For example, drifting figures appear frequently in nineteenth- and twentieth-century literature, and their presence reveals a point at which paradigm, theme, and technique converge. Mario Praz long ago commented upon the disappearance (or eclipse) of the heroic protagonist in nineteenth-century fiction, and only a brief glance is necessary to convince one that *Vanity Fair* is but one of many major novels without a hero.[9] The protagonist of Disraeli's *Coningsby* is thus quite representative of the age when he finds himself forced to confess: 'I float in a sea of troubles, and should long ago have been wrecked had I not been sustained by a profound, if vague, conviction that there are still great truths, if we could but work them out' (bk 3, ch. 5). Disraeli's *roman à thèse* willingly helps Coningsby work out these 'great truths', thus providing the young man with a Tory star by which to guide his vessel.

On the other hand, Dickens, whose *Little Dorrit* places Arthur

Clenham in a similar position, finds no such easy solution. Near the opening of the novel Clenham admits: 'I am such a waif and stray anywhere that I am liable to be drifted where any current may set' (bk 1, ch. 2). Like so many characters in Dickens's later work, Clenham is a curiously passive person – honest, honourable, but decidedly unheroic, very much a portrait of a man without purpose. He resembles many another character in English and American fiction of the nineteenth century (and many an author as well) in the fact that he has cast off a dour Evangelical Protestantism but has found nothing with which to replace it. This state of drifting, of being unable to perceive, much less reach, safe harbour, characterizes Clenham even in the less important aspects of life. Thus while trying to decide whether he should trust Pancks, who has promised to restore Father Dorrit's fortune, he appears 'labouring in this sea, as all barks labour in cross seas, he tossed about and came to no haven' (bk 1, ch. 27). Little Amy Dorrit, wiser than her years, looks at Gowan, Clenham's successful rival for another woman, and 'wondered whether it was with people as with ships, that in too shallow and rocky waters, their anchors had no hold, and they drifted anywhere' (bk 2, ch. 6). Although Gowan, that most unearnest young man, continues to drift, thus ruining his marriage, Clenham is saved by the love of Little Dorrit at the point when he has already begun to encounter disaster.

Dickens provides no universally applicable ideology, except that which Cazamian called the philosophy of Noël: for the novelist the only anchors (or compasses) are love and self-sacrifice. Thus Sidney Carton, who drifts through the dark apocalyptic world of *A Tale of Two Cities*, only finds his destination when he gives up his life to save Charles Darnay. Then, shortly before ascending to the guillotine, he recalls the words of Christ promising everlasting life 'like a rusty old ship's anchor from the deep' (bk 3, ch. 9). Few, however, can obtain such anchors, and even here Carton's love – and not his last second hope of eternal life – prompts self-sacrifice and gives him direction.

These few examples of the drifting metaphor in fiction forcefully remind us once again that such paradigms function as far more than literary decoration, embroidery, or other embellishment upon the main fabric or core of literary structure. At the very least, such a paradigm participates in the basic nature of many individual works of fiction, for it informs their attitude towards plot, character, and theme.

Other intonations of the basic paradigm have similarly complex relations to literary structure. For instance, shipwrecks and comparable situations of crisis often serve in satire, adventure, and science fiction as an effective means of inserting a cast of characters into a strange environment; and although such plot mechanisms rarely function also to convey the full imaginative force of the paradigm, in some works, such as Defoe's *Robinson Crusoe* and Traven's *The Death Ship*, theme and plot device merge. These paradigmatic situations also serve as a means of resolving the problems of a fictional plot. *The Last Days of Pompeii* thus builds towards the moment the volcano erupts, and its great destruction simultaneously punishes the guilty, preserves the innocent, and neatly closes off the fictional world of pagan Pompeii.

Autobiography and fiction and poetry taking the forms of such self-history frequently employ these paradigms similarly. Since the shipwreck and its corollary situations of being stranded, drifting, or cast away are often used as paradigms to communicate experience of personal crisis, they are particularly suited to literary forms that often emphasize the primacy of such experiences. Such paradigms are not mere decorations upon a pre-established narrative or conception of self. Rather, they often serve as a means of discovering – or creating – that self which is the subject (in both senses) of the autobiography. Metaphor always plays a crucial role in this autobiographical self-recognition and self-creation since it provides a ready means of perceiving order in an otherwise inchoate experience. In his study of autobiography and autobiographical fiction, Avrom Fleishman argues that a basic means of 'developing coherent accounts of the self . . . is to choose a metaphor of the self and develop it in a narrative or other sequence, which may be called a conversion of metaphor into myth.'[10]

As one might expect from the way it has pervaded Western thought for several millennia, the paradigm of the life-journey has frequently served as a source of such personal myths. For example, at the close of *The Golden Ass* when Lucius has become an initiate in the worship of Osiris, the high priest congratulates him in terms strikingly similar to those of many Christian authors:

> You have endured and performed many labours and
> withstood the buffetings of all the winds of ill luck. Now at
> last you have put into the harbour of peace. . . . Neither your
> noble blood and rank nor your education sufficed to keep

you from falling a slave to pleasure. . . . But blind fortune,
after tossing you maliciously about from peril to peril has
somehow . . . landed you here in religious felicity.
[trans. Robert Graves]

The one major difference between this use of the voyage paradigm
by Apuleius and that employed by St Augustine in *The Confessions* is
that the Christian self-historian believes an omniscient God, not
'blind Fortune', directed his journey: 'In my pride I was running
adrift, at the mercy of every wind,' he tells God. 'You were guiding
me as a helmsman steers a ship, but the course you steered was
beyond my understanding' (bk 4, sec. 14; trans. R. S. Pine-Coffin).
Under the influence of Augustine, who conceives of himself as a
second Odysseus or second Aeneas, this paradigm continues to be
popular with writers of spiritual autobiographies.

Thus when Charles Haddon Spurgeon, the most popular preacher
in Victorian England, relates his own spiritual history, it appears in
the guise of an imperilled, but ultimately successful, voyage.

> There was an evil hour when once I shipped the anchor of my
> faith; I cut the cable of my belief; I no longer moored myself
> hard by the coasts of Revelation; I allowed my vessel to drift
> before the wind; I said to reason, 'Be thou my captain'; I said
> to my own brain, 'Be thou my rudder'; and I started on my
> mad voyage. . . . It was one hurried sailing over the
> tempestuous ocean of free thought.[11]

At first delighted by the brilliant thoughts he encountered, Spurgeon
ignored the darkening heavens and rushed onward 'with awful
speed' past his old points of belief until, at last, his sceptical course
led him to doubt even his own existence: 'I began to doubt my very
existence; I doubted if there were a world, I doubted if there was
such a thing as myself.' But here at 'the very verge of the dreary
realms of unbelief' the devil

> foiled himself: for the very extravagance of the doubt, proved
> the absurdity. Just when I was at the bottom of that sea,
> there came a voice which said, 'And can this doubt be true?'
> At this very moment I doubted not. Faith steered me back;
> faith cried, 'Away, away!' I cast my anchor on Calvary; I
> lifted my eye to God. . . . I have sailed that perilous voyage;
> I have come safe to land.

Spurgeon's narrative of his own crisis of faith, which turns the ship-voyage topos into an allegory, reminds us how long believers have found it possible – and even necessary – to conceive their lives in terms of this ancient, originally pre-Christian, metaphor.

Like so many nineteenth-century autobiographies, both spiritual and secular, Spurgeon's begins in the condition of belief, moves to a crisis of unbelief, and then resolves that crisis. In contrast, St Augustine, Bunyan, and Newman begin their narratives with an earlier self existing in a state of unbelief and then move towards a true Christian condition. Spurgeon, however, does make the traditional interpretation of his own spiritual crisis and near-shipwreck. Like Crashaw in 'Why are ye afraid, O ye of little faith', he would agree that 'You are the storm that mocks/ Your selves; you are the rocks/ Of your own doubt.' Indeed, the Baptist preacher so emphasizes the element of his own guilt that he transforms the voyage itself into a guilty act, and he can do so only because when he first experienced this situation of spiritual crisis, he was already a Christian in 'safe harbour'. He therefore left safety, truth, and goodness and voyaged, however briefly, towards destruction.

Any reader of Victorian poetry is likely to recognize that Spurgeon's crisis-narrative is the allegorized equivalent of Tennyson's 'The Two Voices'. Although Spurgeon's brief record of crisis begins in belief, and Tennyson's poem in doubt, both works, which are set in the past and hence tell of already achieved spiritual victories, depict the speakers moving through a series of doubts towards self-destruction; at last the doubts themselves prove too absurd, and the progress towards a better spiritual condition is completed. As Tennyson's unnamed speaker tells the voice of doubt, which has been urging suicide, it has failed 'to wreck my mortal ark,/ By making all the horizon dark'. Only after one element in Spurgeon's mind demands, 'And can this doubt be true?' is faith able to seize the helm and steer him back home. Similarly, only after Tennyson's speaker rejects the voice of doubt can the second voice (of hope) be heard – and only then can the speaker turn to nature and rejoice in its rainbow.

In 'That Nature is a Heraclitean Fire and of the Comfort of the Resurrection' Gerard Manley Hopkins makes a somewhat similar use of the shipwreck and imperilled-voyage paradigm to effect a poetic resolution. Unlike Tennyson's 'The Two Voices', Hopkins's poem does not take the form of a dialogue. Instead, it begins with the poet setting forth the flux and transience that characterize earthly existence, after which he mourns the specific fact of man's transience:

Man, how fast his firedint, his mark on mind, is gone!
Both are in an unfathomable, all is in an enormous dark
Drowned. O pity and indignation! Manshape, that shone
Sheer off, disseveral, a star, death blots black out; nor mark
              Is any of him at all so stark
But vastness blurs and time beats level.

Weaving his text from several strands of metaphor, Hopkins combines the notions that light, man's light, disappears into eternal darkness and that his fire is drowned in an 'unfathomable' ocean of darkness. Both analogies are informed by the same structure in which that which is living, bright, or burning is engulfed by a surrounding element, and Hopkins resolves the poetic – and spiritual – tensions he has created by an abrupt turn that emphasizes the elements of the shipwreck paradigm only hinted at obliquely before. After grieving at the fact of man's death, Hopkins takes immediate comfort from the thought of the Resurrection, which comes to him a 'heart's-clarion' that drives away 'grief's gasping, joyless days, dejection'. The thought of it, in fact, saved him from spiritual shipwreck:

Across my foundering deck shone
A beacon, an eternal beam. Flesh fade, and mortal trash
Fall to the residuary worm; world's wildfire, leave but ash:
    In a flash, at a trumpet crash,
I am all at once what Christ is, since he was what I am, and
This Jack, joke, poor potsherd, patch, matchwood, immortal diamond,
          Is immortal diamond.

Combining the voyage paradigm with that of fire and light, Hopkins makes the resurrection of the body his beacon. He then believes he no longer has anything to mourn when the sun, 'nature's bonfire burns on', and yet man, 'her bonniest, dearest to her, her clearest-selvèd spark' is quenched, for the fact of the Resurrection reminds him that man's earthly 'trash' will be burned away, leaving only the 'immortal diamond' of the soul.

Although both more complex and more elegant than either

Spurgeon's account of his spiritual crisis or Tennyson's 'The Two Voices', Hopkins's poem also represents the situation of crisis by means of the same paradigm. What is most interesting to the literary iconologist about 'That Nature is a Heraclitean Fire', however, is not the elements it shares with these other records of spiritual crisis. Spurgeon, who exemplifies a completely traditional and rather old-fashioned use of the metaphor, leaves the listener in no doubt about his interpretation of the voyage. In particular, his continual allegorization of the voyage emphasizes that he was entirely at fault for embarking in the first place. Whereas Spurgeon's narrative of his spiritual voyagings is explicitly related from the vantage-point of the believer, those by Tennyson and Hopkins begin within the experience of spiritual doubt and only later progress to the condition of faith. The transformation of spiritual conditions that both poems dramatize appears centrally in their use of shipwreck or ship-voyage paradigms. For example, Tennyson's speaker announces that the voice of doubt has failed to 'wreck' his 'mortal ark', and he thereby transforms a potentially non-Christian figure of isolation and helplessness into a Christian one of secure faith. This transformation of a central paradigm appears more clearly in Hopkins's 'That Nature is a Heraclitean Fire' because he has preceded the dramatic instant of transformation with oblique introductions of the analogy to drowning and destruction by water. Even more than Tennyson's 'The Two Voices', Hopkins's poem employs the paradigm as a poetic centre, for it not only provides the poetic resolution of the spiritual problems that create the poem's drama but it also thus creates the 'plot' or progress of the poem itself.

This convergence of paradigm, poetic organization, and theme also appears, as one might expect, in *In Memoriam.* When Tennyson's close friend Arthur Henry Hallam died in 1833, the poet felt himself stripped of all sustaining belief and plunged into crisis. Stunned, without direction, he found himself, as he explained in the fourth section of *In Memoriam,* drifting hopelessly 'within a helmless bark'. Hallam's death placed everything in his life – his conception of himself, his poetry, his relation to other people – in crisis as he began to doubt all his most basic beliefs. When friends tried to console him by pointing out that such tragic, wasteful deaths were a common occurrence, such attempts at consolation only made him doubt religion even more. Pointing out the fact 'That loss is common would not make/ My own less bitter, rather more:/ Too common!'

Tennyson then sketches a series of such deaths, one of which takes place at sea:

> O mother, praying God will save
>> Thy sailor, – while thy head is bow'd
>> His heavy-shotted hammock-shroud
> Drops in his vast and wandering grave. [sec. 6]

Waiting for the ship to return Hallam's body so it can be buried in English soil, Tennyson becomes drawn to the vision of his friend as a castaway, for as he thinks that all who loved Hallam wish him buried at home, he compares that final resting place, not to a possible one in Vienna, where his friend died, but to the ocean floor:

> O to us,
> The fools of habit, sweeter seems
> To rest beneath the clover sod. . .

> Than if with thee [the ship] the roaring wells
>> Should gulf him fathom-deep in brine;
>> And hands so often clasped in mine,
> Should toss and tangle with shells. [sec. 10]

After thus placing both himself and Hallam within an imaginative landscape of shipwreck and disaster, the poet then tries unsuccessfully at this early stage in *In Memoriam* to find some means of transforming his 'helmless bark' into an ark of salvation. In the twelfth section, for example, he describes himself in terms borrowed from the dove sent forth from the ark:

> Like her I go; I cannot stay;
>> I leave this mortal ark behind,
>> A weight of nerves without a mind,
> And leave the cliffs, and haste away

> O'er ocean-mirrors rounded large,
>> And reach the glow of southern skies,
>> And see the sails at distance rise,
> And linger weeping on the marge,

And saying; 'Comes he thus, my friend?
  Is this the end of all my care?'
  And circle moaning in the air:
'Is this the end? Is this the end?'

And forward dart again, and play
  About the prow, and back return
  To where the body sits, and learn
That I have been an hour away.

Having encountered in his daydream the ship bearing Hallam's body, the poet then returns to 'where the body sits', but this second body is his own and now appears a corpse. Having imaginatively travelled in spirit, he returns with no inspiriting hope but only more recognitions of death. This dove found nothing that could support life.

This metaphoric element in the poem does not find resolution until section 103, which relates that Tennyson 'dreamed a vision of the dead,/ Which left my after-morn content'. He dreams that he lives in a hall surrounded by maidens who represent the Muses.

They sang of what is wise and good
  And graceful. In the centre stood
A statue veiled, to which they sang;

And which, though veiled, was known to me,
  The shape of him I loved, and love
  For ever: then flew in a dove
And brought a summons from the sea.

Boarding his vessel, he finds Hallam there waiting to greet him, and just before they leave, he discovers that his poetic faculties are to come, too. Tennyson, who now believes once again, not only feels sure that he will be reunited with Hallam and that he will reach his own heavenly destination but also knows his poetry has a role in his life worthy of that destination.

Unlike his own 'The Two Voices' and Hopkins's 'That Nature is a Heraclitean Fire', *In Memoriam* does not find its central resolution in this transformation of the shipwreck paradigm. *In Memoriam*, which is an extraordinarily complex poem, is composed of many such metaphors and their transformations, and although this one contributes to the main effect, it is not its entire source as in the briefer lyrics. One such crucial motif in the poem is that of the hand. In the opening section Tennyson inquires,

> . . . who shall so forecast the years
> And find a loss a gain to match?
> Or reach a hand through time to catch
> The far-off interest of tears?

In the sections that constitute the rest of the poem, Tennyson returns again and again to this notion of a vitalizing, sustaining hand, which in essence represents the presence of both God and Hallam. In his grief he thinks of his friend's hand tossing 'with tangle and with shells' (sec. 10); and when he thinks of loss, he thinks of the absence of that beloved hand. Hands, touching, and similar paradigms occur repeatedly throughout the poem, but the most important instance of them appears in the climactic section 95, which records Tennyson's mystical experience. After reading Hallam's letters once again, the poet felt

> The dead man touched me from the past,
> And all at once it seemed at last
> The living soul was flashed on mine.

The hand that could reach through time and for which he had longed in the poem's opening section can only be that of either Hallam or God. Under their sponsorship, Tennyson not only feels himself reunited with his friend but also writes a poem that sets forth the presence of good in the midst of evil, life in the midst of death, and God in the midst of this world in which entire species become extinct.

Tennyson's mystical experience, which transforms the paradigm of the hand, turns out to have a surprising amount in common with the situation of shipwreck. Both are situations in which Tennyson found himself impinged upon by external forces that threatened to end his life as he knew it, but the mystical experience, of course, took a benign form.[12] The length of *In Memoriam,* which permits Tennyson to develop several such main paradigms, also permits him to transform one into another.

In Memoriam has been discussed recently so well and at such length that I do not wish to go into the matter of all its paradigms, motifs, and systems of transformations again.[13] What I do wish to point out, however, is that this great poem, which has had an extraordinary influence on British and American poetry, has much to reveal to the student of literary iconology. *In Memoriam* exemplifies, for instance, the continued use of ancient paradigms, and it also shows how they may take new forms. Furthermore, it reveals the relation between paradigm transformation and autobiographical literature; and at the same time, it permits us to perceive that paradigms in autobiographical and other literature can function as organizational principles, plot devices, and means of rhetorical and philosophical resolution.

In *The Act of Reading: A Theory of Aesthetic Response,* Wolfgang Iser describes the way the author's ideas emerge during 'the reading process, in the course of which the reader's role is to occupy shifting vantage points that are geared to a prestructured activity and to fit the diverse perspectives into a gradually evolving pattern.'[14] As even this brief discussion of *In Memoriam* and the other works at which we have looked should suggest, they employ paradigms and paradigm transformations as a primary means of directing the reader's activity. In particular, they all begin in a situation of doubt and then dramatize the speaker's sudden accession to faith by means of such paradigms. The reader both understands and experiences these works only when he recognizes that the meaning of the paradigm has shifted. Kuhn likens the exchange of scientific paradigms to a religious-conversion experience, and taking a hint from him, we may observe that a great many literary works control and direct the reader by encouraging him to effect precisely such a paradigm exchange. Paradigms are means of interpreting the world, and therefore to exchange paradigms requires that one change one's interpretation of things. By employing series of paradigms that can fit into two different codes or systems, writers during the past two centuries have frequently made their readers enact what was to them a fundamental situation – that in which a person must *make an interpretation.* Carlyle's *The French Revolution, Latter-Day Pamphlets,* and *Chartism,* Ruskin's *Modern Painters, The Stones of Venice,* and writings in political economy, Tennyson's *In Memoriam* and *Idylls of The King,* Hopkins's *The Wreck of the Deutschland,* and countless autobiographies and writings of the sage, such as those by Cioran, Nietzsche, Mailer, and Didion, all attempt to make the reader accede to their acts of interpretation by making him participate in the hermeneutic process.

This brief examination of the way paradigms function within literary works suggests that one must revise Iser's useful theories of reader response in an important way. Writing primarily as a student of the novel, he has formulated a theory that, in its present form, has severe limitations. According to Iser, his theory of the reading process

> is best exemplified by the novel, which is a system of perspectives designed to transmit the individuality of the author's vision. As a rule there are four main perspectives; those of the narrator, the characters, the plot, and the fictitious reader. [p. 35]

To these four perspectives, as Iser calls them, I would propose adding a fifth, that of the paradigm system. As *In Memoriam* and many prose autobiographies demonstrate, whatever plot these works might possess is far less important in the reader's experience of each one than the development, transformation, and exchange of paradigm systems. Furthermore, brief lyrics, such as Hopkins's 'That Nature is a Heraclitean Fire', and other non-narrative literature often have neither characters nor plot. Their organization takes the form of logical, rhetorical, or other discursive modes; and again, paradigms often play major roles. In fact, these systems of paradigm development and transformation provide the lyric and non-narrative equivalent to plot. In addition, there are many works of fiction, such as those by Dickens, Faulkner, and Broch, in which such paradigm systems are usefully considered as another of Iser's 'perspectives', my fifth to be added to his initial four. Any novel other fictional work with numerous chararacters, such as Browning's *The Ring and the Book,* can employ various paradigms in dialogue spoken by different characters or in the narrator's statements and descriptions. When this is the case, one finds it more efficient to consider these paradigms as composing their own system, rather than treat each as a means by which the individual characters express themselves.

These brief observations are intended merely to suggest how complex is the individual paradigm's relation to the work in which it appears and the traditions in which they both participate. Iconology, which is the study of situations, paradigms, and figurations in the arts, thus has much to offer not only the art, literary, and cultural historian but also the critic and theoretician of literature as well.

NOTES

Chapter One: Images, Situations, and Structures

1   *Romantic Art in Britain: Paintings and Drawings 1760–1860* (Philadelphia, 1968), p. 192. For another discussion of the Turnerian vortex, see Jack Lindsay, *J. M. W. Turner: His Life and Work* (London, 1966), pp. 120–3.

2   William Feaver, *The Art of John Martin* (Oxford, 1975), which contains illustrations of works by the artist referred to below, provides valuable background information on his pictures and comparisons with his contemporaries.

3   *Centennial Review,* 23 (1979), p. 229.

4   Alexandra R. Murphy, *Visions of Vesuvius* (Boston, 1978), p. 6. This catalogue provides illustrations of works depicting both the volcano itself and its destruction of the ancient cities.

5   'Pascal's Sphere', *Other Inquisitions,* trans. R. I. C. Sims (New York, 1966), p. 8. Ernst Robert Curtius, *European Literature and the Latin Middle Ages,* trans. Willard R. Trask (New York, 1953), pp. 128–30, provides an essential introduction to the metaphorics of nautical (and many other kinds of) tropes. Together with Borges, Curtius's remarks on topoi furnished the original impetus for this study, which has also benefited from T. S. R. Boase, 'Shipwrecks in English Romantic Painting', *Journal of the Warburg and Courtauld Institutes,* 22 (1959), pp. 332–46; Lorenz Eitner, 'The Open Window and the Storm-tossed Boat: an Essay in the Iconography of Romanticism', *Art Bulletin,* 37 (1959), pp. 281–90; W. H. Auden, *The Enchafed Flood: Three Critical Essays on the Romantic Spirit* (New York, 1957); Roger B. Stein, *Seascape and the American Imagination* (New York, 1975).

6   Surely one reason for the prevalance of such analogies in Western thought is that all action (and all discourse containing description or presentation of action) inevitably takes the form of conflict, progress, or a combination of them – all of which forms encourage spatialization. See Angus Fletcher, *Allegory: Theory of a Symbolic Mode* (Ithaca, 1964), p. 151, for an argument that the battle and progress provide the two fundamental forms of allegorical narrative.

211

7 W. J. T. Mitchell, 'Spatial Form in Literature: Toward a General Theory', *Critical Inquiry,* 6 (1980), pp. 539–67, argues convincingly that spatialization occurs in all literature and not, as Joseph Frank suggested in his seminal work, 'Spatial Form in Modern Literature' (1945), just that of the modernists. See also Louis O. Mink, 'History and Fiction as Modes of Comprehension', *New Directions in Literary History,* ed. Ralph Cohen (London, 1974), pp. 107–24.

8 Sebastian Brant's fifteenth-century *Narrenshiff* popularized the topos of the Ship of Fools. Edwin H. Zeydel's translation (1944), which is available in a reissue (New York, 1962), contains a bibliography and reproduces the original woodcuts. For the use of this analogy by a nineteenth-century novelist, see Edward H. Rosenberry, 'Melville's Ship of Fools', *PMLA,* 75 (1960), pp. 604–8. For the Ship of State, see the section 'Political and social shipwrecks and castaways', pp. 109–20 below.

9 Translated by Charles S. Singleton, *Commedia: Elements of Structure* (Cambridge, Mass., 1954), pp. 24–5. The original text appears in *De doctrina christiana (On Christian Doctrine),* bk 1, sec. 5.

10 Before examining the situation of shipwreck in more detail, one should recognize that it is very commonly employed as a structural device. The tale of adventure, the romance, and the satire all frequently use shipwrecks – or in more recent years, aircrashes – to remove a character from his or her social, political, and moral context and insert him or her into an alien world. Sidney's *Arcadia* and Shakespeare's *The Tempest* both use shipwreck as a way of thus introducing characters into a new setting, and *Gulliver's Travels,* in which the poor protagonist finds himself at various times abandoned, wrecked, and cast away, exemplifies the satirist's manipulation of this device. When a shipwreck is used for such narrative purposes, however, it rarely also functions to create that sense of being in the world that is here our main concern. A major exception, of course, is *Robinson Crusoe,* a work that manages to combine the devices of the adventure story with its much emphasized theological import. But such combinations are the exception and not the rule.

11 *The Structure of Scientific Revolutions,* 2nd edn (Chicago, 1970).

12 'Introductory', *Studies in Iconology: Humanistic Themes in the Art of the Renaissance* (New York, 1962), p. 19.

13 My *Victorian Types, Victorian Shadows: Biblical Typology in Victorian Literature, Art, and Thought* (London, 1980), pp. 204–31, contains a detailed discussion of both orthodox and ironic intonations of this scriptural episode concerning Moses' vision of the promised land of Canaan. By the late nineteenth century, many secular analogues to this Pisgah sight take the form of a prospect of shipwreck.

Swinburne's 'Evening on the Broads', Mallarmé's 'Brise Marine', and Pessoa's *Ode Maritima* exemplify combinations of the structures of these two situations.

14 The prison metaphor is discussed in Victor Brombert, 'The Happy Prison: A Recurring Romantic Metaphor', *Romanticism: Vistas, Instances, Continuities,* ed. David Thorburn and Geoffrey Hartman (Ithaca, 1973), pp. 62–79; Ronald Paulson, *Emblem and Expression: Meaning in English Art of the Eighteenth Century* (Cambridge, Mass., 1975), pp. 64–8; Lorenz Eitner, 'Cages, Prisons, and Captives in Eighteenth-Century Art', *Images of Romanticism: Verbal and Visual Affinities,* eds Karl Kroeber and William Walling (New Haven, 1978), pp. 13–38.

15 In 'The Hermeneutics of Symbols and Philosophical Reflection', which examines the evolution of Judaic conceptions of evil, Ricoeur provides an interesting instance of paradigm change. Pointing out that the Old Testament variously considers sin as a stain, weight, or deviation, he argues that

a symbol is first of all the destroyer of a prior symbol. Thus we see the symbolism of sin take shape about images which are the inverse of stain images; in place of exterior contact, it is now deviation (from the target, the straight path, the limit not to be crossed, and so on) which serves as guiding schema. This switch in themes is the expression of an overturning of fundamental motifs. A new category of religious experience is born: that of 'before God,' of which the Jewish *berit,* the Alliance, is the witness. . . . What becomes then of the initial symbol? On the one hand, evil is no longer a thing, but a broken relationship, hence a nothing; this nothing is expressed in terms of the vaporousness and vanity of the idol. . . . But at the same time a new positivity of evil arises, no longer an exterior 'something,' but a real enslaving power. The symbol of captivity, which transforms a historical event (the Egyptian captivity, then the Babylonian captivity) into a schema of existence, represents the highest expression achieved by the penitential experience of Israel. [*The Philosophy of Paul Ricoeur,* eds Charles E. Reagan and David Stewart (Boston, 1978), p. 40.]

16 *Natural Supernaturalism: Tradition and Revolution in Romantic Literature* (New York, 1971), pp. 91–2.

17 *The Structure of Scientific Revolutions,* pp. 84–5, 150–1.

18 Theodore Ziolkowski, *Disenchanted Images: A Literary Iconology* (Princeton, 1977), pp. 6–14, provides a useful survey of definitions of 'imagery', 'theme', 'motif', and 'symbol'. Although Ziolkowski's study, which is basically a historical footnote to Tzvetan Todorov's

Introduction to the Fantastic in Literature, convincingly demonstrates that what Todorov took to be an essential characteristic of the fantastic is in fact something traceable to a specific period in Western thought, his approach to iconology is of very little value. Choosing to limit iconology to the study of paintings, statues, and mirrors in fiction – to images that are physically present in the fictional worlds he discusses – he reduces this discipline to little more than a pun.

19 'Loss of the Sloop Betsy', in *Narratives of Shipwrecks and Disasters, 1586–1860,* ed. Keith G. Huntress (Ames, Iowa, 1974), p. 29. This valuable compendium of shipwreck narratives also contains a very useful introduction that provides much information on sea disasters and literary figures.

Chapter Two: Shipwrecks and Castaways

1 Frank Anderson Trapp, *The Attainment of Delacroix* (Baltimore, 1971), p. 18n, comments upon the importance of the metaphor of the wrecked boat to the artist.

2 Stanfield's untraced picture is illustrated in *Great Victorian Pictures, Their Paths to Fame,* the catalogue for the 1978 Arts Council exhibition organized by Rosemary Treble. See p. 93 for a reproduction of the painting and an anthology of contemporary comments about it.

3 Richard Westall's *The Death of Ophelia* (1793), which is now in the British Museum, is one of the Earliest Romantic versions of this popular subject (illus. in Marcel Brion, *Romantic Art* (London, 1960), facing p. 49). According to the *Art-Journal,* 11 (1849), p. 89, H. Le Jeune exhibited an Ophelia at the 1849 British Institution: 'She is presented in a stooping pose, hanging wreaths upon the boughs within her reach.' The Ophelia theme takes two basic forms. The first, which is exemplified by these two last-mentioned works, represents the girl standing or sitting beside the water about to take her life, as in Arthur Hughes's two versions (1852, City Art Gallery, Manchester – illus. in Raymond Watkinson, *Pre-Raphaelite Art and Design* (London, 1970), pl. 84; and 1865, Toledo Museum of Art – illus. in Rowland and Betty Elzea, *The Pre-Raphaelite Era, 1848–1914* (Wilmington, 1976), nos 3–9); *Ophelia* by A. Ercole (1859, location unknown – see *Art Journal,* 21 (1859), p. 167); the statue by W. C. Marshall, R. A. (1863, location unknown – illus. in *Illustrated London*

News (28 March 1885), p. 328); and Richard Redgrave's version (1858, location unknown – illus. in *Art-Journal,* 20 (1858), pp. 354–5). This form of the Ophelia theme is obviously related to other representations of a mournful young woman by a pool of water, such as Francis Danby's *Disappointed Love* (1821, Victoria and Albert Museum – illus. in Eric Adams, *Francis Danby: Varieties of Poetic Landscape* (New Haven and London, 1973), pl. 1) and Viktor Mikhailovitch Vaznetsov's *Alionushka* (1881, Tretyakov Gallery, Moscow – illus. Aleska Čelebonović *Some Call it Kitsch: Masterpieces of Bourgeois Realism* (New York, 1975), p. 94).

Millais's famous painting, which portrays Ophelia floating in the pool that will soon drown her, exemplifies the second major form of this theme. Trapp, *The Attainment of Delacroix,* pp. 168–9, reproduces the Louvre *Ophelia's Death* by Delacroix (1853), comparing it both to the painting by Millais and to Paul Delaroche's *The Young Martyr* (c. 1853, Louvre). George Clairin also painted an *Ophelie aux Chardons* (c. 1898, Barry Friedman coll. – illus. in Elzea, op. cit., no. 8–17). The dying Ophelia is closely related to another extremely popular subject – the dying Lady of Shalott – which also shares the horizontal arrangement of the figure. John William Waterhouse's *The Lady of Shalott* (1888, Tate Gallery – illus. in Čelebonović, op. cit., p. 95) is thus unusual in depicting the Lady in a seated position; more usual are the identically entitled paintings by William A. Breakspeare (n.d., formerly in the Handley-Read coll. – illus. in the 1974 Fine Art Society catalogue of the collection, pl. 13); John LaFarge (n.d., New Britain Museum of American Art, New Britain, Connecticut – illus. in Elzea, op. cit., nos 3–37); and John Atkinson Grimshaw (1878, The Pre-Raphaelite Trust – illus. in ibid., no. 4–36).

4 Lorenz Eitner, *Géricault's 'Raft of the "Medusa"'* (London, 1972), which contains the definitive discussion of the evolution of the painting, points out that the sighting of the other vessel 'is not part of the rescue, it is, rather, the ultimate ordeal of the shipwrecked men. . . . [It] is a scene of anxiety, disappointment, and resignation, rather than relief' (p. 26). His valuable discussion of the artist's use of compositional devices and juxtaposition of distances to dramatize his point occurs on p. 31.

5 Such treatment of the survivors of shipwreck so disturbed William Falconer, himself a mariner, that he devoted a long passage to the subject in *The Shipwreck.* According to Elizabeth Schneider, *The Dragon in the Gate: Studies in the Poetry of G. M. Hopkins* (Berkeley and Los Angeles, 1968), p. 17, Englishmen were shocked to learn when the *Deutschland* perished that 'no attempt at rescue had been made for some thirty crucial hours; and subsequently the vessel was

looted by the owners of local fishing smacks who, it was said, even
tore rings from the fingers of the dead bodies on board.'

6   For a discussion and bibliography concerning this painting, which
was long misidentified as the untraced *Wreck of the 'Hope'*, see *La
Peinture allemande à l'époque du Romantisme* (Paris, 1976), pp. 64–5.
The painting was purchased in 1843 by J. C. C. Dahl.

7   See pp. 75–84 for a discussion of Falconer's *The Shipwreck*.

8   *The Correspondence of Emerson and Carlyle,* ed. Joseph
Slater (New York, 1964), p. 462. Hereafter cited by page number in
text.

9   Harold Bloom, *The Visionary Company: A Reading of English Romantic
Poetry* (Garden City, N. Y., 1963), p. 195. Keith G. Huntress,
Narratives of Shipwrecks and Disasters, 1586–1860 (Ames, Iowa, 1974),
which also discusses the effect of this famous shipwreck on the
poet, contains an account of it by one of the survivors (pp. 131–7).
For two important discussions of this problem, see E. L. McAdam,
Jr., 'Wordsworth's Shipwreck', *PMLA, 77* (1962), pp. 240–7, and R. C.
Townsend, 'John Wordsworth and His Brother's Poetic Development',
PMLA, 81 (1966), pp. 70–8.

10 *The Dragon in the Gate,* op. cit., p. 16.

11 The cultural expectations against which an event is perceived may
of course provide a dominant interpretation. For example, the
disastrous end of Sir John Franklin's 1845 expedition to the
Arctic, which at its onset contemporaries in Britain and Europe
regarded as a test case in man's quest to prevail over nature,
brought with it an obvious conclusion about human heroism,
power, and place in the universe. As Chauncey C. Loomis, 'The
Arctic Sublime', in *Nature and the Victorian Imagination*, ed U. C.
Knoepflmacher and G. B. Tennyson (Berkeley and Los Angeles,
1977), pp. 107, 110, has written:

> There was a feeling that if Franklin went out into the Arctic and
> mastered it, man would somehow be enlarged in mind and
> soul. Instead, the Arctic had swallowed him, obliterated him.
> . . . In their imaginations, the British people, and other peoples as
> well, had voyaged with Franklin 'toward no earthly pole'. . . .
> [Their imagined Arctic] was an environment within which a
> cosmic romance could be acted out: man facing the great forces
> of Nature and surviving if not prevailing over them. The fate of
> the Franklin expedition soured the romance and at least partly
> subverted the image of the Arctic sublime. It was one thing to
> image the expedition disappearing into the Arctic forever: that
> would have been terrible, but in a way sublime. It was another
> to know that the men of the expedition had died slowly in an

agony of scurvy and starvation. Bleeding gums, running sores, and constricted bowels are not sublime.

None the less, no matter how much the fate of the expedition into the Arctic wastes had shocked contemporary optimism, initial cultural expectations did not indicate whether one should take the sad outcome as an instance of divine punishment on human presumption or simply as one of man's basic isolation and helplessness.

12 My *Victorian Types, Victorian Shadows: Biblical Typology in Victorian Literature, Art, and Thought* (London, 1980), pp. 13–63, provides an introduction to the hermeneutic approach and its effect on British nineteenth-century thought.

13 For other instances of this topos in Milton, see Barbara K. Lewalski, 'The Ship-Tempest Imagery in "Samson Agonistes" ', *Notes and Queries,* 204 (1959), pp. 372–3.

14 *Discussions, critiques & pensées diverses sur la religion et la philosophie* (1844), quoted by H. G. Schenk, *The Mind of the European Romantics* (Garden City, N. Y., 1964), p. 86.

15 See my *Victorian Types, Victorian Shadows,* pp. 205–16.

16 *The Greeks and the Irrational* (Berkeley and Los Angeles, 1964), pp. 16–17. See also Bruno Snell, *The Discovery of the Mind: The Greek Origins of European Thought,* trans. T. G. Rosenmeyer (Cambridge, Mass., 1953).

17 'The Logic beneath "The Open Boat" ', *Georgia Review,* 26 (1972), pp. 330, 334–5.

18 Professor Monteiro suggests that

Crane makes convincingly real to us just how precarious and tentative man's hold upon life actually is. What wastes away in the course of events is the unexamining man's sense of his own self-assurance, comfort, and safety. Drawing upon Schopenhauer, Nietzsche describes the ordinary human situation: 'Even as on an immense, raging sea, assailed by huge wave crests, a man sits in a little rowboat trusting to his frail craft, so, amidst the furious torments of this world, the individual sits tranquilly, supported by the *principium individuationis* and relying on it.' The concept of *principium individuationis* helps us understand how man so orders his portion of experience that he can believe he controls it. The logical categories that he ordinarily lives by – a linear sense of time, meaningful sequences of cause and effect, the measurement of possibilities and probabilities – these, and others, enable him to keep on an even keel for most of his waking hours. . . . Useful as they usually are, these props are the first things to fail him in his crises. [p. 327]

19 Another important version (or transformation) of the castaway appears in the motif of the Babes in the Wood, which, as Barton L. St Armand points out, was 'surely one of the most popular themes of nineteenth-century art and illustration' ('Emily Dickinson's "Babes in the Wood": a Ballad Reborn', *Journal of American Folklore,* 90 (1977)), p. 434. This important study traces the many varying applications and intonations of this version of the castaway or orphan in nineteenth-century literature. It also demonstrates how ballad incident was often combined with scriptural echoes and allusion.

20 Two valuable discussions of the orphan-figure have appeared comparatively recently: Nina Auerbach, 'Incarnations of the Orphan', *ELH,* 42 (1975), pp. 395–419; and John R. Reed, *Victorian Conventions* (Athens, Ohio, 1975), pp. 250–67.

21 Georges Poulet, *Études sur le temps humain* (Paris, 1949) makes a well-known attempt to explore the differing ways Western man has experienced time since the Middle Ages. Since he performs his phenomenological analyses on metaphors and other tropes, Poulet works as an iconologist of sorts. In the title essay of *Beyond Formalism: Literary Essays, 1958–1970* (New Haven, 1970), p. 52, Geoffrey H. Hartman has objected to Poulet's procedure of treating these tropes without regard to limits of genre or even individual works and yet ending up with something very like 'Lovejoy's unit ideas in the history of ideas. . . . it is a curious antiformalism which strains at the gnat of genre distinctions and is obliged to swallow the camel of periodization.' One may defend Poulet by pointing out that his phenomenological analyses in fact furnish us with a description of the codes and paradigms different individuals have employed historically to formulate and communicate various ideas. Therefore, although Poulet himself often falls into the trap of writing as if he were describing a period mind or period consciousness, he actually provides a clear examination of some of the kinds of codes Foucault proposes as the subject of an archeology of knowledge. In fact, we may take him as a Foucault without obfuscation.

22 *Swinburne: An Experiment in Criticism* (Chicago, 1972), pp. 141, 41.

23 See ibid., pp. 35–8, for the poet's anti-perfectibilianism. According to Jerome Hamilton Buckley, *The Triumph of Time: A Study of the Victorian Concepts of Time, History, Progress, and Decadence* (Cambridge, Mass., 1966), p. 57, suspicion that progress might be an illusion formed an important current of Victorian thought. Huxley, for example, began to suspect that

material progress might thus menace the true objects of

humanity. Besides, as Tennyson suggested, reversion no less than advance might be a fact of history; or – as Huxley put it, in terms of biological evolution – 'Retrogressive is as practicable as progressive metamorphosis.' The new archeology, which seemed at one moment to be offering a testimony of steady progress, at the next was furnishing incontestable proof of social retrogression. Prehistoric cave painting, charged with a rich creative energy, had flourished widely, then disappeared altogether, and its power had not been matched in art for millennia. 'Thronèd races' (to use the language of In Memoriam) had clearly degraded; and whole civilizations had vanished – not necessarily to make way for higher cultures. Perhaps the metaphor of ebb-and-flow, most memorably developed in Arnold's 'Dover Beach,' was more adequate a description of the movement of public time than the image of a resolute forward march.

Swinburne's debt to classical thought, particularly his debt to classical stoicism, seems to have made him one of the earliest major Victorian writers to oppose strongly the idea of progress. When dealing with politics, the poet could envisage improvement and movement towards a goal, but when he stood back and considered the history of humanity from a distance, he always emphasized a cyclic, rather than a progressive or meliorist, view of history.

24 Eliot's use of so many Swinburnean images, including those of withering flowers, wreckage, and pain, like his use of the earlier poet's characteristic associative and meditative 'circular' poetic structure, suggests a strong, specific influence at work. Of course, Eliot takes these Swinburnean poetic forms and employs them for very different ends – much as if, in the manner of so many poets, he were showing an earlier poet (or his audience) how one should do things the best way.

25 Eliot, who shares much with Arnold, Clough, Browning, Tennyson, and Swinburne, is at his most Victorian in this religious solution to the problems of human existence, time, and history by reference to the Incarnation. For the theological bases of such attempts, see my Victorian Types, Victorian Shadows, pp. 46–50, 187–8, 192–4. See also J. H. Buckley, 'The Eternal Now', The Triumph of Time, pp. 137–53, and Carol T. Christ, The Finer Optic: The Aesthetic of Particularity in Victorian Poetry (New Haven, 1975), pp. 105–49.

26 Recent scholarship has demonstrated the great degree to which Defoe's fiction draws upon traditional Christian symbolism. See, for example, Maximillian E. Novak, 'Robinson Crusoe's "Original

Sin" ', *Studies in English Literature,* 1 (1961), pp. 19–29; Edwin P. Benjamin, 'Symbolic Elements in *Robinson Crusoe',* *Philological Quarterly,* 30 (1951), pp. 206–11; and Robert W. Ayers, *'Robinson Crusoe:* "Allusive Allegorick History" ', *PMLA,* 82 (1967), pp. 399–407.

27 Baudelaire, for instance, ends 'Le Cygne' thinking 'aux matelots oubliés dans une île', while the hero of Tennyson's *Maud* compares himself to a 'Shipwreck'd man on a coast/ Of ancient fable and fear'. George Eliot's Felix Holt describes Annette, Esther Lyon's mother, as such a castaway 'on a remote island where she had been saved from wreck' (ch. 6), while Dickens describes Arthur Clenham in *Little Dorrit* in much the same terms with his love 'like Robinson Crusoe's money; exchangeable with no one, lying idle in the dark to rust, until he poured it out for Little Dorrit' (bk II, ch. 13). And Raskolnikov from Dostoyevsky's *Crime and Punishment* is seen with Sonia 'mournful and dejected, as though they had been cast up by the tempest all alone on some deserted shore' (Pt V, Ch. 4).

28 Much valuable information on the visual sources of the Ship of State and related pictorial symbolism appears in Sylvia Pressouyre, 'L'Emblème du Naufrage à la Galerie François 1er,', *Actes du Colloque International sur l'Art de Fontainebleau* (Paris, 1975), pp.127–39.

29 Trans. W. O. Henderson and W. H. Chaloner (Stanford, 1968), pp. 32, 50, 34, 37, 33.

30 *On Revolution* (New York, 1965), p. 42. Hereafter cited in text.

31 Quoted by J. A. Froude, *Thomas Carlyle: A History of His Life in London* (London, 1884), 1, p. 231.

32 Trans. Bernard Frechtman (New York, 1957), pp. 22–3.

Chapter Three: Related Paradigms

1 *The Mind and Art of Victorian England,* ed. Josef L. Altholz (Minneapolis, 1976), p. 64.

The theology espoused by most evangelicals, and generally accepted by most others, was a sort of unsystematic and semiconscious quasi-Calvinism, positing the Atonement rather than the Incarnation as the eternal fact of Christianity, and stressing the sterner and harsher Christian doctrines: original sin, reprobation, vicarious atonement, eternal punishment. The

unbalanced emphasis of these essentially unattractive themes
was bound to come into conflict with the sentimental and
humanitarian spirit of the age, itself largely a product of the
religious revival. . . . How could a benevolent and sensitive
conscience accept the morality of a Jehovah who behaved, as the
young Darwin put it, like a 'revengeful tyrant' and who
condemned the majority of his human creatures to an eternity
of torment disproportionate to their wickedness or based on no
personal fault at all? These were the issues which provoked
theological crises in the 1850s.

2 *The Eve of the Deluge* (1865, The Fine Art Society Ltd, London),
painted by W. H. Hunt's friend, William Bell Scott, who was
definitely not a believing Christian, provides an example of a
moralizing treatment of this subject. Scott's painting, which depicts
Noah and his family entering the ark while their neighbours scoff,
emphasizes the sensuality of those destroyed but presents no
obvious instances of cruelty or other sin. The spectator looks past a
man embracing two bare-breasted young women, all of whom
appear on the painting's left, to observe a sceptical drinker
mockingly offer Noah and his family a toast. The patriarch is
shown about to enter the ark above which has suddenly appeared
the only cloud in an otherwise empty sky. Alarmed, one of the
servants points to it, but no one else has yet seen the approaching
danger.

3 W. B. Stanford, *The Ulysses Theme: A Study in the Adaptability of a
Traditional Hero,* 2nd edn (New York, 1964), which I did not come
upon until most of this section was in its present form, provides an
excellent detailed examination of its subject and includes
discussions of the Homeric figure, his relation to his grandfather
Autolycus, and his appearance in the epic cycle and subsequent
classical literature. Stanford also includes a useful introduction to
the Renaissance Ulysses and two chapters, 'The Wanderer' and 'The
Re-integrated Hero', on the Romantic and post-Romantic
appearances of Odysseus. The subject is so admittedly complex
that, although I agree fully with almost all his discussions of
modern figures and the earlier literary background, we discuss very
few of the same works. I especially recommend to the reader the
discussions of the Homeric hero as he appears in Pascoli,
Kazantzakis, and Joyce.

4 F. A. C. Wilson points out that Porphyry symbolizes the birth of
the soul on

its journey from the Isles of the Blessed in a celestial boat (the
'vehicle' in which the soul was thought to be contained): during

the life the soul is tossed about on the sea of emotion and passion; after death, living backwards through time, it recrosses the sea and returns to the island paradise from which it set out. All this symbolism can be read into the *Odyssey,* where the fruitless wanderings of Odysseus over the hostile sea are taken to symbolize the life of the unregenerate soul; his arrival at the holy city of Phaecia, where it is perpetual spring, is read to mean the conversion of the soul to the intellectual life; and his return to Ithaca, to symbolise the soul's restoration to heaven, its native land, which can only be accomplished by virtue of the intellectual life. [*W. B. Yeats and Tradition* (New York, 1958), pp. 211–12]

I would like to thank Professor Michael Goldman, now of Princeton University, for pointing out this passage to me many years ago when I first became interested in the journey-of-life topos.

5 Stanford, *The Ulysses Theme,* p. 276n, contains a bibliography of critical discussions of this problem.

6 Tennyson's statements and much other necessary information about the poem are conveniently assembled in Christopher Ricks's Longmans Annotated English Poets edition of the *Poems* (London, 1969), pp. 560–6.

7 'Tennyson's "Ulysses" – A Re-interpretation', *Critical Essays on the Poetry of Tennyson,* ed. John Killham (New York, 1967), pp. 164–73.

8 In addition to this passage, which appears in 'The Hesperid Aeglé' chapter in *Modern Painters,* vol. 7, Ruskin also offers theological interpretations of the rainbow in 'Byzantine Palaces' in *The Stones of Venice.* We may take Ruskin, who is a particularly complex case, as a type of Victorian attitudes towards the rainbow (and exterior nature as well), for he first calls in the *The Stones of Venice* for a time when people will again read nature in terms of what he calls 'the language of types'; but by the last volume of *Modern Painters,* when he has lost his faith, he is already attacking ideas of a beneficent nature. None the less, he still cites the older tradition for his arguments, and one finds it difficult to determine precisely what he believes literally and what he is using for rhetorical effect. At any rate, we know from his earlier letters, diaries, and writings that he once definitely held such notions of sacramental nature.

9 *Baroque and Rococo Pictorial Imagery: The 1758–60 Hertel Edition of Ripa's Iconologia,* ed. E. A. Maser (New York, 1971), pl. 100 (no pagination). The words quoted are by the editor, who has based them upon the commentaries in earlier editions. For other rainbows, see the plates for 'Air' (8) and 'Peace' (79).

10 Miriam Allott quotes the poet's agreement with Charles Lamb as a

note to *Lamia* in her edition of the *Poems* in the Longmans Annotated English Poets series (London, 1970), p. 645n. She also suggests, mistakenly I think, that Keats in *Lamia* refers to the rainbow in Revelation 4: 2–3, but since that second rainbow (which is an antitype of the one in Genesis) has not yet come into existence, it must refer to the first seal of the covenant.

11 Marjorie Hope Nicolson, *Newton Demands the Muse: Newton's 'Opticks' and the Eighteenth-Century Poets* (Princeton, 1946), which begins with the famous lines from Keats, examines the stimulating effect Newton's discoveries had upon earlier writers.

12 *The Art-Union Journal,* 9 (1847), p. 286. Significantly, the landscape with a rainbow used to illustrate this episode functions quite convincingly since the reader has adapted himself to the world of fantasy.

13 Tennyson, *Poems,* ed. Christopher Ricks, p. 1,480.

14 *Studies in Early Impressionism* (New Haven, 1973), pp. 1–2.

15 In addition to the examples mentioned at various places in the text, one may cite the following: Joseph Wright, *Landscape with a Rainbow* (*c.* 1794–5, Derby); Thomas Girtin, *Rainbow over the Exe* (before 1802, Huntington Library, San Marino, California); Turner, *Fall of the Rhone at Schaffhausen* (1806, Boston Museum of Fine Arts) and various watercolours and studies; William David, *The Rainbow* (n.d., Walker Art Gallery, Liverpool); A. W. Hunt, *A November Rainbow – Dolwyddelan Valley, 1865* (Ashmolean Museum, Oxford); and Ruskin, an undated *Landscape with Rainbow* now in a private collection.

Such aesthetic uses of the rainbow occur also in literature. For examples of nineteenth-century word painting of the rainbow in Coleridge and Francis Kilvert, see E. D. H. Johnson, *The Poetry of Earth: A Collection of English Nature Writings* (London, 1966), pp. 120–1, 361–2. For Ruskin, see *Fors Clavigera,* letter 42, where he quotes from his 1873 diary.

16 See my *William Holman Hunt and Typological Symbolism* (New Haven and London, 1979), pp. 104–12.

17 For much of the information in this paragraph I am indebted to David C. Huntington, *The Landscapes of Frederic Edward Church* (New York, 1966). Mason I. Lowance, 'Typology and Millennial Eschatology in Early New England', *Literary Uses of Typology from the Late Middle Ages to the Present,* ed. Earl Miner (Princeton, 1977), pp. 228–73, contains the essential background for such an interpretation of American painting.

18 *Caspar David Friedrich,* trans. Sarah Twohig (New York, 1974). One may point out that in one of this artist's rainbow landscapes – *Mountain Landscape with Rainbow* (*c.* 1810, Essen) – he uses a device

analogous to that of the fantasy. As Börsch-Supan points out, in this picture 'the fact that the rainbow can be seen at all is completely illogical, for it would normally be visible only if the source of light was behind the observer' (p. 88). In other words, such an obviously non-realistic treatment of this natural phenomenon signals us to read the picture symbolically – as long, that is, as we make the admittedly dangerous assumption that the rendering of an optical impossibility is intentional.

19 *Art-Journal,* 22 (1860), p. 169.

20 'HOPE rediscovered, a shipwreck by Francis Danby', *Burlington Magazine,* 121 (1979), p. 584. Rodgers, whose discoveries confirm my earlier speculations in *Nature and the Victorian Imagination* (1977) that the lost painting employed the rainbow ironically, does not, however, accept that the ambiguities in Danby's picture are intentional, and he concludes that they are simply the result of the artist's ineptitude.

21 Information about *The Wreck Buoy,* which was originally painted in 1809 and then extensively repainted in 1849, appears in *Sudley: The Emma Holt Bequest,* a catalogue compiled by Mary Bennet and Edward Morris (Liverpool, 1971), pp. 75–6. It contains a bibliography of the extensive writing on this picture and references to similar subjects in Turner. For my discussion of this artist I am also indebted to John Gage, *Colour in Turner: Poetry and Truth* (New York, 1969); and Jack Lindsay, *The Sunset Ship: The Poems of J. M. W. Turner* (London, 1966) and *J. M. W. Turner: His Life and Work* (London, 1966).

Chapter Four: Iconology and Technique

1 None of these rhetorical difficulties afflicts *The Wreck of the Deutschland,* which takes the five Franciscan nuns as innocent victims of the sea disaster. The poet places most of the blame for the wreck upon the German government, which had exiled the nuns, but his primary elegiac resolution comes in his discovery that the nun who called for Christ was an antitype of the Virgin, for by calling to her Saviour she also gave birth to the word of God, as had Mary before her. Having made this rather extraordinary leap of faith, Hopkins can then respond affirmatively to his own question, 'is the shipwreck then a harvest?' (st. 31) and admiringly turn to God. 'master of the tides,/ Of the Yore-flood' (st. 32).

2 The writings of this school of moral philosophy, psychology, and aesthetics are conveniently contained in *British Moralists, being Selections from Writers Principally of the Eighteenth Century,* ed. L. A. Selby-Bigge, 2 vols (Oxford, 1897). See also Walter Jackson Bate, 'The Sympathetic Imagination in Eighteenth-Century English Criticism', *ELH.* 12 (1945), pp. 144–64; and my *The Aesthetic and Critical theories of John Ruskin* (Princeton, 1971), pp. 146–61.

3 On Sterne, see John Traugott, *Tristram Shandy's World: Sterne's Philosophic Rhetoric* (Berkeley and Los Angeles, 1954), and my 'Tristram Shandy and the Comedy of Context', *Brigham Young University Studies,* 7 (1966), pp. 208–24, and reprinted in *Laurence Sterne, Wege der Forschung,* ed. Gerd Rohmann (Darmstadt, 1980).

4 *Poetics,* 5 (1971–2), p. 12. Hereafter cited in text.

5 *Géricault's Raft of the 'Medusa'* (London, 1972), p. 26. Hereafter cited in text.

6 In a lecture delivered at the Frick Museum, New York City, in 1966, Professor McCoubrey demonstrated Turner's elaborate reference to contemporary political affairs in both *The Slave Ship* and *Tapping the Furnace.* These discussions will be incorporated in a forthcoming work.

7 See Jack Lindsay's edition of Turner's poems. *The Sunset Ship* (London, 1966), pp. 46–9; and my *Aesthetic and Critical Theories,* op. cit., pp. 439–42.

8 The absence of a divinity who watches over the victims of shipwreck appears with particular clarity in Géricault's *Raft of the 'Medusa'* because, as Eitner suggests, the artist violated certain codes and expectations of the audience. First, the artist broke radically with contemporary art when he created a major public image without traditional religious or political meanings – something especially blatant because he chose a large canvas of the size previously reserved for statements of political and religious belief. Second, Géricault omitted any sort of secular or heavenly divinity, which were conventionally included in such works. The painters of the Napoleonic era, particularly Gros, had glorified the emperor by making scenes of human suffering the setting for imperial pomp. According to Eitner,

> Gros made this subordination of human suffering to a higher, political interest naively clear in the horizontal subdivision of his canvases: above the victims of war agonizing in the lower foreground, the Emperor and his retinue pass like a celestial vision.

Géricault omitted from the *Raft* all devices for placing human suffering in an ideological context.

Its drama has no heros and no message. No God, saint, or monarch presides over the disaster; no common cause is in evidence; no faith, no victory justifies the suffering of the men on the Raft: their martyrdom is one without palm or flag. It is as if Géricault had taken the foreground of human misery from one of the Gros' pictures and omitted the apotheosis above. [p. 51]

The artist, in other words, makes his point by violating two codes or conventions, the first that large works were reserved for statements of ideological import sanctioned by church or state, and the second that such works which represented human suffering should contain an ideological justification of them. By omitting both expected features, Géricault forcefully created an image of human isolation and helplessness which proclaims the absence of such usual explanations.

9   *The Hero in Eclipse in Victorian Fiction* (London, 1966). Also published as *The Disappearance of the Hero in Nineteenth-Century Fiction*.

10 'Personal Myth; Three Victorian Autobiographers', *Approaches to Victorian Autobiography,* ed. George P. Landow (Athens, Ohio, 1979), p. 216.

11 This version of Spurgeon's spiritual near-shipwreck appears in 'The Bible', *Sermons* (London, 1860), I, pp. 28–9; all subsequent quotations in the text below are taken from this same passage. The preacher reused the same language with only a few additions and embroideries in his *Autobiography* (Edinburgh, 1962), I, pp. 66–9.

12 Tennyson's resolution of the problems posed for a believer by the shipwreck paradigm by means of a mystical experience anticipates Hopkins's strategies in *The Wreck of the Deutschland* in which such intrusion of the divine upon the human occurs twice, first to the poet himself at his conversion (secs 2–4) and then to the nun (secs 17–9, 24). The poet's comprehension of the nun's cry to Christ as a new creation of the word of God comes to him as a 'beacon of light' – the same figure used in 'That Nature is a Heraclitean Fire'.

13 A. C. Bradley, *Commentary on 'In Memoriam'* (London, 1903); Jerome H. Buckley, *Tennyson: The Growth of a Poet* (Cambridge, Mass., 1960); John D. Rosenberg, 'The Two Kingdoms of *In Memoriam', Journal of English and Germanic Philology,* 58 (1959), pp. 228–40; E. D. H. Johnson, *'In Memoriam:* the Way of a Poet', *Victorian Studies,* 2 (1958), pp. 139–48; Carlisle Moore, 'Faith, Doubt, and Mystical Experience in "In Memoriam" ', *Victorian Studies,* 7 (1963), pp. 155–69; John R. Reed, *Perception and Design in Tennyson's 'Idylls of the King'* (Athens, Ohio, 1960), pp. 11–25; Christopher Ricks, *Tennyson* (London, 1972);

and James R. Kincaid, *Tennyson's Major Poems: The Comic and Ironic Patterns* (New Haven and London, 1975).

14 Trans. David Henry Wilson (Baltimore, 1978), p. 35. Hereafter cited in text.

INDEX